INSTRUC

to accompany

LITERATURE AND THE WRITING PROCESS
Backpack Edition

Elizabeth McMahan
Illinois State University

Susan X Day
University of Houston

Robert Funk
Eastern Illinois University

Linda S. Coleman
Eastern Illinois University

Longman

Boston   Columbus   Indianapolis   New York   San Francisco   Upper Saddle River
Amsterdam   Cape Town   Dubai   London   Madrid   Milan   Munich   Paris   Montreal   Toronto
Delhi   Mexico City   Sao Paulo   Sydney   Hong Kong   Seoul   Singapore   Taipei   Tokyo

Instructor's Manual to accompany McMahan/Day/Funk/Coleman, *Literature and the Writing Process, Backpack Edition*

Copyright © 2011, Pearson Education, Inc.
All rights reserved. Printed in the United States of America. Instructors may reproduce portions of this book for classroom use only. All other reproductions are strictly prohibited without prior permission of the publisher, except in the case of brief quotations embodied in critical articles and reviews.

1 2 3 4 5 6 7 8 9 10–V036–13 12 11 10

Longman is an
imprint of

www.pearsonhighered.com

ISBN 10: 0-205-82612-1
ISBN 13: 978-0-205-82612-4

Anthology of Poetry

CONTENTS

Paired Poems for Comparison

A Portfolio of War Poetry

Instructor Resource Center

Register or log in to the Instructor Resource Center to download textbook supplements from our online catalog or request premium content for your school's course management system.

GETTING REGISTERED

To register for the Instructor Resource Center, go to **www.pearsonhighered.com** and click **"Educators."**

1. Click **"Download teaching resources for your text"** in the blue welcome box.

2. Request access to download digital supplements by clicking the **"Request Access"** link. s

Follow the provided instructions. Once you have been verified as a valid Pearson instructor, an instructor code will be emailed to you. Please use this code to set up your Pearson login name and password. After you have set up your username and password, proceed to the directions below.

DOWNLOADING RESOURCES

1. Go to http://www.pearsonhighered.com/educator and use the "Search our catalog" option to find your text. You may search by Author, Title, or ISBN.

2. **Select your text** from the provided results.

Literature and the Writing Process, Backpack Edition, 1/e
McMahan, Day, Funk & Coleman
©2011 | Longman | Paper; 800 pp | Not Yet Published
ISBN-10: 0205730728 | ISBN-13: 9780205730728

3. After being directed to the catalog page for your text, click the **Instructor Resources** link located under the **Resources** tab.

   Clicking the Instructor Resources link will provide a list of all of the book-specific print and digital resources for your text below the main title. Items available for download will have a  icon.

4. **Click on the View Downloadable Files** link next to the resource you want to download.

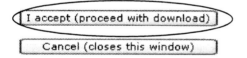

   A pop-up box will appear showing which files you have selected to download. Once you select the files, you will be prompted to login with an Instructor Resource Center login.

5. Enter you login name and password, and click the **"Submit"** button.

6. Read the terms and conditions and then click the **"I accept"** button to begin the download process.

   I accept (proceed with download)

   Cancel (closes this window)

7. **"Save"** the supplement file to a folder you can easily find again.

Once you are signed into the IRC, you may continue to download additional resources from our online catalog.

Please "Sign Out" when you are finished.

www.myliteraturelab.com

MyLiteratureLab^{TM} gives you and your students access to a wealth of online resources that bring literature to life as well as writing and research resources that help students succeed. You will save time by managing assignments and grading in one convenient place, and your students will benefit from having 24/7 access to terrific resources.

Resources. The Resource area contains instruction, multimedia tutorials and exercises for a wide array of literature, writing, grammar and research topics. Students can use this area on their own for self-study or instructors can point students to specific tools. Here is a sampling of the features in each section:

* **Literature**: Longman Lectures, Interactive Readings and Timelines, full-length films, "Writers on Writing" videos, glossaries of literary terms, literary element resources, and robust activities.

* **Writing**: Instruction in the writing process, writing about literature, the effective use of sources, and a library of sample papers.

* **Grammar**: Diagnostics, video tutorials and thousands of exercise sets.

* **Research**: Avoiding plagiarism and evaluating sources tutorials, citation diagnostics and exercise sets, step-by-step instruction in writing a literary research paper, samples, and much more.

eAnthology. Two hundred additional selections are available with this interactive eAnthology, which is organized by genre and alphabetized within each genre. In addition to providing more selections, the eAnthology is an excellent study aid: students can search, highlight, and take notes.

Longman Lectures. Narrated by our textbook authors and select interested professors, these compelling "lectures" include background information about the author and work, and an engaging multimedia reading. The students are then walked through interpreting the work and given instruction in writing about it.

Interactive Readings. For a variety of key works, students can click on highlighted sections of text to read helpful explanations and see critical thinking questions. These aids guide their reading and increase their understanding of the work.

Writers on Writing. Students will gain inspiration for their own writing from exclusive interviews with noted contemporary authors, including Rita Dove and Alberto Rios, as each discusses practicing the craft of writing.

Diagnostics and Study Plan. Students can improve their grammar skills outside of classroom time through MyLiteratureLab's grammar diagnostics, which produce personalized study plans. The study plan links students to multimedia instruction in a given topic and practice opportunities. Instructors and students can track progress via the Gradebook.

Composing. This dynamic space for drafting and revising, includes a "Writer's Toolkit" that provides students with writing, grammar, research, and online tutoring help in one convenient place. With all of this online help, students are likely to turn in better papers. They will also be saving paper!

Commenting. MyLiteratureLab^{TM} offers two flexible commenting tools that will reduce the amount of time spent grading papers: pre-loaded "Common Error" comments on key grammar topics and "My Comments," which enables instructors to save the comments they make over and over.

Peer Review. Students can also comment on each other's papers within MyLiteratureLab,^{TM} making peer review projects easier to execute—and paperless.

Gradebook. Built specifically for courses with a heavy writing component, the MyLiteratureLab^{TM} Gradebook makes it easy to capture, assess, and manage student submissions and practice results.

Media Resources Featured in
MYLITERATURELAB.COM myliteraturelab

FICTION

Toni Cade Bambara *The Lesson*: About the Author, Longman Lecture, Comprehension Quiz, Essay Questions

Raymond Carver About the Author, Bibliography

Kate Chopin *The Story of an Hour*: About the Author, Critical Overview, Bibliography, Longman Lecture, Comprehension Quiz, Essay Questions

Louise Erdrich *The Red Convertible*: About the Author, Comprehension Quiz, Essay Questions

William Faulkner *A Rose for Emily*: About the Author, Critical Overview, Bibliography, Critical Essay and Questions, Comprehension Quiz, Essay Questions

Nathanial Hawthorne *The Birthmark*: About the Author, Critical Overview, Bibliography, Comprehension Quiz, Essay Questions

Ernest Hemingway About the Author, Bibliography

Shirley Jackson *The Lottery*: About the Author, Critical Essay, Comprehension Quiz, Essay Questions

James Joyce About the Author, Bibliography

D. H. Lawrence About the Author

Bharati Mukherjee *A Father*: About the Author, Comprehension Quiz, Essay Questions

Joyce Carol Oates *Where Are You Going, Where Have You Been?*: About the Author, Critical Overview, Bibliography, Longman Lecture, Comprehension Quiz, Essay Questions

Tim O'Brien *The Things They Carried*: About the Author, Longman Lecture, Comprehension Quiz, Essay Questions

Flannery O'Connor About the Author

John Steinbeck *The Chrysanthemums*: About the Author, Comprehension Quiz, Essay Questions

John Updike *A & P*: About the Author, Critical Overview, Bibliography, Interactive Reading, Evaluation Questions, Student Essay, Critical Essay, Writing Prompts, Comprehension Quiz, Essay Questions

Alice Walker *Everyday Use*: About the Author, Critical Overview, Longman Lecture, Bibliography, Student Essay, Comprehension Quiz, Essay Questions

Eudora Welty *Why I Live at the P.O.*: About the Author, Longman Lecture, Lecture Questions

POETRY

Matthew Arnold "Dover Beach": Audio

Elizabeth Bishop "One Art": About the Author, Critical Overview, Bibliography, Longman Lecture, Critical Essay and Questions

Gwendolyn Brooks "We Real Cool": About the Author, Critical Overview, Bibliography, Interactive Reading, Critical Essay and Questions, Comprehension Quiz, Essay Questions

Robert Browning "My Last Duchess": About the Author, Longman Lecture, Audio Essay, Video, Critical Essay, Student Essay

Billy Collins "Introduction to Poetry": About the Author, Critical Overview, Bibliography, Evaluation Questions, Writing Prompts

E. E. Cummings "anyone lived in a pretty how town": About the Author, Critical Overview, Bibliography, Audio, Critical Essay, Comprehension Quiz, Essay Questions

Emily Dickinson "Because I Could Not Stop for Death": About the Author, Critical Overview, Bibliography, Longman Lecture, Lecture Questions, Comprehension Quiz, Essay Questions

"Wild Nights-Wild Nights!": Critical Overview, Audio

John Donne "Death Be Not Proud": About the Author, Critical Overview, Bibliography, Audio

"A Valediction: Forbidding Mourning": Critical Overview, Evaluation Questions, Writing Prompts

(continued)

INTRODUCTION

This Instructor's Manual reflects our belief that a student-centered classroom provides the best environment for learning. We have found peer involvement useful in helping students to discover a thesis, to invent ideas, to improve first drafts, and to catch editing errors. We also consider class discussion the best method of encouraging literary understanding. Students can begin by making connections between their own lives and the literature they read. Once they become engaged and interested, they can proceed to analysis and evaluation.

They will finally learn to interpret literature by continually asking themselves pertinent questions about the works as they read. Our text provides a list of such questions for each genre (designed to elicit meaning from any piece in that genre). You will want to encourage your students to use these lists whenever they read selections in the three anthologies (on short stories, poetry, and drama).

In this Instructor's Manual we supply responses to the discussion questions and to the exercises in the writing chapters, and possible answers to the post-reading questions in the literature anthologies and portfolios. Your students may come up with different but equally good answers. We frequently offer suggestions for classroom activities that involve using a workshop situation (with students divided into groups helping each other solve problems in writing about or interpreting literature). We also include commentaries on all the selections in the anthologies and portfolios, along with additional questions for discussion and writing, as well as suggestions for "Making Connections" among selections by both theme and form. At the beginning of each part, we offer "Activities for Creative and Critical Thinking" for each literary genre.

Getting Started

On the first day of class, you need to initiate the class activities you will want to use during the semester: if you want students to speak, write, and work in groups, you need to do those things today. We like to begin with a round-robin introduction in which each person (including the instructor) gives his or her name, one interesting statement, and one boring statement about his or her life. Before we start, we emphasize that the purpose is for everyone to learn everyone's name, which is easier when we have a little information to connect with the name. If you use this method, announce that you will ask a few people to name everyone when the exercise is over (though missing a few doesn't mean flunking). This activity helps to break down inhibitions and sets a friendly tone.

Because it's important to get students writing from the start of the course, you might use an activity that involves writing to help students get acquainted. Pair students up and have them converse with each other for ten minutes or so. If you want, write these questions on the board for the pairs to use in their conversations:
1. What does everybody know about you?
2. Is there anything that very few people know about you? What is it?
3. What would you like your classmates to know about you?

Tell them to take notes, and give them five more minutes or so to write up a brief paragraph about their partner. Then ask them to read their paragraphs to the class—or collect the paragraphs and read them aloud to the class (disregarding errors, of course).

1

These two activities will ease the way into using group work and peer review. They may take time from routines like going over the syllabus, but they are more valuable in the long run. Remember, students are going over syllabi in four or five other classes concurrently, and not much of that will stick anyway. If you close with a specific assignment, your students will be assured that you do have a plan. Discussing the syllabus may be more sensibly done in the second or third session when the class membership is more stabilized.

Reading and Writing Right Away

At the end of the first class, you should give a specific assignment. For example:

> Read the first story in the book, "Eveline," pp. 3–7, and be prepared to discuss your reactions to the story.

If you want the students to do some writing for the next class, ask them to write at least two paragraphs on Eveline, the title character: What do they think of her? You can also ask them to react to the ending: Were they prepared for the way the story ended? What questions do they have about it? Or give them a choice. Explain that short writings like this will be done frequently throughout the course to aid discussion and focus students' thoughts. When the students come to class, divide them into small groups (from three to six, depending on your class size) and have them read their papers to each other and try to come to a consensus about Eveline and/or the story's ending. This consensus will be reported to the class as a whole. Reconvene the class and listen to the reports. These discussions will lead naturally into assigning the rest of the chapter for the next class meeting.

Using Reading Journals

Many instructors have their students keep a reading journal: a record of their impressions of, thoughts about, and responses to the literary works they read. A journal is an excellent place for students to experience the process of writing. Journals don't involve the usual pressures associated with most college writing assignments, and they provide a low-risk opportunity for student writers to pursue their ideas and explore their thoughts.

If you decide to assign reading journals, you have several ways to go about it. You can ask students to keep a journal in which they record reactions to and thoughts about assignments and reading selections. These entries can then be used as a springboard for class discussions or as prewriting for writing assignments. Journal entries might also be written in class during the last ten or fifteen minutes as a follow-up to a discussion or to get ready to discuss a different idea the next time. You can also provide prompts for writing that encourage students to make connections between the readings and their own experiences.

Many instructors collect and read their students' journals every week or so, although you can set several deadlines throughout the semester when you will pick up journals. You can stagger the deadlines, collecting journals from only certain students at any one time. You don't have to read and respond to every entry, but you need to make the journals seem worthwhile or the work will be slack. You can give bonus points for substantial entries or base a grade on a minimum length. We have found that assigning at least 10 percent of the semester grade to a journal and setting a minimum number of entries (e.g., three one-page entries per week) for a C works rather well. You can reward

2

those students who write more and deduct from the grade of those who don't write enough.

RESOURCES FOR TEACHING LITERATURE

Useful Works for Teachers of Literature

Adler, Mortimer J., and Charles Van Doren. *How to Read a Book*. New York: Simon, 1972. Print.

Bevington, David. *How to Read a Shakespeare Play*. New York: Blackwell, 2006. Print.

Brunel, Pierre, ed. *Companion to Literary Myths, Heroes, and Archetypes*. Trans. Wendy Allatson, Judith Hayward, and Trista Selous. London: Routledge, 1996. Print.

Bryer, Jackson R., and Mary C. Hartig, eds. *The Facts on File Companion to American Drama*. 2nd ed. New York: Facts on File, 2010. Print.

Bunge, Nancy L. *Finding the Words: Conversations with Writers Who Teach*. Athens: Ohio UP, 1985. Print.

Eagleton, Terry. *How to Read a Poem*. New York: Blackwell, 2006. Print.

— *Literary Theory: An Introduction*. 2nd ed. Minneapolis: U of Minnesota P, 1996. Print.

Forster, Thomas C. *How to Read Literature Like a Professor: A Lively and Entertaining Guide to Reading Between the Lines*. New York: HarperCollins, 2003. Print.

Guerin, Wilfred L. et al. *Handbook of Critical Approaches to Literature*. 4th ed. New York: Oxford UP, 1999. Print.

Harmon, William. *A Handbook to Literature*. 10th ed. Upper Saddle River: Prentice, 2005. Print.

Kimmelman, Burt, ed. *The Facts on File Companion to American Poetry*. New York: Facts on File, 2005. Print.

Lipschultz, Geri. "Fishing in the Holy Waters." *College English* 48 (1986): 34–49. Print.

McMahan, Elizabeth, Robert Funk, and Susan Day. *The Elements of Writing About Literature and Film*. New York: Macmillan, 1988. Print.

Shaw, Valerie. *The Short Story: A Critical Introduction*. London: Longman, 1983. Print.

Werlock, Abby H. P., ed. *The Facts on File Companion to the American Short Story*. New York: Facts on File, 2000. Print.

Young, Gloria L. "Teaching Poetry: Another Method." *Teaching English in the Two-Year College* 14 (1987): 52–56. Print.

Online Resources for Teachers of Literature

Electronic Resources for Literature Teachers. http://people.ku.edu/~kconrad/eleclit.html
   A diverse collection of select resources, including sample literature sites, online journals of interest to teachers of English, and online teaching resources.

Literary Resources on the Net. http://andromeda.rutgers.edu/~jlynch/Lit/
   Maintains a generous collection of literature syllabi and other course materials.

World Lecture Hall. http://web.austin.utexas.edu/wlh/
   Publishes links to pages created by faculty worldwide who are using the Internet to deliver course materials. For anyone interested in online courseware.

PART I
COMPOSING: AN OVERVIEW

Chapter 1 The Prewriting Process [pp. 3–17]

In this opening chapter, we focus on analytical reading—on giving careful attention to the literary text and asking pertinent questions about it in order to derive a thorough understanding of the meaning. At the same time, we assume that students will be writing about this work, so we introduce them to several useful invention techniques that will help them discover what they want to say about the piece when they get ready to write.

Who Are My Readers? [p. 7]

The issue of audience can be a tricky and elusive one for many students. Writing a class paper presents a special problem in audience awareness. They know they are writing for the instructor, who is their most artificial and most attentive reader. They know the teacher is responsible for evaluating the students' work and will read their essays no matter how bad or good they are. But the writing that students do in class should prepare them for writing they will do in other situations and for other audiences. They need to get beyond the captive and limited audience of an instructor and learn how to write for an audience of general readers.

The general reader—also called "the universal reader" or "the common reader"—is essentially a fiction, but a very useful one. It is helpful for students to imagine a reader who is reasonably informed and generally attentive, one who will keep reading the paper so long as it is interesting and worthwhile. If students can focus on such a reader, they can gauge how much detail and background information to provide. The general reader knows a little about many things, but lacks specific information on the topic the writer wants to present. In the case of writing about literature, it's very helpful to ask, "How well do my readers know the literary work?"

The best way we know to help students develop and refine their audience awareness is to use student writing groups. (See pp. 49–51 in the main text and pp. 20–21 in this manual for suggestions on the use and operation of peer groups.) Sometimes we assign a short paper in which students are to explain or interpret a piece of literature for younger readers or for readers who have not read the selection. Or you might ask students to choose a favorite selection and write a recommendation for readers who aren't familiar with it, as in a movie or book review. The goal is to interest the audience in the reading but not spoil it for them.

Here is a checklist of questions that may help students to analyze their audience and define their purpose, especially if they are working in groups:

1. How well do my readers know the work? What details and information will I need to supply? What questions will they be likely to have?
2. Will my readers be interested in my ideas? How can I get them interested?
3. Will my readers be in agreement with my interpretation? Do I have to be careful not to offend them?
4. How do I want my readers to respond? What do I want them to get from my essay?

4

Prewriting Exercise (letters to and from Eveline) [p. 8]
The purpose of this activity is to teach students the concept of audience. But from reading, or hearing the students read, their letters, you will also be able to see how well they understand the characterizations in the story.

Prewriting Exercise (about purpose) [p. 9]
These four assignments may prove too taxing for students to complete individually. Instead, you may want to assign this section to groups of three or four students to complete as a project—checking, revising, and approving one another's work.

Reading and Thinking Critically [pp. 9–10]
Not all reading is critical reading. Asking questions while reading is the best way to develop the abilities to analyze, make inferences, synthesize, and evaluate. You can also suggest some of these other techniques to promote critical thinking and reading:
- Make predictions as you read.
- Note any changes of opinion you have as you read and reread.
- Pay attention to patterns—and to elements that disrupt the patterns.
- Look for any significant shifts in meaning, tone, plot, point of view, etc.
- Mark passages that are especially memorable, ones that you might use in a paper.
- Identify the selection's most important images, symbols, and scenes.
- Think about the writer's options; imagine ways the writer could have done something differently.
- Compare the selection with other works that are similar in some way; make comparisons to movies, songs, TV shows, or advertisements.
- Look away from the text occasionally and jot down your reactions.
- Freewrite for five to ten minutes immediately after reading a selection.
- Think about how you would describe this work to a friend or relative.

Self-Questioning (inventing ideas) [p. 10–11]
Here are some possible responses to the invention questions:
1. Eveline's home life is dreary, routine, and oppressive.
2. In her new life with Frank, Eveline expects to gain freedom, respect, adventure—and maybe love.
3. Since Eveline apparently knows very little about Frank or Buenos Ayres, her expectations seem to be based mainly on hopes and wishes.
4. The dust is a symbol of the dry stagnation of Eveline's life.
5. Dusty cretonne, a yellowing photograph of a priest, a broken harmonium, a "coloured print of the promises made to the Blessed Margaret Mary Alacoque" (which would be promises of lifelong virginity): these suggest decay and the denial of a vital life.
6. Eveline is "over nineteen." Probably she is around twenty years old, a time when one usually reaches adulthood and is making life decisions.
7. Eveline's father is an alcoholic, selfish, demanding tyrant, who—like most of his kind—has moments of tenderness. His being in "a bad way" means that he is drunk.

5

8. Eveline sometimes thinks of him as an overgrown child in need of care, like the rest of her siblings. But she also fears his violence and resents his making her beg for money to feed the family.

9. Eveline's mother led a "life of commonplace sacrifices closing in final craziness." Eveline identifies so closely with her mother that she has adopted her dead mother's self-sacrificing role in the family.

10. Eveline feels sorry about the pitiful quality of her mother's life and respects her memory. But at the same time, she wants to avoid being trapped into simply reliving her mother's dreary existence.

11. Eveline's mother, influenced by her religion, believes that pleasure in life must be paid for later with pain. When she says, "The end of pleasure is pain," she may be thinking of sexual pleasures, which, for a woman, can end in the pain of childbirth and the toil of caring for the child. She seems to be simply worn out by having too little money to care for too many children.

12. Eveline's father knows about good-for-nothing men who make promises they may not keep, and sailors have a reputation for having "a girl in every port." Her father also has a good reason for wanting his daughter to stay at home instead of marrying, since she takes care of him and his young children.

13. Frank is purposely not well defined in the story. He seems cheerful and devoted, but Eveline has not known him long: "It seemed a few weeks ago."

14. Eveline surely has a romanticized view of what married life with Frank will be like. Yet her father might justifiably be concerned that she is too inexperienced to marry and move to a foreign land.

15. Eveline has been a virtual slave to her father, seemingly because she promised her dying mother "to keep the home together as long as she could." But the modern reader sees her as having quite fulfilled her duty to her father by now.

16. Eveline holds conflicting views that she has a "right to happiness" and that she has a duty to keep her promise to her mother to serve the family. Her sense of duty to others wins out over any sense of her right to a life of her own.

17. Although she feels affection for her brothers, one is dead and the other is gone all the time decorating churches.

18. Eveline is "like a helpless animal," paralyzed by the lights of an oncoming car. She seems incapable of exercising free will. She is afraid of freedom, the unknown, and the spiritual consequences of breaking her vow to her mother.

19. Eveline's terror paralyzes her and overwhelms any other emotion she might feel at the dock. Also, Frank has seemed to be more a symbol of freedom than a real person. To respond with "love or farewell or recognition" would require that she see him as a human being.

20. Answers will surely vary here. One might say that running away to a new life is Eveline's one chance for happiness, and she refuses it—rightly or wrongly—out of fear. Others might say that eloping to Buenos Ayres with a lighthearted drifter whom she barely knows is not the wisest decision a woman could make.

Directed Freewriting / Problem Solving / Clustering [pp. 11–15]

The material generated through these invention methods will be similar to the information resulting from the questions above. You may find that one technique works best for you and that your students prefer another. Encourage them to try the various methods so that they will have more options for discovering ideas to write about.

Finding the Theme / Stating the Thesis [pp. 15–17]

You will surely want to discuss this essential material with your students and be sure they understand the difference between a *topic* and a *thesis statement*. Tell them also not to worry if at first they cannot discover the theme of a piece. It takes practice in analytical reading to develop the ability to see how the parts of a literary work dovetail to reveal the meaning of the whole. We offer further help with determining theme in later chapters.

Making Connections

→Compare Eveline to Connie in "Where Are You Going, Where Have You Been?" Consider their reactions to the men who want to take them away from home? Which one made the smarter decision?

Chapter 2 The Writing Process [pp. 18–31]

Organization, which requires hard, clear thinking, is one of the most difficult elements of the writing process for students to handle. Most writing specialists agree that compiling a formal outline is unnecessary, but most also agree that devising some plan is essential. Students should understand, though, that the plan can always be modified as the writing proceeds.

The plan can be as simple as recording the main points of the essay in the order to be followed. But we feel strongly that these points should be stated as sentences, not merely as topics, in order to make clear the direction of the writer's thoughts (as well as to make sure that those thoughts *have* some direction). Students who merely jot down topics sometimes experience difficulty in keeping their essays unified, because as they write, their ideas veer off in directions not relevant to the thesis.

In this chapter, we suggest ways to organize an essay about a literary work and offer advice about how to develop the ideas in this plan.

Writing Rituals May Help in Getting Started

Most experienced writers perform—perhaps unconsciously—little rituals that help them get started. Some people, for instance, always write in the same place—in a comfortable chair, at a desk, at the kitchen table, perhaps lying on the living room rug. It does not matter where a person writes, but having an established place may help to get the process going when writing needs to be done. Some people sharpen pencils before they start or find a favorite pen. Some always compose at the keyboard. Some get themselves a cup of coffee or a soft drink to keep their strength up during this arduous undertaking. You may want to discuss writing rituals with your students. If they have none, suggest that they try to establish some just in case these preparations may help to spark the writing process.

Arguing Your Interpretation [pp. 18–19]

Here is a chance to relate writing about literature to good principles of writing in general. With your class, discuss the meaning of these terms: claims, evidence, reasoning, and refutation. Look for an editorial or letter to the editor in the school or community newspaper as an example, and invite students to assess the elements of the piece's argument.

Building an Effective Argument [pp. 20–21]

For many people *argument* is a negative term. Perhaps it makes them think of unpleasant shouting matches and bitter disagreements. We hear and see these nasty, noisy clashes on the radio and TV all the time. But these are not examples of good arguments. They substitute volume and name calling for reasoning and evidence. So it's important for students to see that arguing is a constructive process, one in which they identify an issue for possible debate, take a position on that issue, analyze their position, and try to persuade others that their position is worth sharing or at least reasonable. The general procedure we outline on page 19 will guide them through this process. This plan is one they can use throughout college.

Be sure to make the connection that persuading readers of a point of view on a literary work is similar to persuasion of any sort. Literary critics may have some advantage because the readers usually do not already have firm opinions of their own: a good argument can stand on its own rather than working upstream against preexisting judgments.

Questions for Consideration (using adequate detail) [p. 22]

We think the sample paragraph is adequately developed. Here are the details used to support the main point (the topic sentence):

- Eveline's brothers and sisters are grown.
- Her mother is dead.
- Her father will be alone.
- He has a drinking problem.
- He is getting old.
- She thinks he will miss her.
- She feels she is abandoning her father.
- She has written to him to ease the blow.
- The letter soothes her conscience.

Students may mention the following additional details as possible support for the main idea of the paragraph:

- Tizzy Dunn and the Walters (possibly former friends of her father) are gone; also gone is the priest who was his school friend.
- "Latterly he had begun to threaten her"; she apparently forgets this fear—or discounts it, even though "now she has nobody to protect her."
- "Sometimes he could be very nice"; she remembers when he took care of her one day when she was sick and when he played with the children on a picnic long ago.

The writer introduces personal opinion in the final sentence: "Eveline *seems to* feel . . . "

Most students will probably agree that the interpretation is valid, but some may disagree about whether Eveline's younger brothers and sisters (entrusted to her care by her dying mother) are indeed "grown up" by the time she considers leaving with Frank. Some might argue also that Eveline writes the letter to her father, not out of consideration for his feelings, but as a means of avoiding a bitter confrontation with him.

8

Class Activity on Introductions and Conclusions [pp. 23–26]

You will want to be sure your students understand all the material in this chapter—especially the section on distinguishing critical details from plot details so that they can successfully maintain a critical focus in their papers. But since an effective opening and closing are crucial to the success of an essay, you may want to give your students extra practice in writing these special kinds of paragraphs.

Ask your students to devise a thesis statement for a paper about a work of literature they have read recently. Then have them write only the introduction and conclusion for such a paper. After they have completed their paragraphs, you could have them exchange papers and do peer evaluation. Write the following questions on the board and ask your students to respond (concerning a fellow student's paper) in writing.

ABOUT THE INTRODUCTORY PARAGRAPH:
1. Is the main point of the (intended) paper made clear?
2. Is the topic introduced gracefully? Or is it too bluntly stated?
3. Is the thesis itself interesting? Or is it too obvious?
4. Would you want to continue reading a paper that began with this introduction?

ABOUT THE CONCLUSION:
1. Does it simply repeat the introduction?
2. Does it convincingly establish the main point of the paper?
3. Does it have an emphatic final sentence?

Ideas and Suggestions for a First Writing Assignment

You may want your students to apply some of the procedures for prewriting and drafting that they have been studying in these first two chapters. We suggest having them write a draft of an essay about Kate Chopin's "The Story of an Hour" [pages 215–16]. Here are some directions you might give them:

1. Read the story.
2. Then turn to Chart 6-1 at the end of Chapter 6, and see how many of the questions you can answer after a single reading. But do not be discouraged if you can respond to only a few.
3. Reread the story again, paying attention to the details. Then look once more at the questions in Chart 6-1 to see how many more of them you can answer.
4. Use one or more of the prewriting techniques discussed in Chapter 1 to come up with ideas for writing. You can use self-questioning, directed freewriting, clustering, or whatever works for you.
5. Then devise a thesis (or claim), and draw up a list of details to develop and support it.
6. Write a draft of your interpretation.

If students have problems coming up with an approach to this story, here are some ideas for writing that might help them:

1. In interpreting the story, focus on Mrs. Mallard's life and character to show why she reacts as she does to news of her husband's death. Why was she previously unaware of the "subtle and elusive" thoughts that come to her as she sits in her room? Why do other characters misread her reaction?
2. Focus on the imagery—the appeals to the senses—that Chopin uses to surround

9

Mrs. Mallard. Write about how the sights, sounds, smells, and sensations contribute to the reader's understanding of Mrs. Mallard's experience.

You can, of course, also use the questions for discussion and writing that follow the story [p. 217].

Other stories in the Anthology of Short Fiction that might provide students with interesting characters to analyze or respond to are Richard Wright's "The Man Who Was Almost a Man," Sherwood Anderson's "Hands," Tillie Olsen's "I Stand Here Ironing," John Updike's "A & P," and John Steinbeck's "The Chrysanthemums."

Chapter 3 Writing a Convincing Argument [pp. 32–47]

This chapter expands the concept, introduced in Chapter 2, that interpreting a literary work involves making an argument. As a way of thinking about how the elements of argument apply to interpreting literature, a discussion of a controversial work or an element in a work might be useful. We don't mean a classroom debate on an issue, but an exploration of where we get our opinions and why we accept some interpretations and not others. Here's a reading and writing activity you might use (or adapt); you might want to assign it before assigning the rest of the chapter:

Have students read the story at the end of the chapter, "Love in L.A.," and write a paragraph (or a page) in which they express their reactions to Jake, the main character. Tell students to be prepared to share their writings with the class. You could also use a class Web site to carry out the first part of this activity. Some questions you might pose: What do you think of Jake? What kind of person is he? Is he a positive or negative character? What are his good and bad qualities? Do you know people like him? Would you consider having him as a friend? If you were Mariana, would you have given your number to him? Then ask several students to read their assessments of Jake out loud. Or put them in groups of four or five to read and discuss their interpretations. Chances are they will not agree about Jake: some will like him more than others do. Then ask them to explain how they arrived at their opinions. At this point you might ask them to go back and look at the story again—to find particulars that support and explain their reactions. Also ask if the reactions of other students have caused them to rethink their feelings about Jake.

The point of this activity is not to reach agreement about Jake but to illustrate that interpretations vary and to encourage students to analyze why and how they form opinions about what they read. After reviewing and discussing the rest of the chapter, use the sample student essay to show how one student explained and supported his interpretation of Jake.

Interpreting and Arguing [p. 32]
An interpretation will be more effective if it is controversial, but it doesn't have to be controversial in the usual sense, like the arguments for and against capital punishment. Both the student papers in Part I (on "Eveline" and "Love in L.A.") argue for interpretations that few people would come to harsh words over. But there are other ways to interpret these stories, and an awareness of this fact gives the process of writing about literature some dynamic tension. Once students have roughed out their interpretations,

10

have them ask this question: What other way(s) can this selection be interpreted? Even if they never directly refute other views, the question will help firm up their own opinions.

Identifying Issues [pp. 32–33]

Many students won't be familiar with writing a literary essay that addresses an issue. But identifying an issue—and formulating a claim (or thesis) about that issue—will help students to write papers that do more than summarize content and make obvious points.

In Chapter 3 we define an issue as a question with no obvious or clear answer. You'll want to give students plenty of practice in asking questions about literary works, a prewriting process that's explained and illustrated in Chapter 2 of the main text. This questioning is a vital part of argumentative writing. You can illustrate the value of identifying issues by referring to the debates on some current hot topics. For instance, a key issue in the debate about capital punishment is whether or not the death penalty acts as a deterrent to violent crime. How you answer that question will determine the way you argue your position on this topic. An issue, then, is a pivotal point around which an argument develops. Here are some other debates and possible key issues:

> Immigration: What effects do illegal immigrants have on the economy?
> Same-sex marriage: How will gay marriage affect the nuclear family?
> Abortion: When does life begin?
> Capital punishment: Does the death penalty deter crime?

You don't need or want to debate these topics. You just want to demonstrate what an issue is and how it determines the direction of the discussion.

Issues in literature aren't necessarily as clear-cut as they are for social problems and political debates, but the interpretation of a literary work will often depend on answering one or two key questions. In Chapter 5, we show how two students identify several important questions in developing their interpretations. The questions and writing prompts that we provide throughout the book will guide students to issues they can use for arguing their interpretations. Here are some examples:

"Good Country People"	What does [the story] say about uniqueness and imperfection? [p. 200]
"The Lesson"	Why doesn't Sylvia get the point of the lesson? Why is she angry enough to want "to punch somebody in the mouth"? [p. 317]
"The Red Convertible"	Why does Lyman send the car into the river? Why are the car's lights left on? [p. 331]
"My Papa's Waltz"	What is the speaker's attitude toward his father? [p. 345]
"Mending Wall"	How does the speaker feel about walls? [p. 412]
"Execution"	What is the speaker's attitude toward his coach? Do you think he likes or admires him? [p. 445]
Othello	How do race and racism contribute to Othello's downfall? [p. 670]
Trifles	Describe your reaction to the decision made by Mrs. Peters and Mrs. Hale to hide the dead bird from the men. Did they do the right thing? [p. 733]

Chapter 17, "Writing About Dramatic Structure," offers additional instruction about defining and using issues in a literary interpretation [pp. 521–22].

Making Claims [p. 34]

As we point out in the main text, a paper's main claim is the same as its thesis, a term that students may be more familiar with. We think the term *claim* is stronger because it implies that the writer must prove something: a claim is debatable, but a thesis statement might not be. In addition to the main claim, writers make smaller supporting claims, which are analogous to "topic sentences" in the terminology of a conventional academic composition.

If you work with students to identify key issues in a selection and to phrase those issues as questions, then it's usually easy to see that claims are the debatable answers to those questions. Sometimes a student may come up with a claim first. It's helpful, then, to ask, "What key question about the work does your claim answer? What issue does your argument resolve?" We think that the more students understand the relationship between issues and claims, the better able they'll be to argue their interpretations. You should probably not expect students to produce full-blown arguments early in the semester. It's more realistic to start by giving them plenty of practice in formulating issues and experimenting with making various claims about the literature they read.

Using Evidence [pp. 34–35]

We're tempted to say that writers can never have enough evidence to support their claims. That's an overstatement, of course, but we have found that it's important (and often necessary) to challenge students with questions like, "Why do you think that?" and "Where did you get that idea?" It's also important to let students know that you are not denigrating or dismissing their interpretations; you just want them to recognize the value of using solid evidence to support their ideas.

There are two pitfalls that you may want to help students avoid in their use of evidence. The first is quoting or summarizing long passages from the literary selection, which often amounts to padding and usually detracts from the main argument. Audience awareness is the key to avoiding this problem: remind students that their readers have already read the selection and don't need extensive quotations and detailed plot summaries to see where the interpretation comes from.

The second potential pitfall is relying too much on the ideas and opinions of others. Many instructors limit the use of background materials and secondary sources, especially early in the semester. The first two student papers that we present in Part I (at the end of Chapters 3 and 4) were written by students who used only the primary text to develop their interpretations. In Chapter 5 we demonstrate how one of those students expanded and substantiated her initial observations by using quotations and paraphrases from the published criticism about the work she had interpreted.

Using Reasoning [pp. 35–36]

Reasoning is essential to interpretation; it involves making connections and drawing conclusions. We don't think it's necessary to spend time studying enthymemes, syllogisms, or logical fallacies in a course on writing about literature. As we point out in the main text, reasoning simply means *explaining* how the evidence relates to the claims.

12

Inexperienced writers will sometimes point to pieces of evidence and assume that their readers will understand what the evidence shows. The examples we present on pp. 36–37 in the main text illustrate the basic pattern of making a claim, citing the evidence, and explaining how the evidence supports the claim. Without that last step, the interpretation doesn't get made.

Answering Opposing Views [p. 37]
Some people think that any mention of a different opinion or an alternative position weakens their interpretation. But in many cases a weak argument can be made stronger by recognizing and using alternative interpretations to advance one's own position. In Chapter 13, "Writing About Persona and Tone," we demonstrate how looking at different reactions to the speaker in "My Papa's Waltz" can lead to the formulation of a productive thesis or claim about the poem and its tone.

The two examples on page 37 in Chapter 3 illustrate how the student writers use opposing views to set up their own interpretations. The rhetorical formula is a rather simple one: "Other readers may think . . .but I think. . . ." But it is not enough, of course, just to acknowledge or describe the opposing view; one has to *argue* against it—i.e., to present a convincing interpretation, with evidence and reasoning.

Organizing Your Argument [pp. 38–41]
In this section we present an all-purpose outline for arguing an interpretation [p. 38] and several variations (or alternate approaches). We think that outlining is an important step in presenting a clear interpretation. That's why we present the sample plans for two student papers [pp. 38, 39]. We also show how to flesh out an outline by subdividing the major claim into minor supporting claims and indicating the specifics that support these claims [p. 39]. We also believe strongly in the value of making an outline of the first draft—as a way of checking the arrangement of ideas and the sufficiency of the evidence. See pages 51–53 in Chapter 4, "The Rewriting Process."

Using the Inductive Approach [pp. 38–40]
The inductive method is the easiest way to develop an interpretation of a literary work, primarily because it mirrors the way that most people read and respond to a selection. The major requirement for a strong inductive argument is that the evidence be sufficient and relevant. Just a few points and quotations won't sustain an interpretation. A prewriting activity, like freewriting or clustering, will help to expose an inadequacy of evidence. Rereading with the major and minor claims in mind—and taking notes—are essential steps in using the inductive process.

Making a Counterargument [p. 40]
A favorite strategy of literary critics is to review the major interpretations of other critics, refute and reject them in some way, and then offer the writer's own new and improved interpretation. Obviously, this approach will work only if the critic is familiar with a wide range of other interpretations. For most student writers this would mean doing research and reading a number of secondary sources. The example that we give in the main text [p. 40], however, is built on hypothetical (but reasonable) answers to the key issues in "Eveline." Students can get some interpretations to argue against from class discussions and small group work. But when they consult secondary sources, they may have to look

again at their claims and revise their interpretations extensively, as Wendy Dennison did in her essay on "Eveline" [see Chapter 5, pp. 87–92].

As a short essay assignment, a journal activity, or an essay exam, challenge students to write a counterargument in response to an interpretation that you give to them. For example, ask them to argue against the claim that Jig, the young woman in the story "Hills Like White Elephants" [pp. 240–42], will give in to her lover and have an abortion. Or argue against the claim that the Duke in Browning's "My Last Duchess" [p. 457] unwittingly reveals too much of his cruel nature and has blown the chance to get a new duchess with a big dowry. At the end of Chapter 13 [pp. 353–56], you will find a student response to the poem "To an Athlete Dying Young," which you can also use in a counterargument assignment.

Arguing Through Comparison [pp. 40–41]

Comparisons of literary selections, or of elements within selections, can be effective in clarifying and advancing an interpretation. But merely comparing one theme or one character to another isn't necessarily meaningful. A successful comparison, like any successful argument, begins with a clearly articulated, focused, and significant claim. You'll want to stress that comparisons should make a point, that they should support a claim. The examples on pages 40–41 focus on comparing the main characters from two different stories, but the goal in both cases is to identify important insights about the characters and to explain the themes these characters exemplify.

Clear organization is also crucial to the success of a comparison argument. On pages 40–41, we explain and illustrate the two major options for organizing a comparison: the block pattern and the alternating pattern. A third option is to mix the two patterns, presenting most of the comparison in a block pattern and then summarizing the minor claims in an alternating pattern, which will highlight and emphasize the key similarities or differences. Whatever approach a writer takes, outlining—both before and after composing a draft—will save everyone a lot of grief.

Sample Student Essay [pp. 41–44]

This essay of about 550 words is a model for your students to examine and perhaps follow. The annotations in the margins identify claims, evidence, refutation, and conclusion, elements discussed in the text directly before the sample paper. The story "Love in L.A." follows the student paper, and if you wish you can have students read this very brief piece before the paper. However, we believe that reading the paper will spark students' interest in the story. After reading both, they can decide whether they agree with Carter's interpretation.

One way to discuss the paper is to look at the general statements, such as "Jake's self-concept is built on lies," and then have students identify the specific details that Carter uses to support each one. This impresses upon your class that each generalization needs specific support. For instance, how do we know that "Mariana isn't buying any of his lines"? What other support could Carter use as evidence of Mariana's unspoken thoughts?

You can also note the way the conclusion ties back into the introduction. It restates the main idea about self-delusion and reuses an image from the introduction, the traffic jam in which nothing is moving forward. In this way, both the major claim and the minor claim are brought together as part of the concluding comments. After students

14

write the first draft of their own papers, they can tinker with the opening and closing to match them up in a similar way.

LOVE IN L.A. by Dagoberto Gilb [pp. 45–47]

One fruitful way to approach "Love in L.A." is through the characterization of Jake, on whom the story focuses. While we are given no physical description of him, we know he's wearing "less than new but not unhip clothes," and we can assume he must be fairly good looking because Mariana, whose brand new car he has just crunched, continually smiles at him. He "sounded genuine," as he cons her into believing his effortlessly smooth string of lies. Jake has no job but fantasizes about the luxurious car he would drive and the exotic lifestyle he would lead if he had the "advantages" of "a steady occupation." In reality, we know he has been at loose ends for quite some time: "one of his few clear-cut accomplishments over the years" is that his aging Buick is "clean except for a few minor dings." The Buick is sturdy, not easily damaged, doesn't sustain even a scratch—just as Jake is untouched by scrapes, like this accident, which he caused through his daydreaming. The setting of the story is apt since Los Angeles is a city famous for its crowded freeways and ubiquitous cars. And although cars are essential for many L.A. residents, for Jake a luxurious new car has become the object of intense longing. Ironically, the freedom he enjoys by being jobless is what keeps him from any realistic hope of achieving his dream. We see throughout the story that appearances and showiness matter to him, but truth and ethics count for nothing. His life is stalled, just like his car on the freeway.

The title perhaps has a double meaning. It may suggest Jake's love for sexy cars as well as his lust for Mariana, neither of which involves real love in any meaningful way. The final paragraph neatly captures the essence of Jake's character. Having dodged his responsibility for the accident, he drives away, reveling in his freedom, dreaming about an "FM stereo radio and crushed velvet interior and the new car smell" that would make his life perfection. But we suspect that he may eventually have an awakening and discover that, in the words of Kris Kristofferson, "Freedom's just another word for nothing left to lose."

Questions for Discussion and Writing
1. Does Jake have anything in common with his Buick? How about Mariana and her new Toyota? Does she share any attributes with her car?
2. What do you think the title means?
3. Do you think Jake might feel guilty about how he scammed Mariana? What might he regret?
4. How much of what Jake says and does is a "performance"—of pretending to be somebody he isn't and trying to fool an audience? How about Mariana? In what ways does she pretend to be someone different and to put on an act for Jake? Write an essay arguing for this interpretation of the story.
5. How does the last paragraph capture the essence of Jake's character?

Making Connections
→Compare Jake with the larcenous Bible salesman in Flannery O'Connor's "Good Country People." Which do you find more unprincipled?

→Compare the encounter between Jake and Mariana to the one between Betty and Bill in the play *Sure Thing* by David Ives.

Chapter 4 The Rewriting Process [pp. 48–70]

Nancy Sommers's award-winning article, "Revision Strategies of Student Writers and Experienced Adult Writers" [*College Composition and Communication* 31 (Dec. 1980): 378–88], reveals that student writers typically do little revising—even when they *think* they have. Their alterations fall into the category of editing—cosmetic changes—rather than a true re-visioning of the writing. So, you will probably need to monitor your students' revising process by looking at drafts and suggesting improvements if you want to be sure that they learn to revise in a meaningful way.

The sample student paper that appears in its first draft in Chapter 2 and in its revised version at the end of this chapter provides a good model of an essay that is much improved by revision. Our student Wendy outlined her first draft and discovered that she had a paragraph that lacked support and a couple of points out of place. Making these changes produced a far better paper, and the effort proved well worth her time, raising her grade considerably.

We are sold on outlining after the writing [see pp. 51–53 in the main text]. Since many writers need to discover and refine their reactions and ideas as they write, they can't make detailed plans before they begin a draft; the after-the-writing outline lets them see whether their first draft is orderly and coherent or whether it wanders around, has underdeveloped paragraphs, and repeats ideas.

The exercises in this chapter concern revision at the sentence level—not as crucial as global revision but still essential for effective writing.

Revising in Peer Groups [pp. 49–51]

Not all teachers are comfortable with using student writing groups, but the practice has several significant advantages: students develop a greater sense of audience; they become more involved in the class; they see writing that is better and worse than their own; and the instructor doesn't have to do all the work of leading discussions and responding to papers. Here are some general recommendations and points to consider concerning pairs and groups:

1. Think carefully about whether you want students to stay with the same partner or group for most of the semester or change around. Stable groups promote more rapport and commitment, but they can grow stale or develop interpersonal problems.
2. Have students stay with the same partner for peer review of essays, but occasionally put pairs together or tell students to solicit a second (or even a third) opinion from another partner. If peer advice is contradictory, as it sometimes is, allow the students to decide which suggestions to follow. Doing multiple peer responses will virtually assure that everyone gets some good advice. And sorting out the bad feedback from the good is a valuable learning experience.
3. Provide structure for the groups or pairs, especially in the early stages. Suggest a goal for the peer response work, such as: "Check to see whether your partner's

16

essay has a good, clear thesis," or "Look for places where a concrete example or detail would help." Let groups know whether their goal is to report back to the class or to brainstorm ideas for writing outside of class.

4. Be active during pair and group work—don't sit behind the desk. Wander around and eavesdrop or sit in on a group once in a while. Be open to individual questions as you walk around the classroom.

Peer Evaluation Checklist [p. 50]

These questions are designed to help students learn to evaluate their own or other students' papers. We have found that learning to be good editors helps students to become good writers. You might find it useful to duplicate this checklist, leaving spaces so that your students can write directly on the sheets during peer evaluation sessions.

Combining for Conciseness: Sentence Combining Exercise [pp. 58–59]

Responses will vary, of course.

1. The second common stereotype, usually symbolizing sexual temptation, is the dark lady.
2. As the title suggests, Kate Chopin's short story "The Storm" shows how the characters react during a cyclone.
3. Because Emily Dickinson's poetry can be extremely elliptical, readers often have difficulty discovering the literal meaning.
4. There are three major things to consider in understanding Goodman Brown's character: what the author tells us about Brown, what Brown himself says and does, and what other people say to and about him.
5. Most of the humorous incidents that inspire Walter Mitty's fantasies fall into two groups, the first illustrating his desire to be in charge of the situation.

Varying the Pattern [pp. 59–60]

Emphasis is usually achieved when the most important information is placed near the end of the sentence. Advise your students to shift less important modifiers (whether words, clauses, or phrases) to the front of the sentence. For example, in the first sentence of the exercise, "when she was a child" should be moved out of the emphatic or "stress" position at the end and placed somewhere earlier in the sentence. The most important information (and the most surprising) is that Wharton was "not allowed to have paper on which to write" and that should be placed at the end of the sentence.

Exercise on Style [p. 60]

Students will be able to combine sentences in several ways; here are some likely constructions:

1. Edith Wharton, who was born into a rich, upper-class family, was, as a child, not allowed to have paper on which to write.
    Or: Born into a rich, upper-class family, Edith Wharton, as a child, was not allowed to have paper to write on.
2. Because her governesses never taught her how to organize ideas in writing, she had to ask her friend Walter Berry to help write her book on the decoration of houses.
3. When she was 23 years old, Edith married Teddy Wharton, who always carried a

17

one-thousand dollar bill in his wallet—just in case she wanted anything.
4. Although her good friend Henry James helped her to improve her novels, Wharton's books invariably sold far more copies than his.
5. Following World War I, she was presented the highest award given by the French government—the Legion of Honor—for her refugee relief activities.

Exercise on Passive Voice [p. 62]

Answers may vary somewhat.
1. Creon brutalizes Antigone because of her struggle to achieve justice.
2. Antigone's tirade against his unbending authority did not convince Creon.
3. The play pitted male against female.
4. Society may experience considerable benefit if someone wins even a small point against a tyrant.
5. Creon's exercise of iron-bound authority causes the tragedy.

Exercise on Word Choice [p. 63]

Responses will vary, of course; here are some possibilities:
1. The first sentence of "A Good Man Is Hard to Find" foreshadows the grandmother's violent end at the story's conclusion.
2. The family's conversations reveal their self-absorption and ignorance.
3. Lying, untruths, and self-deception abound in this story.
4. Three sinister-looking strangers approach the family after their car accident.
5. Each character speaks in a comically disturbing idiom.

Chapter 5 Researched Writing [pp. 71–101]

We placed this chapter in the first part of the book so that it will be available whenever you and your students are ready to undertake researched writing. We strongly recommend that you assign and discuss Chapters 1 through 4, but we think you may want to skip over Chapter 5 and come back to it later, after students have written about literature on their own.

One of the challenges of researched writing is deciding how much weight to give to secondary sources. Even experienced writers are intimidated by the views and opinions of critics and scholars; they feel they don't have anything to say about a literary work that hasn't already been said. This feeling often results in a researched essay that amounts to little more than a compilation of quotations and paraphrases with very little input from the student writer. For this reason, we suggest that you follow the procedure illustrated by the sample student paper in Chapter 5: have students write a draft of their argument or interpretation before they consult secondary sources. That's what our student Wendy Dennison did with her analysis of "Eveline," and we think it's a good way to ensure that a student's own ideas and opinions will not get lost in the time-consuming business of finding sources and documenting them. In this paradigm, students use secondary sources to expand and support their understanding of a literary work, not as a replacement for their own thoughts.

Focusing the Coverage

Another common problem with research assignments is the tendency to take on a topic that is too broad for the time frame and the available sources. Beginning with a response statement or preliminary draft will help to keep the coverage manageable. Another approach (which also works for writing that does not rely on research) is to identify a problem to be solved and focus it with a *thesis question* to be answered. Students will write with greater engagement if they can discover some problem concerning a literary work, one that genuinely interests them and that they can set out to solve in their writing and research. For example, someone writing about *Fences* [Chapter 18] might wonder, as many readers do, how to interpret the paradoxical and contradictory nature of the play's protagonist, Troy Maxson. A question that focuses this problem might be phrased like this:

> Is Troy Maxson a hero or a failure, is he to be admired or pitied?

And the thesis statement would then involve the writer's solution of the problem:

> Troy Maxson is a modern hero who overcame racism and economic adversity, but alienated his son and betrayed his wife.

Helping Students Complete a Documented Paper

Most students find procrastination a major problem when they attempt to write using secondary materials. Setting a clear schedule with well-defined checkpoints along the way will help these students enormously. Here is a list of checkpoints you might want to have them meet. Assign your own dates.

1. Discuss chosen topic in conference with you—at least, those who are having trouble deciding on an approach.
2. Turn in thesis question or problem for approval.
3. Prepare a preliminary draft of the argument or interpretation to get feedback from peer groups and instructor. Another option is to have students turn in an outline or plan for approval at this point.
4. Turn in a preliminary bibliography so you can check for relevance and form.
5. Bring to class a substantial number of note cards or electronic notes—to be sure they are making progress and handling paraphrases and quotations appropriately.
6. Pass out open-book quiz on MLA style; a sample quiz is included at the end of this chapter in this manual.
7. Bring a section of the rough draft along with note cards or electronic notes to class—or have them bring notes and actually write a section in class—so that you can check how well they are integrating sources and how accurate their documentation is.
8. Bring a draft of the paper to get feedback from peer groups.

Also call your students' attention to the suggestions about conducting research [pp. 71–77], taking notes [p. 77–80], devising a working outline [pp. 80–81], writing a first draft [p. 81], organizing notes [pp. 81–82], and rewriting and editing [pp. 85–87]. These brief discussions reinforce the importance of following a process and emphasize the notion that good writing develops in stages.

Using the Online Catalog [p. 73], Indexes and Databases [pp. 73–74]

The library's computers provide an overwhelming number of sources and service options. With so many possibilities, it's important that students take an orientation course if they haven't already done so. You may want to arrange a tour or an orientation session with your school's librarian. Many libraries can tailor their presentations to fit the needs of a specific assignment, so even students who already know how to use the online services can benefit from such a session. Libraries are also constantly updating their resources, so each year new research tools are available. Students will also have to spend some time with these data systems to find out how they work and how useful they are. But it's time well spent. Once students get the hang of it, they will be able to research a topic with astonishing ease and thoroughness.

Using the Internet [pp. 75–77]

The Internet and the Web give students access to a great deal of information that is often more current than anything available in printed sources, and the Web's hypertext feature allows them to explore a topic quickly and thoroughly. Nonetheless, there are a couple of serious pitfalls in using the Web that you might want to point out.

First, it's difficult to know how to judge the vast array of information that's available. Students will find research reports, online journals, and government publications. But they will also find unsupported opinion, propaganda, inaccurate information, and tasteless junk. Anyone can publish on the Web; there is no editorial board to screen the material. So, researchers must apply sound judgment in evaluating each of their electronic sources, just as they would the print sources that they find in the library. Encourage students to check the information against other sources, and carefully consider the credentials—and the biases—of the person or organization supplying the data. The suggestions [on pages 76 and 77] will help them. In addition, your librarians may have created and posted additional vetted, discipline-specific Web site recommendations. You many want to institute a policy of not allowing the use of Internet-only sources without approval.

Second, searching on the Internet, especially on the World Wide Web, can eat up a lot of valuable time. Because it's easy to move from site to site through numerous interlinked sources, it's possible to spend hours browsing the Web. Students' time might be better spent reading their source materials, taking notes, and writing the paper. To avoid wasting time, students should always go to the Web for specific purposes, skim the sites first, and note the size and downloading time of a document before printing it out. (The slow downloading time on some equipment can consume a lot of time.)

Using Reference Works in Print [p. 77]

Scheduling a library tour may provide a student's first trip to the library and can introduce the class to the print and other materials the university makes available to students. A quick scavenger hunt activity can be a useful start to good library habits.

Working with Sources [pp. 77–81]
We still think that note cards are a productive way to record secondary source material. They're highly portable and can be easily arranged and rearranged when it comes time to construct a working outline. But the electronic age has made the note card method seem outdated and inefficient. Today's students may prefer to highlight useful passages from photocopied or downloaded sources and type them into a computer file. They can then use the cut-and-paste function to group ideas and to help them visualize the arrangement they might follow in their paper. If they have also typed out the sources of these quotations and/or paraphrases in MLA style, they can then cut and paste them alphabetically on the Works Cited page.

Using a Research Notebook [pp. 78, 79]
A Research Notebook, though a more significant investment of time at the research stage, becomes a history of students' actions and thinking for the final paper. Students find themselves shaping their ideas and theses as they progress and are set to write a draft at the end of the process.

> You can instruct students to begin their notebooks with these entries:
> 1. Write down your topic and record your thoughts about it. Explain why you are interested in the topic and what you want to learn about it.
> 2. Discuss the topic with your instructor and with others who might be familiar with it. Record their reactions, and use their feedback to explain how you can limit the scope of the topic to make it more manageable.
> 3. Formulate several questions that you will try to answer with your research.
> 4. Outline your search plan: Where are you likely to find relevant information? What kinds of sources will you be using? Which ones will you look at first? Which indexes and databases should you use?

Then, as students read and take notes, they use the divided-page format to record the results of their research.

Instructors who use this method of conducting research think it is more efficient than starting with index cards because a student can keep all the information in a single convenient place, which the instructor can check from time to time to monitor progress and give advice. More important, the response side of the notebook shows the evolution of the student's thinking and lets her articulate questions that arise as she reads and processes the information from secondary sources. This procedure steers the student away from a cut-and-paste style of research writing because it encourages synthesis and analysis throughout the project. At the same time, it also helps writers to identify which ideas are their own and which ones they picked up along the way—an important distinction that guards against inadvertent plagiarism and allows them to claim their own views and contributions with confidence.

Summarizing, Paraphrasing, and Quoting [p. 80]
Most students will benefit from practice on how to write an acceptable paraphrase. If you want, photocopy a page or two from a critical article, perhaps about a work that you've

already covered in class. Ask students to write paraphrases of two passages from these works of criticism; you can even specify the passages to work on. To get students in the habit of best practices, you might include instructions on appropriate attribution and citation methods at this stage. Have them prepare their individual paraphrases and then meet in groups to compare results.

Devising a Working Outline [p. 80]

Even professional writers disagree about the value of outlining. But whatever your thoughts and feelings about outlines, you need to consider their advantages as an efficient way for your students to create and evaluate the organization of their writing. Sometimes an outline is a good way for students to move from the prewriting and early research stage to making a draft. Such an outline can focus thinking, keep writers on track, and get them to think about how well the parts of an interpretation fit together. Or for writers who want to get their ideas down on paper right away, they can outline after they complete their first drafts to check for inadequate and inconsistent coverage—and decide where to place support materials from secondary sources. See pages 51–53 in the main text for more detail on the use of after-writing outlines.

Realize, too, that outlines come in many forms, some more flexible than others. Sometimes a simple listing of main points and their relevant supports will give all the direction a writer needs. For the more complicated task of researched writing, you may want your students to construct a formal outline that lays out the main ideas in full sentences and breaks them down into detailed subdivisions. Such outlines take time and effort, but they provide a solid basis for writing a complete and nearly finished draft. Whatever form you require of your students, let them know that any outline they make is a tentative plan that can be revised as they draft and redraft their writing.

Integrating Sources [pp. 82–84]

Stress that all three parts of in-text citations are crucial because readers need to know where the writer's own ideas stop and the views and opinions from the sources begin—and end. Advise students not to be afraid to let their sources show—that's the whole point of a researched essay—and encourage them to use lots of attributions to introduce and highlight their research (see p. 83). It will help if you give students a number of models to study and replicate. Some teachers use anonymous examples from student papers they've collected from previous classes. One of our colleagues uses an in-class exercise in which students select three note cards (or entries printed out from their computer file) on a particular subtopic or subject heading, each from a different source; they then write a paragraph on that subtopic, summarizing the main points and integrating quotations and paraphrases. The instructor then has students meet in small groups to review the effectiveness of these paragraphs; she also collects the paragraphs and uses them, usually in conference, to help students improve their skills at synthesizing researched materials.

Avoiding Plagiarism [pp. 84–85]

Students often commit plagiarism, both intentional and unintentional, because they are pressed for time and feel unsure of their own ideas and interpretations. The best way to counter these problems is to take students through all the steps of the writing process—prewriting, writing (drafting), revising, and editing—and to monitor them at each step. That's why we like to have students draft an essay in which they work out their own thoughts and opinions first (even if it's just in directed freewritings), and then consult secondary sources to support their views (as the sample documented essay in the main text illustrates). Use the list of checkpoints given earlier in this manual (pp. 24–25), and collect or review the materials produced at each point (notes, research notebooks, outlines, source cards, drafts, and so forth). A simple checkmark system or a grading rubric sheet can help you keep track of the progress a student makes on the way to completing the final version. Including a peer-review step also helps to ensure that students are working on the essays themselves, especially if you require them to make peer evaluations in writing and to submit these written evaluations with their revised drafts. Make sure that students understand that successfully completing all the stages of the process, including writing a peer response for someone else, will be part of the final grade.

Explanation of the MLA Documentation Style [pp. 93–101]
This section gives details on what to include in parenthetical citations and how to prepare the list of works cited. We have included sample entries for the most commonly used sources. Note that the *MLA Handbook for Writers of Research Papers*, (7th ed., 2009) now recommends italic type, especially in source citations.

Citing Online Publications [pp. 98–100]
For complete, authoritative explanations of the MLA style for citing sources from online sources and the World Wide Web, see the *MLA Handbook for Writers of Research Papers* (7th ed., 2009). The MLA also provides guidelines and updates of information on their Web site at www.mla.org. An excellent online guide for citing electronic sources can be found on the Library of Congress Web site at www.loc.gov/teachers/ usingprimarysources/mla.html. This page is especially good for citing unusual sources; it also provides links to a number of other citation guides on the Internet.

Quiz on the MLA Documentation Style
The following brief test—or it could function as a worksheet—will bring to your students' attention the details essential to accurately using MLA documentation.

Part I. Write correctly spaced and punctuated Works Cited entries using the following fabricated sources:
1. A third edition of a book named Grammar Is Fun by Oliver M. Battleax. The book was published by the Prentice Hall Book Publishers in New York, New York, in 1984.
2. An essay called Springsteen's Special Magic by Carla Mayhem in a collection of essays about rock and roll. The collection, edited by Tipper Gore, is entitled Jump On It, Baby. It came out in May 1988, published by Macmillan Publishing Company in New York City. The essay on Springsteen appears on pages 24 through 28.
3. An article called Madonna as Social Icon that was published in Cultural Currents in the summer of 2000 in volume 7 of that periodical (meaning a scholarly journal or magazine). Written by Camille Pretentious, the piece appeared on pages 27 through 32.

4. An article from the first page of section C in the New York Times of April 13, 1998. Entitled How to Train Your Bad Puppy, it was written by Morris E. Rich. It appeared on the New York Times Online database and was accessed through Nexis-Lexis Academic computer service on February 4, 1999.

Part II. Fill in the blanks.

The MLA style does away with _____ in source documentation. Instead, the author of the source and the appropriate _____ number are given within the paper, surrounded by _____. The author's name and the page number are separated by a_____, not a comma. Just the page number is cited if the author's _____ is mentioned in your sentence. The Works Cited list, at the _____of your paper, is organized according to the_____.

Here are the answers to the above quiz.

Part I:

Battleax, Oliver M. *Grammar Is Fun*. New York: Prentice, 1984. Print.

Mayhem, Carla. "Springsteen's Special Magic." *Jump On It, Baby*. Ed. Tipper Gore. New York: Macmillan, 1988. 24-28. Print.

Pretentious, Camille. "Madonna as Social Icon." *Cultural Currents* 7 (2000): 27-32. Print.

Rich, Morris E. "How to Train Your Bad Puppy." *New York Times Online* 13 April 1998, sec C. *Lexis-Nexis Academic*. Web. 4 Feb. 1999.

Part II.

The MLA style does away with <u>footnotes</u> in source documentation. Instead the author of the source and the appropriate <u>page</u> number are given within the paper, surrounded by <u>parentheses</u>. The author's name and the page number are separated by a <u>space</u>, not a comma. Just the page number is cited if the author's <u>name</u> is mentioned in your sentence. The Works Cited list, at the <u>end</u> of your paper, is organized according to the <u>author's last name</u>.

PART II
WRITING ABOUT SHORT FICTION

Chapter 6 How Do I Read Short Fiction? [pp. 105–110]

Although you may not have time to assign all of the papers suggested in the following chapters on fiction, poetry, and drama, we think it advisable to assign your students to read every chapter in order to receive an adequate understanding of all the fundamentals of literary analysis. Each chapter also presents a practical approach to writing about literature and includes explanations of various revising and editing techniques.

   At the end of this brief introduction to the study of short fiction, your students will find the useful list of "Critical Questions for Reading the Short Story" [p. 110]. These questions can serve as an invention heuristic to develop material for writing about any of the stories included in the anthology.

Writing Activities for Creative and Critical Thinking
The following projects will help students to integrate their reading of and writing about short stories. These are suggestions for exploratory writing, for playing with texts and language—designed to deepen an awareness of the cognitive and imaginative processes involved in reading literary texts. You can use these activities at any point in your students' study of short fiction.

- Write a continuation of a short story. Tell what happens next.
- Rewrite the ending of a short story. Choose a point in the action and change the direction of the plot.
- Rewrite the story from the point of view of a minor character.
- Change the gender or age or race or sexual orientation of a character from a story and rewrite the story—or a selected scene—accordingly.
- Work out the shots for filming a short story. Or prepare a script for dramatizing a key scene from a short story: describe the set and the characters; write the dialogue and the stage directions.
- Select a character from a short story and write a letter to him or her. You might offer some advice or express your support. Or write a letter *from* a character, in which he or she explains something to the reader (or the author).
- Select a character from a story and write an advertisement in which this character would endorse a product or service. Describe the ad and write some dialogue for the character to speak. Explain why you picked this particular product or service for the character to endorse.
- Write a letter to the author. Tell the author what you think of the story, or ask him or her to explain something about the story to you and your classmates.

Chapter 7 Writing About Structure [pp. 111–29]

Although we focus in this chapter on discovering and writing about structure in a literary work, we believe that acquiring an understanding of how fictional pieces are designed should help students learn to structure their own essays. We suggest that whenever you discuss the pattern that underlies a literary work, you need to remind your students that the principle of structuring an essay is essentially the same, so that they can consciously relate this new understanding to their own writing.

In this chapter we discuss the most common forms of narrative structure, with cross-references to poetic structure in Chapter 15 and dramatic structure in Chapter 17. Since the structure of short stories is usually concealed (or underlying), students who plan to write about the structure of a work need to focus on plot and look for underlying clues: flashbacks, space breaks, patterns of repetition, contrasting details, beginnings and endings—and, of course, the title. These elements, then, can provide the framework for the student's own essay on the structure of a literary work.

Pre-Reading Activity

Ask students to come up with different senses and definitions of the verb *carry*. You might consult a dictionary and prepare a list of meanings for them to consider. *The American Heritage Dictionary* gives 26 transitive definitions and 5 intransitive ones. Ask students to look for as many uses of the word as they can discover when reading the story. What does "carrying" mean to the soldiers? Why do they carry so many different items?

THE THINGS THEY CARRIED by Tim O'Brien [pp. 113–25]

This powerful story about the Vietnam War uses the things—both tangible and emotional—the soldiers carry to convey the unbearable burden of that senseless war. The listing begins with personal items, then moves to weapons and equipment—"whatever seemed appropriate as a means of killing or staying alive." Most telling are the intangibles that he takes up last: fear, exhaustion, disease, "emotional baggage," memory, even "the weight of the sky." About their battle equipment, they felt "a silent awe for the terrible power of the things they carried." As Bobbie Ann Mason observes, it all adds up to "the weight of America's involvement in the war." The central incident involves the company's first casualty. From start to finish, the story is punctuated with details of that sudden and senseless death. The main character, Lt. Jimmy Cross, carries a heavy burden of self-imposed guilt, since he holds himself responsible for Lavender's death. He thinks he failed to maintain strict discipline in his squad because he had been distancing himself from the grim realities of the war by fantasizing about a girl back home. At the end we see him focused on duty to his men, determined never to be caught off guard again, as he relinquishes love for leadership, and the squad resumes "the endless march, village to village, without purpose, nothing won or lost." But the actual loss is unbearable.

Finding Patterns [p. 125]

Once students have written their responses to our questions, you may wish to discuss their answers in class. Here are some suggested responses:

1. Each part of the story describes some burden the soldiers carry, which are material, emotional, psychological, and existential "things."
2. Blank linear spaces separate parts of the story visually. There are eleven parts. To save time, you could assign pairs or triads one part each and ask them to title their sections, and then write the titles on the board. While giving the parts titles, students

26

will realize that the different "things they carried" serve as themes for the parts.

3. Jimmy Cross's date with Martha is the earliest episode described, and that is done in retrospect. Mainly, all of the episodes take place on April 16 and the morning of April 17, the tunnel mission and its aftermath:

    Date with Martha to *Bonnie and Clyde*

    First week of April—Jimmy gets good-luck pebble from Martha

    Mid-April—Mission to clear tunnels in Than Khe area

    April 16—Lee Strunk goes into the tunnel, Ted Lavender goes to pee, Jimmy daydreams about Martha, Lee comes back up and during celebration, Lavender is shot in the head

    April 16—Men smoke Lavender's dope while waiting for helicopter to take his body away

    April 16—Chopper takes Lavender's body away

    April 16—The soldiers burn Than Khe

    April 16—Soldiers march for hours

    April 16, evening—Jimmy digs foxhole and weeps, Kiowa retells Lavender's death

    April 17—Jimmy burns Martha's letters and photos and makes new resolutions

4. Jimmy's thoughts of Martha structure the beginning and ending of the story. The changes in his feelings about Martha are part of the overall change he undergoes, mostly through his guilt about daydreaming of her when Lavender got shot in the head. Students can point out many clues that show how Jimmy, through most of the story, makes more of the relationship with Martha than exists in reality. However, he shows doubt about his own fantasies, so he is not totally deluded about the thinness of their real relationship.

5. The soldiers we meet in the story are

    Jimmy Cross
    Dave Jensen
    Henry Dobbins
    Ted Lavender
    Norman Bowker
    Rat Kiley
    Kiowa
    Mitchell Sanders
    Lee Strunk

You might choose to assign pairs or triads of students to find information in the story about one of these characters, and then pool their findings in a class discussion. O'Brien leaves out the majority of detail about their home lives, perhaps to emphasize their disconnection and alienation from civilian life in the U.S. They seem suspended like snapshots in an unreal setting, though we are allowed glimpses of their individuality, particularly from descriptions of the things they carry, and from their individual responses to Ted Lavender's death.

6. The story of Lavender's death is retold six times, each time with richer detail (both factual and emotional). The men's reactions to the death reveal their characters and illuminate the situation in Vietnam. Lavender's death is important in tipping the balance of Jimmy Cross's ambivalent feelings about Martha and his attitude toward leadership of the group.

Grouping Details [p. 126]

The assignment of identifying a repeated element of the story (a scene, theme, or event) and then finding supporting details lends itself well to in-class activity. Students will be aware of recurring elements from the Finding Patterns questions.

First go over the Martha theme and the details listed on page 126. Read the thesis that grows from these. Ask students, "What is the difference between the list of related details and the thesis?" The answer is, of course, that the thesis makes an assertion or claim about the meaning and details; it puts forth an interpretation of Jimmy Cross and the change he undergoes.

Now take another recurring element and brainstorm a list details as a class. Write the list on the board. Suggested elements include Ted Lavender's death, psychological burdens, idiosyncratic items the soldiers carried, ways of dealing with stress and danger. Then, develop a thesis sentence that evolves from the details identified.

Integrating Quotations Gracefully [pp. 128–29]

You may want to advise students at this point to consult Chapter 5 on researched writing. Our instruction there is directed toward integrating quotations from secondary sources into an essay, but the technique (except for acknowledging the sources) is the same. They will find in that chapter many further examples of graceful ways to combine quoted material with their own writing. Since students usually have not read much criticism (or, for that matter, any prose that incorporates quotations from other sources), they need to be provided with as many examples as possible.

Making Connections

→Read Alice Walker's "Everyday Use" beginning on page 157. What is similar about the structure of "Everyday Use" and "The Things They Carried"?

→Compare and contrast structure, settings, and themes in "The Things They Carried" and "The Red Convertible."

→Compare this story with the poems in the Portfolio of War Poetry, especially "Dulce et Decorum Est" and "Six National Guardsmen Blown Up Together."

Web Sites

→*Tim O'Brien's Home Page.* Provides a wide assortment of resources, including research links for students. **www.illyria.com/tobhp.html**

→A reading guide to *The Things They Carry*, including study questions. **www.readinggroupguides.com/guides_T/things_they_carried1.asp**

Discovering and interpreting images and symbols is a skill that takes time to learn. If students in high school have been involved in discussions of these important elements, they will take to it enthusiastically and perhaps even go a bit wild. You may need to encourage those who are unfamiliar with looking beneath the surface of a literary work. Remind them to look for recurring images and find associations that give symbolic meaning. Everyone will probably profit from consulting Cirlot's *A Dictionary of Symbols* or any of the other useful books mentioned on page 132 of the text.

Pre-Reading Activity
Discuss *rituals*. A ritual can be a prescribed form or order for conducting a religious or solemn ceremony, but it can also be any detailed method of procedure that's followed faithfully and regularly. Ask students if they have any of their own rituals—like getting ready for a date, preparing for an athletic event, cleaning their room. Why do they follow a set procedure? Is there an element of superstition in these (or most) rituals?

Interpreting Symbols [pp. 139–40]
1. Personal responses will vary. This would be a good topic to consider in a pre-reading discussion, although the subject matter might be sensitive. Students might prefer to write on this question in their reading journals.
2. The townspeople know that the unlucky person who draws the black dot will be killed, but whether they understand the social purpose of the ritual is left vague. The implication is that the people don't want to face the cruelty of their actions. The ritual seems to be reenacted out of fear and a blind adherence to tradition.
3. The uncertain history of the lottery suggests that the violent ritual has been around for a long time and that the townspeople don't care to examine their behavior, and its origins, too closely. The precise meaning of the lottery is not important to the townspeople; what is important is the tradition that binds them together and focuses their repressed aggression on a single object. That Mr. Summers asks a question that everybody knows the answer to underscores the mindless nature of the ritual: they go through the motions without reflecting on what they're doing and why they're doing it. A stylized question-and-response formula is part of many religious rituals.
4. The black box is a symbol of the tradition the townspeople follow. The color black conventionally signifies evil. The box is clearly an icon (i.e., a sacred or revered image), as the details of its history suggest.
5. The stones mentioned at the story's opening foreshadow the ending and add an unspecified but threatening note to the early description. Historically, stoning was the fate of outcasts from a community (as in the Christian story of Mary Magdalene, who was saved by Jesus from being stoned as a harlot). Though the outcasts had supposedly violated the community's rules or laws, many times they served as scapegoats. Mrs. Hutchinson is an extreme example of a scapegoat, since she has not transgressed.
6. Although the characters are not fully developed, they do present a variety of viewpoints. (The fact that few of them have first names suggests that they are types.)

29

Old Man Warner (who is always called "Old Man") serves as a rigid conservative who doesn't approve of any change in the traditional ritual (perhaps partly because he has escaped the black dot for 77 years). Mr. Summers, whose sunny name is surely ironic, is a civic booster who enjoys his priestlike role in the ritual; he represents the dutiful liberal who bends the rules a little but never questions the value of tradition. Mr. and Mrs. Adams can be seen as ineffectual radicals who point out that some communities are giving up the lottery but who do nothing to change their own community. Mrs. Hutchinson, ironically, is a well-liked, cheerful woman who seems to enjoy the ritual (until the end), though she forgets about the date and arrives late (which also seems ironic). The name *Hutchinson* may be significant for its association with Anne Hutchinson (1591–1643), a religious liberal who became one of the founders of Rhode Island after her banishment from Massachusetts Bay Colony. Hutchinson stressed individual intuition in finding salvation; she also criticized the Massachusetts Puritans for their narrow concepts of morality. Although Tessie Hutchinson does not stand up to her community, it is interesting that her name recalls a New Englander who was once tried and banished for speaking out against established authority. This historical association may also suggest parallels between "The Lottery" and the Salem Witch Trials.

Exercise on Thesis Statements [p. 140]

This exercise works well in small groups of three or four because the discussion of each revision will bring up criticisms and suggestions beyond what each individual could generate alone. Answers will vary, but here are some possible revisions:

1. Shirley Jackson's "The Lottery" presents a compelling indictment of the practice of blaming innocent people for society's ills.
2. The ritual of the lottery itself serves as a symbol of a society dominated by unexamined tradition.
3. The impact of Shirley Jackson's "The Lottery" depends largely on the contrast between the placid, ordinary setting and the horrifying conclusion.
4. The characters in "The Lottery" symbolize the conflict between tradition and progress.
5. Shirley Jackson's "The Lottery" explores the dangers of conformity and mob action.

Ideas for Writing [p. 141]

The responsive writing suggestions ask students to examine their understanding of and experience with two key concepts in the story—traditional rituals and scapegoats. These assignments can be used to stimulate discussion and generate material for further writing.

Each of the critical writing assignments calls for a general statement (thesis) supported by analyzed examples. You may want to talk through a sample essay or outline of this type before your students begin to write [see Chapter 4].

Sample Student Paper [pp. 143–53]

Here are some possible responses to the questions in the margins of the finished version:

Todd dropped "incongruities" from the thesis because he discusses only one incongruity, and it's a supporting detail rather than the main point.

The opening sentence was revised for conciseness and exactness.

30

"Jackson does this" was vague and general; "Jackson creates tension" uses more precise language and makes a definite point.

Todd improved the opening sentence of the second paragraph by identifying the black box as the "controlling image" and specifying the connection of the box to death. Both of these revisions sharpen the point of the topic sentence.

Changing "grew" to "growing" makes the series ("faded," "splintered," "growing shabbier") grammatically parallel (they're all participles).

Adding the information about the townspeople's failure to see the need for change makes this sentence more relevant to the general thesis.

The elimination of sarcasm is an improvement because the opening had not prepared the reader for a sarcastic tone; thus, the passage was confusing in the uncorrected draft.

The word "selfishness" narrows the focus of the paragraph to a specific aspect of human nature.

Todd moved the last paragraph of the draft because it was one more example of Jackson's use of symbols, not a conclusion.

He replaced the informal "in a nutshell" to keep the tone consistently serious.

The last two sentences in the final version refine and reflect the thesis from the opening paragraph, bringing the analysis full circle and giving it a sense of unity and closure.

Making Connections
→Compare the use of symbolism in "The Lottery" with the use of symbolism in "Everyday Use" by Alice Walker.

Videos
→"The Lottery." 18 minutes, color, 1969. Available from Filmic Archives.
→"A Discussion of the Lottery." With Dr. James Burbin. 10 minutes, color, 1969. Available from Filmic Archives.
→"The Lottery" and "A Discussion of 'The Lottery'" together on laser disc. Available from Filmic Archives.

Audio
→"The Lottery." Read by Shirley Jackson and Maureen Stapleton. 1 cassette. Available from Caedmon Records.

Chapter 9 Writing About Point of View [pp. 154–66]

When reading fiction, we often overlook the fact that we're seeing the world through someone else's eyes—eyes that control our view of the plot, characters, and setting. And behind these eyes is the author, manipulating events and providing or withholding information. It's important to make students aware of point of view and to understand that writers choose a point of view to achieve particular effects.

What Is Point of View? and *Describing Point of View* [pp. 154–55]

No brief summation of point of view can account for all the variations and subtleties of this narrative technique. Our system should be sophisticated enough to introduce students to the main uses of point of view, but they may need further explanation as they encounter the numerous refinements in prose fiction.

One way to get students to see how point of view affects writing is to have them develop a brief narrative from more than one point of view. For example, ask them to describe a break-up scene between an engaged couple from the personal point of view of one of the people involved (first-person); then ask them to render the same scene in a more objective way or in a way that does not give access to the consciousness of either person. You can also have students rewrite the opening paragraphs of a first-person story (e.g. "A & P" or "I Stand Here Ironing" or "Why I Live at the P.O.") from a different point of view, or have them rewrite a third-person opening (from "Seventeen Syllables" or "Where Are You Going, Where Have You Been?" for example) in first person. This experiment in composition can become a valuable group activity in which comparisons of different versions may raise productive observations about point of view and its effects.

Looking at Point of View [p. 156]

The basic question to ask about the first-person narrator is this: Why does Walker choose to tell the story through Mama's point of view? One reason is that Mama knows the background that Walker wants us to know. She knows what happened to Maggie and Dee in the past; she also knows the history of the quilts, which are symbolically important in the story. In other words, she supplies the facts about the history and heritage that Dee wants to reinterpret. For instance, she knows that Dee was named after her Aunt Dicie, not after her oppressors—which sets up the wonderfully comic exchange they have about Dee's name. Her practical, down-to-earth presence punctures Dee's pretensions; she's the necessary other side of the cultural conflict that the piece is based on. Since we have no access to Dee/Wangero's inner life, we have to understand her indirectly through details that Mama observes but doesn't interpret, such as the hair, the names, the handshakes, and the iconography of the everyday objects.

The irony of the story is that Mama does understand her heritage, which is one of putting useful items to everyday use and enjoying their beauty in that context. Perhaps she also understands to some extent what Dee/Wangeroo is up to—and simply resists. It's a kind of passive-aggressive thing, where she pretends to misunderstand, as, for instance, when she garbles Asalamalakim's name, referring to him as Hakim-a-barber: "I wanted to ask him was he a barber, but I didn't think he was, so I didn't ask." When it comes to interacting with her visitors, she becomes a great comic character.

Mama—uneducated, large-boned, snuff-dipping, and "man-working"—seems to fulfill the stereotypical image of African Americans that the Black Nationalists (represented by Dee/Wangero, Hakim-a-barber, and the farmers down the road) were trying to change. So, it is tempting to conclude that Mama represents Walker's point of view in the cultural conflict. Clearly we are meant to sympathize with Mama and cheer her on when she gives the quilts to Maggie. But in a 1973 interview, Walker explains that

32

her feelings are more complex:

> I really see that story as almost about one person, the old woman and two daughters being one person. The one who stays and sustains—this is the older woman—who on the one hand has a daughter who is the same way, who stays and abides and loves, plus the part of them—*this autonomous person,* the part of them that also wants to go out into the world to see change and be changed. . . . I do in fact have an African name that was given to me, and I love it and use it when I want to, and I love my Kenyan gowns and my Ugandan gowns, the whole bit, it's part of me. But on the other hand, my parents and grandparents were part of it, and they take precedence.

Pre-Reading Activity
Discuss the meaning and importance of *heritage*. What do students consider their heritage to be? Do they have any possessions or heirlooms that have been passed down in their family? Are these items strictly personal or do they have any larger cultural significance? You might follow up this pre-reading activity with a post-reading discussion of Responsive Writing idea number 3 (p. 164).

Analyzing Point of View [p. 163]
These answers are not definitive; good answers will vary.
1. Mama is a strong, hardworking, down-to-earth woman who can "kill and clean a hog as mercilessly as a man." Some might see as weaknesses her second-grade education, her being 100 pounds overweight, and her lack of "a quick and witty tongue," and perhaps Mama does too. But we see that she has a lively sense of humor and that, given the way she lives, her lack of education and her surplus of pounds have not in any way held her back. We admire her. Being called only Mama, as well as the absence of any mention of a husband/father, emphasizes her authority as the matriarch of the family.
2. Maggie is probably too shy and too nice to make an effective narrator. She would probably cut Dee too much slack. And Dee/Wangero is blind to her family heritage, so she would present a very biased perspective. She would, in fact, be an unreliable narrator, if she were telling the story.
3. Certainly we feel sorry for Maggie—disfigured, lame, "not bright," and with low self-esteem—but we are taken by her sweet disposition and gentle nature. She is a foil (almost the exact opposite) for Dee/Wangero, who is intelligent, physically attractive, and well educated—but we are revolted by Dee's cruelty and selfishness. We deplore Dee's behavior when the house burned and are put off by her condescending attitude toward her mother and sister. We cheer for Mama when she gives the quilts to Maggie.
4. The past tragedy of the fire is crucial in understanding the character's actions: the heartlessness of Dee/Wangero and the shy goodness of Maggie. We are not told how the house caught fire, but Dee/Wangero's satisfaction in seeing it burn casts suspicion on her, especially considering her thoroughly despicable character. There is, of course, no evidence that she set the fire. Walker pared down what she presents in the story and gives us just enough to understand the situation and the conflict.

33

5. The African names, dress, and hairstyles stem from the Black Nationalist movement of the 1960s in which black people in this country were encouraged to go back to their African roots, to adopt the African culture and heritage. Hakim-a-barber is in the story mainly for comic effect.

6. Dee/Wangero wants the quilts as icons representing her ancestry, as works of art, but Mama gives them to Maggie who lovingly remembers the actual women who made them. The quilts for Maggie will not be symbols but a living heritage.

7. The major conflict in the story concerns the clash between two cultural heritages. Dee/Wangero has embraced her African ancestral roots, but Mama, who knows nothing of this culture, sees value only in her personal heritage. Most readers will think that Mama has the better understanding of family heritage since she gives the symbolic quilts to Maggie.

8. The title, "Everyday Use," could apply to the practical use of the artistically groomed yard as a living room, to Mama's real-life competence, to the bare-bones house, to the lovely benches and churn, and finally to the priceless quilts. So, if the theme involves learning to see the cultural value and beauty of everyday things, we see that the quilts go not to the exotic Dee/Wangero but to the very everyday Maggie.

Ideas for Writing [p. 164]
You might want to ask all of your students to write briefly on the first prompt under "Ideas for Responsive Writing." This prewriting will serve to sharpen their understanding of point of view as they move to the more challenging critical writing assignments, all of which involve exploring point of view in one way or another.

Sharpening the Conclusion [pp. 165–66]
The advice in this section is aimed at getting student writers to understand and create stress or emphasis—that is, to end their writing on a strong point. Even the best writers have to control the flow of their ideas in a way that will lead to a strong, emphatic closing. Writers can improve their conclusions in a number of ways:

    a. trim the ending by cutting less important phrases and clauses;
    b. shift the important ideas or points to the end;
    c. break up long sentences and end with a relative short one;
    d. extract the best idea and isolate it in the last sentence—the clincher.

Sometimes these experiments lead to gimmicky, even irrelevant endings, but students will probably gain from the experience of manipulating the arrangement of their ideas and words. One more revision won't hurt them.

Making Connections
→Compare the characters in "Everyday Use" with the characters in the play *Fences*. Also compare how these two works handle the value of home and the importance of heritage.
→Analyze the symbolic function of hand-stitched quilts in revealing theme in "Everyday Use" and Susan Glaspell's *Trifles*.

Audio
→Interview with Alice Walker. 45 minutes. Available from American Audio Prose Library.

→"Alice Walker." Biography of the author. 33 minutes, color. Available from Films for the Humanities & Sciences.
→"Alice Walker: A Portrait in the First Person." The author talks about her life and works. 28 minutes, color. Available from Films for the Humanities & Sciences.

Web Sites

→*Anniina's Alice Walker Page*. Provides links to online resources, including articles, interviews, essays and criticism, bibliographies, reviews, and excerpts from Walker's works. **www.luminarium.org/contemporary/alicew/**
→*Voices from the Gap: Women Writers of Color*. Includes photographs and illustrations with a biography, bibliography, and links to interviews and essays.
http://voices.cla.umn.edu/artistpages/walkeralice.php

Chapter 10 Writing About Setting and Atmosphere [pp. 167–83]

In this chapter we deliberately chose the word *atmosphere*, instead of *mood*, since *mood* is often used (perhaps mistakenly) to mean the same thing as *tone*, which is an altogether different concept in literary criticism. *Tone*, as we understand the term, is the attitude of the author toward the written work. Typically a *tone* might be amusing, light, warm, sympathetic, facetious, sarcastic, ironic, satirical, biting, scathing, or sentimental. But *atmosphere*, which is closely associated with the setting of a work, is created to stir feeling in the reader, as Faulkner does in "A Rose for Emily" by taking us into the attic of Miss Emily's house where a "thin, acrid pall as of the tomb seemed to lie everywhere upon this room decked and furnished as for a bridal." Shirley Jackson creates a deceptive, ironically chilling atmosphere in "The Lottery" by setting her story of ritual execution on a sunny summer's day.

Pre-Reading Suggestion

Encourage students to visualize the three main characters, to imagine what they look like and sound like. What do they wear? How do they walk? Some students may even draw sketches of the three men. Also ask which actors they would cast in the roles of Tub, Kenny, and Frank, should the story be filmed.

Prewriting Exercise [pp. 178–79]

1. This prompt might be expanded to develop a responsive essay for this story. The different season would change a lot of the details: Tub would probably sweat profusely and have trouble breathing, for example. And the absence of hunting rifles would require a big change in the way the plot develops, although a fishing trip that includes a lot of drinking and going out on the water could still end disastrously. The primary character interactions would likely remain the same.
2. The first ten paragraphs encapsulate the relationships and personalities of the characters. Kenny drives far too fast, blares the horn, jumps the curb, and makes more than a token attempt to run over Tub. Kenny and Frank are an hour late to pick up Tub, letting him wait in the cold dawn, and then Frank snaps at Tub for

complaining about it. Frank's irritability is further indicated by his insistence that Tub stop rubbing his hands together. We see Tub as a weakling, easily bullied by his mates and dropping items from his food stash as he stumbles out of the truck's way. All three men see nothing risky about driving into the countryside in freezing cold with a hole in the windshield, showing the poor judgment that ultimately ends in death.

3.   The snow and cold provide an uncomfortable backdrop to the action from the very beginning of the story. The severe weather turns what might be mere foolishness into dangerous behavior. It also makes the men more touchy and irritable than they might be if they were comfortable. On a plot level, Frank and Tub's stops to get warm on the way to the hospital sign Kenny's death warrant.

4.   a.   An occasion like a hunting trip is often associated with bonding between masculine men, some type of expression of their natural instincts. The trip is also typically an escape from the demands of women and civilization. While Tub, Kenny, and Frank do some male bonding on the trip, it is fraught with cruelty and pettiness rather than manly virtue. They are not free of the influence of women (see 4.e.), and their uncivilized behavior has no natural nobility.

b.   The characters are distinct early on. Kenny is an unfunny practical joker, insensitive and crude; Tub is fat and impulsive and serves as the outsider for the others; Frank is irritable, morose, and distracted by his affair with the babysitter.

c.   The first indoor scene, in the farmer's house, reveals that the man asked Kenny to shoot the dog when Kenny knocked to ask whether they could hunt on his land. This revelation is important because by making killing the dog part of a joke, Kenny fooled Tub into thinking he himself was about to be shot. In a sense, Kenny's tomfoolery leads to his own murder. The second indoor scene is the tavern where Frank and Tub stop on the way to the hospital. This scene includes the revelation that Frank is having an affair with the fifteen-year-old babysitter and intends to leave his wife. The scene ends on the macabre note of the two men extolling the virtues of friendship as their third friend lies in the snow bleeding to death outside. A further grotesquerie: the men carelessly leave the directions to the hospital behind at the tavern. The third indoor scene occurs at the roadhouse where they stop again. The revelation of this scene is that Tub has no glandular reason for being so fat: he just eats all the time, and even his wife doesn't know his secret.

d.   Frank's ordering the pancakes for Tub is difficult to interpret. There is some element of cruelty in the way Frank prepares the pancakes and insists on Tub's gluttony. It could be that Frank enjoys encouraging someone else who has trouble curbing an out-of-control appetite. On the other hand, it may seem to Tub like an act of acceptance and permission to be himself.

e.   Frank's babysitter girlfriend has clearly influenced him, at least superficially. We frequently hear him say things in terms that are out of character and sound vaguely like a fifteen-year-old's wisdom, yet indeed reflecting more empathy than Frank has had before. The fact that Roxanne has been able to affect him even this much indicates her power over him. Her wisdom has not gone very deep, as we see in scenes like the one where he glorifies friendship and then goes outside to berate his dying pal for thrashing around in pain. Frank and Tub are both guilt-ridden over the secrets they keep from their wives. The farmer's wife understands her husband's feelings about the dog better than he admits, and she is the one who gives the shortcut directions that might have saved Kenny's life.

f. Tub's sudden shooting of Kenny is quite shocking because it comes so fast and unexpectedly, even though we know that Tub has reason to resent Kenny. The men's occasional acts of thoughtlessness and cruelty to each other are shocking, such as Kenny and Frank's lack of concern when Tub gets lost at the creek and their driving off without him, making him run and jump in the back of the moving truck. The pancake scene is shocking in its strangeness and ambiguity. Finally, the last scene, in which Frank and Kenny take the blankets off the dying Kenny and laugh about his final practical joke, is very shocking, though we are certainly prepared for their brutishness.

Ideas for Writing [pp. 180–81]
Encourage students to read carefully and make notes on all of the writing suggestions before deciding which one to use for their essay. All of the topics will encourage insight into the story.

Improving Style: Sentence-Modeling Exercise [pp. 181–83]
Because sentence modeling may be new to your students, you can help them get the idea by writing one of the sample sentences on the board and marking the parallel elements. Also let them know that they need not imitate the sentence structure precisely but should try to come close enough to catch the cadence of the balance that makes the model sentences impressive.

Making Connections
→Discuss the idea of masculine folly in Wright's "The Man Who Was Almost a Man," Wolff's "Hunters in the Snow," and Updike's "A & P."

Audio
→*Tobias Wolff interview with Kay Bonetti* (1985). 57 minutes. Available from American Audio Prose Library.

Online Resource
→*The Salon Interview.* Wolff talks about his short stories. www.salon.com/ dec96/interview961216.html

---

Chapter 11 Writing About Theme [pp. 184–203]

Students often have more difficulty in *stating* theme than in *understanding* theme. Many common literary themes can be expressed in familiar maxims (such as, "People who live in glass houses shouldn't throw stones" or "You should practice what you preach"); but in writing about literature students need to learn to phrase themes in a more mature and thoughtful manner. They usually need practice in order to master the technique.

Every time you begin the study of a literary work, you might try having your students write an in-class statement of the theme in a sentence or two. At the start of the semester, you can have them compose their theme statements after having discussed the selection, but later in the semester, have them write before the class discussion—in order to judge how well they are learning to understand and express the theme of a work on their own. Collect these impromptu writing samples and read them aloud to the class, asking the students to discuss the virtues and shortcomings of each one. At the end, reread the two or three that everyone agrees are the most effective. In these exercises, stress the importance of precise word choice and clear sentence structure.

Pre-Reading Activity

The question at the beginning of the first responsive writing topic (p. 200)—about "good country people" being the "salt of the earth"—might make a good prompt for a brief pre-reading assignment. Have students respond in writing to this question and, if you have time, let them compare responses before they read the story. You can also collect the responses and have students reread them after they have read and discussed "Good Country People"; then give them an opportunity to expand or revise their initial reactions and to compare their views with O'Connor's.

GOOD COUNTRY PEOPLE by Flannery O'Connor [185–98]

Irony and satire prevail in this story. The title suggests the comforting, if inaccurate, notion that the country life produces vigorous, well-balanced people with a sense of purpose and community. None of the characters in this story exhibit any of these traits. Each employs sets of clichés with which to measure one another and their world. The result is psychological blindness. Joy/Hulga's mother, Mrs. Hopewell, avoids having to think by being armored with empty platitudes. "Everybody is different" is her motto, although she clearly disapproves of people who *are* different. Her crony, Mrs. Freeman, completes the gossiping, countrified cliché festival. Hulga, with a bad heart, a wooden leg, and no future, considers herself a nihilist. Her extensive education has not enabled her to find or construct a better existence. She despises the country myths, but winds up being taken in by them anyway when she meets Manley Pointer, a genuine walking philosophical void, against which her philosophy has no defense. His cynical courtship results in Hulga's being left without a leg to stand on and with blurry vision, physical equivalents to her inner state.

Figuring Out the Theme [pp. 198–99]

Leading questions on the story elements will vary; here are some possibilities:
1. What does "country people" mean in this story? Does the title apply to all the characters in the story? Are they all "good"? Is it an ironic title?
2. Why is Hulga still living at home? How well off are the Hopewells? Does their economic status affect the way they live and think?
3. Why does Joy want to be called Hulga? Why does Mrs. Freeman call her Hulga even though her mother doesn't? Is Manley Pointer's name a sexual pun? Why does Mrs. Hopewell tolerate Mrs. Freeman? Are Mrs. Hopewell and Mrs. Freeman parallels or foils? Why are Mrs. Freeman's daughters mentioned but never seen? Why does

38

Hulga dress the way she does? Why does the author describe Manley's clothes in such detail? What does this description convey about him? What does Mrs. Freeman's name suggest about her character? Is she free in a way that Hulga and her mother are not?

4. Is Hulga's leg symbolic of her artificial or incomplete character? Is it the cause of her personality problems? Is there some symbolic connection between her artificial leg and her heart problem? Is Manley's Bible a symbol of hypocrisy? Is it meant to parallel Hulga's leg? How sincere is Mrs. Hopewell when she says that "Everybody is different. . . . It takes all kinds to make the world. . . . Nothing is perfect"? How well does Mrs. Hopewell actually tolerate differences and imperfections?

5. What does it mean that Hulga shows interest in Manley? Why does Hulga want to seduce Manley? Why is Manley obsessed with Hulga's artificial leg?

6. Why are Hulga and Manley drawn to each other? Why do they play a series of jokes on each other? How are these deceptions related to the theme? What are we to make of Manley's blatant hypocrisy? How will Hulga's encounter with Manley affect her?

7. What does the narrator mean that "Mrs. Hopewell had no bad qualities of her own but she was able to use other people's in . . . a constructive way"? Is that an ironic remark? Why does Manley's gaze seem "somehow familiar" to Hulga? Why does the narrator say about Hulga's reaction to her first kiss that, "Some people might enjoy water if they were told it was vodka"? Or is that Hulga's comment to herself?

8. Why did the author add two more paragraphs concerning Mrs. Hopewell and Mrs. Freeman? What is the purpose of these final paragraphs? What do they contribute to Hulga's story?

Stating the Theme [p. 199]
Students will state the theme in various ways. Here are some possible responses:

Although people may acknowledge that "everybody is different" and that "it takes all kinds to make the world," differences and individuality are not readily accepted in our society.

Sometimes people have to have their illusions and defenses destroyed before they can learn to see and accept themselves.

"Good Country People" explores the spiritual blindness and moral hypocrisy of modern America.

Ideas for Writing [p. 200]
Use the responsive writing topics about Manley Pointer and Hulga as the basis for a critical analysis of either or both of these characters. See pages 107–08 in Chapter 6 for advice on analyzing character.

The use of "glosses" forces students to consider what they are saying at each stage of their paper. You may want to use the overhead projector or distribute a brief sample to demonstrate how to add glosses to a paper. This technique is a variation of outlining the first draft, a revising procedure that was explained in Chapter 3.

Making Connections

→Compare Hulga Joy with Eveline (in Joyce's story of that name) and Connie (in "Where Are You Going, Where Have You Been?" by Joyce Carol Oates. What problems do they have in common? How do they differ in their attempts to deal with what they feel are oppressive family situations?
→Compare Manley Pointer with Jake in "Love in L.A."

Web Site

→*Comforts of Home.* A site dedicated to Flannery O'Connor, containing biographical material; recent news about O'Connor and her works; and links to online essays, offline essays, and other sources. **www.mediaspecialist.org/index.html**

ANTHOLOGY OF SHORT FICTION

The following brief analyses and possible responses to the questions in the main text may prove useful to you in teaching the stories included in this anthology and in formulating writing assignments derived from them.

THE BIRTHMARK by Nathaniel Hawthorne [pp. 204–15]

Hawthorne himself once wrote, "I am not quite sure that I entirely comprehend my own meaning in some of these blasted allegories." While "The Birthmark" is not as heavily allegorical as some of his works, we can certainly see the characters as representing concepts. Alymer is an archetypal hubristic scientist attempting to play god. The removal of the birthmark, he says, "will be my triumph, when I shall have corrected what Nature left imperfect, in her fairest work." Georgiana, of course, is that "fairest work," flawed by the birthmark, "that sole token of human imperfection," which signifies her "liability to sin, sorrow, decay, and death." Aminadab "represents man's physical nature," and serves as a foil for Alymer, who is "a type of the spiritual element." Students may need to be made aware that Hawthorne in this story uses the term "spiritual" not in a religious sense, but to indicate Alymer's affinity for the occult, as he attempts through alchemy to "acquire a power above nature." It is Aminadab, the man of the flesh, who delivers the prescient warning to Alymer, "If she were my wife, I'd never part with that birth-mark." The story can certainly be seen as condemning the vaunting pride of Alymer, as he persists in his folly despite knowing the danger and, even more importantly, knowing that many of his previous experiments have failed (including the shocking one in which a flower, "lovely" like his wife, is blighted by her touch). Hawthorne's cautionary tale of man's attempt to surpass the laws of nature may bring to mind a number of questionable scientific advances: the development of the atomic bomb, germ warfare, and other weapons of mass destruction, as well as one currently relevant to the story, the controversy over cloning human cells.

Possible Responses to *Questions for Discussion and Writing*

1. Responses will vary, but students may suggest that Alymer represents the intellectual, the spiritual, the superstitious in human nature. Aminidab clearly represents man's physical nature. Georgiana represents ethereal beauty as well as selfless devotion. Alymer is flawed by his egotism, his vaunting pride that makes him seek to play God and "correct what Nature left imperfect." Aminidab, being a foil for Alymer, is perhaps too incurious, too unquestioning, too much a creature of the senses. Georgiana, who seems to have no mind of her own, is flawed by an excessive devotion to her husband that borders on the demented.
2. The shape of the birthmark reminds us that it was placed there by the hand of God or of Nature and hence must not be tampered with.
3. The major conflict in the story involves Alymer's struggle to attain control over Nature, to achieve accomplishments on a level with the God-head.
4. Hawthorne's allegory stresses the folly of vaunting pride, of elevating science to the level of a religion, of considering himself capable of controlling Nature. Science today treads a fine line between being the salvation of humankind and of destroying it. Consider the advances in medicine, the marvels of engineering, the convenience of automobiles and air travel. Consider also the disastrous floods caused by damming rivers, the yearly highway death toll, the inventions of poison gas and the atom bomb.
5. The story provides ample evidence to support the argument that Georgiana is complicit in her own death. She encourages Alymer in his "scientific" endeavors to produce a potion to remove her birthmark, even though she knows full well that all of his previous recorded experiments have failed. She tells him calmly, "I shall quaff whatever draught you bring me; but it will be on the same principle that would induce me to take a dose of poison, if offered by your hand." Her inordinate love of her husband borders on lunacy and proves her undoing.

Additional Questions for Discussion and Writing

1. Write an essay about Alymer's character as a mixture of "deep science" and superstition.
2. What is the function of Aminadab? Explain how he functions as a foil to Alymer.
3. Do you think Alymer is the victim of forces beyond his control?
4. In January 2002, the President's Council on Bioethics selected this story for discussion in determining the ethical implications of human cloning. Go to the Council's Web site (www.bioethics.gov), click on Bioethics in Literature, and scroll down to the questions on "The Birthmark." Discuss what you think Hawthorne's position would be if he were a member of the President's Council on Bioethics.

Audio
→"The Birthmark." 1 cassette, 63 minutes. Read by Walter Zimmerman. Distributed by Jimcin Recordings.

Making Connections

→Compare Alymer's obsession with that of Paul in D.H. Lawrence's "The Rocking-Horse Winner." Do you find either obsession morally defensible?

THE STORY OF AN HOUR by Kate Chopin [pp. 215–17]

Brilliantly crafted to entice readers into empathizing with Mrs. Mallard, this brief work is a tour de force. Chopin makes it clear that the widow who rejoices in her new freedom did not consciously arrive at this perception. Instead, in a state of "suspension of intelligent thought," this "thing" came to her even as "she was striving to beat it back with her will—as powerless as her two white slender hands would have been." The ironic ending is also foreshadowed in the first line by the reference to Mrs. Mallard's "heart trouble," a trouble that acquires a double meaning as the story progresses. The major theme is the same as that of *The Awakening*—the constriction of a woman's life by marriage in the late nineteenth century.

Possible Responses to *Questions for Discussion and Writing*

1. Mrs. Mallard's heart trouble is literally heart disease, but she also appears to suffer emotional "heart trouble" since she feels not lost but liberated upon hearing of her husband's death.
2. Many of the images suggest that her life experiences will be expanding: the open window, the open square, "trees all aquiver with spring life" (suggesting rebirth as nature comes back to life), the delicious breath of rain" (water being symbolic of spiritual rebirth), someone singing, birds twittering, "patches of blue sky" (all positive, life enhancing images)—except, at the end of the passage, the clouds piling up in the west, suggesting tragedy, even death, since every day dies in the west; these concluding dark images can be seen as foreshadowing her husband's death (or her own).
3. The "joy that kills" in the final line could mean that Mrs. Mallard dies from the joyous shock of seeing her husband alive, or more likely, the agonizing shock of seeing her dream of freedom vanish.
4. A feminist reading of the story might state the theme as a plea for equality in marriage instead of a union like the Mallard's in which one "powerful will" exerts control over the other person.
5. Some students may devise a claim that Mrs. Mallard in not a sympathetic character but is heartless, even cruel, since she is elated to hear the news of her husband's death. Others, though, may support a claim that she is a woman who was repressed in her marriage and thus is justifiably relieved to find herself free to live now as she chooses. There is evidence to support either claim.

Additional Questions for Discussion and Writing

1. What do you think Louise Mallard's married life was like? Compose some diary entries in which Mrs. Mallard describes and comments on her relationship with Brently.
2. Find out about Kate Chopin's life and marriage. How autobiographical is this story?

Making Connections

→Compare Mrs. Mallard with Elisa in "The Chrysanthemums" by Steinbeck. What do these wives have in common? How do they differ?

Videos

→"The Joy That Kills." 56 minutes, color. Available from Films for the Humanities & Sciences.
→"Kate Chopin: Five Stories of an Hour." Five versions of the story. 26 minutes, color. Available from Films for the Humanities & Sciences.

HANDS by Sherwood Anderson [pp. 217–21]

You may want to explain the story's context when your class begins to discuss "Hands." It comes from *Winesburg, Ohio*, a collection of twenty-three stories held together by a common small-town location. Characters from one story appear in the others, as George Willard appears in this one.

    "Hands" is relevant today, as ever, when communities are roused to point accusing fingers at individuals whom they perceive as dangerous to young people. Like Adolph Myers/Wing Biddlebaum, these individuals might well be gifted eccentrics who have not mastered the codes of ordinary social behavior. The fact that even Wing never seems to understand what he was accused of (homosexual advances toward his students) certifies his innocence of such aggression. His actual sexual orientation is not really important, though students may find evidence in the comparison of Wing to "the finer sort of women" and in his dream of young men at his feet.

    The action of the Pennsylvania men and its repercussions in Wing's life are the substantial issues of the story. The first rumor started in an enamored student's dreams, which the half-witted boy could not distinguish from reality, and the first action against Wing came from a saloonkeeper, whose view of human nature could understandably be negatively distorted. Wing finds himself in exile, ridiculed by the young people he loves and hiding his talents except from George Willard (who is the voice of broadmindedness in Winesburg in several stories).

Possible Responses to *Questions for Discussion and Writing*

1. Wing Biddlebaum's decaying house, perched "on the edge of a ravine," is similar to his precarious position in the little town where he lives. The field that has been "seeded for clover" but produces only weeds is symbolically like his successful teaching career, which he lost because of small-town gossip and ignorance. The image of the "cloud of dust that floated across the face of the dying sun" suggests the young people's lack of spirituality and human kindness as they needlessly hassle the old man. The whole scene leads into the earlier story of Wing's torment when he was called Adolph Meyer. The major theme of the story is implicit in that episode, as Anderson shows us the cruelty and ignorance that lie beneath the peaceful serenity of a small town in the heartland of America.

2. Poetry often contains an element of the mystical seldom found in prose. And Wing Biddlebaum's hands are mystical; they seem not under his control: "The hands alarmed their owner" and earlier had caused tragedy to befall him.
3. The men of the Pennsylvania town caused Adolph Meyer to flee and were even prepared to hang him because they thought he was homosexual. His touch "caressed" the children, and his voice was "soft and musical." The men should, of course, have questioned the first report since it came from a boy who was "halfwitted" and had only imagined the "strange hideous accusations." Anderson perhaps chose the town's saloonkeeper as the one who stirred up the confrontation because saloonkeepers in that day were usually uneducated and were not themselves considered upstanding citizens.
4. Wing is trying to tell George not to waste his life in the backward town he happened to be born in. When he tells the young man he "must begin to dream," he means that he must use his imagination to figure out a way to enlarge his life experiences. Anderson has left the content of Wing's teachings vague in order to avoid limiting in any way the young man's chances of expanding his horizons.
5. The final image of Wing as a penitent receiving the host fits perfectly the role he has played throughout the story. He has been harassed (perhaps persecuted) for innocent behavior by small-minded people who wrongly perceive him as a threat. The tone at the end is solemn, even religious, as Wing Biddlebaum receives a benediction in his humble surroundings.

Additional Questions for Discussion and Writing
1. The introduction to the stories in *Winesburg, Ohio*, is titled "The Book of the Grotesques." Find out what the term *grotesque* means as a literary device. (Flannery O'Connor also used *grotesques* in her fiction.) Then discuss Anderson's use of the grotesque in "Hands."
2. Do you think Adolph Meyers's physical contact with his students was inappropriate? How would such contact be viewed in your community today?
3. What is the role of George Willard in this story?

Making Connections
→Compare Wing Biddlebaum with the speaker in Tillie Olsen's "I Stand Here Ironing." What oppressive circumstances affect each of these characters? What were their responses?

THE ROCKING-HORSE WINNER by D. H. Lawrence [pp. 222–32]
This story has fairy-tale elements and an age-old theme: wealth does not equal love or happiness. The family atmosphere Lawrence builds is one charged with damaging values, such as the attribution of failure and success to luck, the son's belief that his mother's love is something he must acquire, and the "whispering voices" that insist there is never enough money, even after Paul begins to bring in his winners.

In the midst of such a family, a child is likely to take blame and responsibility upon himself or herself, often in unrealistic ways. Thus, Paul decides that he will acquire luck by an act of will, and thereby gain the love and happiness he has mistakenly connected to luck. He finds himself undertaking a series of tasks to win the prize, just as happens in fairy tales, and the tasks become more difficult. The final one kills him.

The real prize, the love and happiness of his mother, is never achieved. Lawrence suggests that some inherent defect in the mother has set off the fatal course of events, and in the end her heart "turned actually into a stone." Today's students may remark on the sexist assumptions of the story—the cold mother, rather than the ineffectual father or the other exploitative adult men or some systemic family failure, is the villain.

Possible Responses to *Questions for Discussion and Writing*

1. The supernatural elements are so smoothly and unobtrusively integrated into the story that they hardly seem unbelievable at all. These elements are used because they are essential to the plot and serve to illuminate the theme that equating wealth with love and happiness can prove illusory.
2. When Paul manages to attain money for his avaricious mother, she only wants more. The voices become louder because Paul feels he must acquire yet more and more. To Paul, money represents his ability to gain his mother's love; to his mother, money represents her ability to maintain her lavish lifestyle.
3. The two criticisms can be reconciled because neither can be proved; a person could reasonably endorse one theory or the other.
4. Paul must die in the end because he is a scapegoat atoning for his mother's greed (and also because the plot requires it; he'll soon outgrow that rocking horse).
5. This is a challenging topic, but students may want to pursue a claim that gambling lies at the root of the evil in this story, or that the neglectful father is at least equally responsible for his son's demise, or that Uncle Oscar and Bassett should have been more aware of the boy's desperation and secured help for him.

Additional Questions for Discussion and Writing

1. Write an essay examining this story as a critique of money, greed, and capitalism.
2. Why does Lawrence treat inanimate objects (such as the house, the rocking horse, the big doll) as lifelike? What effect does this personification have on you as a reader?
3. What secrets do the characters keep from one another? How do these secrets relate to the story's main themes?
4. Write an analysis of the story in which you focus on one of these themes: the isolation of the human spirit, the difficulty of achieving self-understanding, the desire and need for approval, the consequences of misplaced priorities.

Making Connections

→Compare the family's behavior in Lawrence's story with the family dynamics presented in Mukherjee's "A Father."

Videos

→*The Rocking-Horse Winner.* 30 minutes, color, 1977. With Kenneth More. Adapted by Julian Bond. Directed by Peter Modak. Available from Learning Corp. of America.
→*The Rocking-Horse Winner.* 91 minutes, b&w, 1949. With John Mills, Valerie Hobson; directed by Anthony Pelissier. Available from Films for the Humanities & Sciences.

A ROSE FOR EMILY by William Faulkner [pp. 233–39]

Commentators have discussed "A Rose for Emily" in terms of conflict between the North (Homer Barron) and the South (Emily Grierson). But, if indeed there are allegorical implications, the story seems more reasonably to present the crumbling of the old aristocracy as it is absorbed by the new mercantile society. The story can profitably be approached through its structure, since without the deliberate disruption of the time scheme, Faulkner would lose the impact of the final line. But the character of Miss Emily is clearly important, as is an understanding of the title. Faulkner revealed that, "here was a woman who had had a tragedy, an irrevocable tragedy and nothing could be done about it, and I pitied her and this [story] was a salute . . . to a woman you would hand a rose." Her father, by driving away her suitors, has deprived her of the only role in life allowed her by society. Thus, when she finds another man, she wants to keep him. Faulkner explained it this way:

> She picked out probably a bad one, who was about to desert her. And when she lost him she could see that for her that was the end of life, there was nothing left, except to grow older, alone, solitary; she had had something and she wanted to keep it, which is bad—to go to any length to keep something; but I pity Emily [because] her life had probably been warped by a selfish father.

Thus, though Miss Emily Grierson is patently insane (insanity runs in her family, remember), we nonetheless admire her dignity, her pride, her endurance—and can perhaps see her not just as a "fallen monument" but as a tragic heroine.

Possible Responses to *Questions for Discussion and Writing*

1. Faulkner achieves suspense by disrupting the chronology. We hear about the offensive smell in section II before we've even heard about Homer Barron; in section IV we find out that Homer's gone missing and that Miss Emily's long hair has gone gray, but not until the end of the story do we get the shock of the strand of long gray hair on the pillow next to where Homer's rotting corpse lay.

2. The narrative voice is that of a townsperson, probably a male, who speaks from a limited omniscient point of view. Conveying the viewpoint of the entire town, he uses the royal "we," in this case perhaps more accurately described as the public "we" or the citizens' "we."

3. Miss Emily is clearly proud but at the same time pathetic. Her pride stems from the once exalted position held by her once wealthy family in this small community. She lives in the past because the mighty have fallen. But we, and the narrative voice of the townspeople, now find her sadly pathetic because she is friendless, isolated, and out of contact with reality, comporting herself with genteel arrogance as if she were still the town's leading citizen.

4. Homer Barron is a hale fellow well met. He's a good worker, has an honest job, and gets along fine with all who know him. But the townspeople do not consider him worthy of Miss Emily because he's working class, and they like to think of the Griersons as aristocrats. Miss Emily, perhaps desperate by now to be married, seems to think Homer will do just fine.

46

5. A strong claim can be argued that Emily's father, by driving away her many suitors when she was a beautiful young belle, left her alone and bereft after his death, unable to create a satisfying life for herself.

Additional Questions for Discussion and Writing
1. Explain the function of dust and decay in the story.
2. Readers and critics disagree about the meaning of the word *rose* in the title. Locate several different interpretations of the title, and then write your own interpretation, incorporating the ideas of others into your discussion.

Making Connections
→Examine "A Rose for Emily" and Shirley Jackson's "The Lottery" as modern horror stories. How does the use of horror in these stories differ from its use in popular entertainment?

Video
→"A Rose for Emily." 27 minutes, color, 1983. Available from Pyramid Film & Video.

Audio
→"Collected Stories of William Faulkner." Read by Wolfram Kandinsky and Michael Kramer. Vol. 2 contains "A Rose for Emily." Available from Books on Tape.

HILLS LIKE WHITE ELEPHANTS by Ernest Hemingway [pp. 239–43]
This story consists mainly of dialogue, which often seems trivial, even pointless. We learn practically all we know of the characters (which is really very little) through what they say. But the understatement is so subtle that we only gradually realize that beneath the small talk lies a very serious argument: the unnamed male speaker wants the woman (Jig) to have an abortion, which she resists. In the end, the man manipulates "the girl" (as Hemingway insists on calling her) to agree to the operation, although it appears that she is not completely swayed by his words. The speeches, if read carefully, do reveal a difference in personalities: the man seems literal-minded, irritable, unthinking; the woman seems more sensitive and emotional.

The description outside the dialogue is highly suggestive. The landscape seems to mirror the two choices that the woman faces: a dry, sterile landscape ("no shade and no trees") on one side of the train tracks and a peaceful fecundity ("fields of grain and trees along the banks of the Ebro") on the other side. The setting of a railroad junction serves to reinforce the crossroads motif.

Possible Responses to Questions for Discussion and Writing
1. The point of view is objective, consisting primarily of conversation with a brief description of the setting and an occasional indication of an action, almost like a stage direction. The reader is expected to figure out who the characters are, what is being discussed, and what possibilities might result from their discussion.
2. The repetition of the number two and the parallel, nonintersecting lines, all suggest that these are two separate people with different values and objectives who profess to

love each other and are trying to resolve their problem, but it seems apparent that they may eventually end up going their separate ways.

3.   This story focuses on a male/female relationship in which the dominant male seeks to convince the reluctant woman to have an abortion. The abortion is the central issue in the story simply because the conflict would not exist if the woman were not pregnant. The lack of communication results from their both being firmly committed and unyielding in their opposing viewpoints. At the end, the woman insists, "I feel fine now," but we have no concrete reason to believe she has actually changed her mind. She may have just gotten tired of arguing.

4.   The white elephants in the title can be seen in two different ways, like the story itself. A white elephant in an Asian or African culture is a valuable creature that would be treasured by anyone who possessed it (as a desired baby might be). But a "white elephant," in a garage sale, for instance, is something unwanted that the possessor would like to get rid of (as an unwanted baby might be). The fetus that Jig carries is clearly wanted by her but unwanted by her lover.

5.   Hemingway leaves both questions unanswered, but either response can be reasonably argued. It seems sensible to speculate that if Jig gets an abortion, the two will probably remain lovers—at least for a while. But if she keeps the pregnancy, then the decision becomes more problematic. Will the man stay with her if she ignores his wishes? If so, how long? We know he does not want to become a father.

Additional Questions for Discussion and Writing

1.   Write the backstory for this episode: How old are these people? Where are they from? What do they do for a living? How did they meet? How long have they known each other? What kind of relationship have they had? What differences are there in age, experience, social status? What has led them to this point in their relationship?

2.   Why does the woman say they can't have the whole world, that they can't go anywhere they want, that "It isn't ours any more"? Who's taken it away and why can't they ever get it back again?

Making Connections

→Compare Jig to the wife in Steinbeck's "The Chrysanthemums." What similarities can you find in their relationships with their men?

Video

→"An Introduction to Ernest Hemingway's Fiction." Lecture. 45 minutes, color. Available from Filmic Archives.

THE CHRYSANTHEMUMS by John Steinbeck [pp. 243–52]

Elisa Allen is good with flowers, like her mother before her, but she is vaguely anxious and unfulfilled. Elisa is strong and mature, at the height of her physical strength, but there is no appropriate outlet for her energies. She is like the Salinas Valley she lives in: a "closed pot," shut off by the fog from the sky and from the rest of the world. Her urge to fulfill her nature is directed into the chrysanthemums, which bloom profusely (in contrast to her own barrenness—she has no children).

48

The men in the story feel none of Elisa's unfulfillment. They take the opportunities of the male world for granted. Henry Allen has sold his cattle for a good price and is celebrating by taking his wife out to dinner. The itinerant repairman is temporarily down on his luck, but he recognizes an easy mark when he sees one. He flatters Elisa and hands her a line about chrysanthemums for a lady he knows down the road. Both men disappoint Elisa. Her husband's reward of a trip to town is just a concession to allow her to accompany him for his entertainment. After Elisa does her hair and puts on make-up and her prettiest dress, the only compliments that her husband can offer is that she looks "nice" and "strong" and "happy." And when Elisa sees that the tinker has cruelly discarded her chrysanthemum sprouts, she is too disheartened even to attend the prizefights (where she might get some satisfaction of seeing men hurt each other, as they have hurt her). At the end of the story, Elisa is "crying weakly—like an old woman"; her strength and energy have been completely depleted.

Possible Responses to *Questions for Discussion and Writing*

1. The chrysanthemums can, of course, symbolize all of the ideas listed plus any more reasonable connections that your students can come up with.
2. Since the fog "sat like a lid on the mountains and made of the great alley a closed pot," we understand that Eliza is isolated "from all the rest of the world." The foothill ranch where she and Henry live is "bathed in cold pale sunshine," suggesting perhaps that any passion in her life has by now cooled and faded.
3. Eliza craves attention and acknowledgment of her sexuality from both men, but neither responds satisfactorily. As she talks to the tinker, "her breast swelled passionately"; "kneeling there, her hand went out toward his legs" and "her hesitant fingers almost touched the cloth." There is a clear undercurrent of desire in her actions. She later makes herself attractive for Henry, as she prepares for what appears to be like a date with him, but he ruins the romantic mood by complementing her appearance as "nice" and "strong" and happy"—not the way she hoped to be perceived. As a way to get some business, the tinker feigns interest in the chrysanthemums and concocts a story about taking a sprout to another of his customers down the road. (Eliza sees later that he has thrown the flower away, but kept the pot.) Her husband manipulates Eliza by complimenting her on her "gift" with plants, hinting that she might be able to help run the farm, and suggesting they go to Salinas for dinner and a movie.
4. See the previous answer.
5. Eliza would probably like to break some men's noses and bloody their chests—or see them hurt each other as they have hurt her. But she backs down and settles for wine with dinner.

Additional Question for Discussion and Writing

→Two different ways of life are presented in this story. Identify and discuss them.

Making Connections

→Compare Elisa and Tome Hayashi of "Seventeen Syllables" by Hisaye Yamamoto. How do these women cope with their less-than-satisfactory husbands? Would you say that they are strong women who refuse to be defeated? Explain.

→"The Chrysanthemums." Film guide with purchase. 24 minutes, VHS. Available from Pyramid Film & Video.

THE MAN WHO WAS ALMOST A MAN by Richard Wright [pp. 252–61]

This story concerns a poor black youth, Dave, whose need for acceptance and respect as a man is identified in the opening paragraph with possession of a gun: "One of these days he was going to get a gun and practice shooting, and they [the older field hands] couldn't talk to him as though he were a little boy." Almost seventeen, Dave's feelings of inferiority are clear reflections of the attitudes of those around him: he is referred to as a "boy" at least five times in the story, his mother compares him to hogs, and he feels exploited like an animal ("They treat me like a mule"). Wrapped up in his longing to assert his manhood is Dave's anger at being thought of as a "nigger." His mother calls him a "nigger" and he himself regards the other field workers as "niggers"—examples of the way that Dave and his family have internalized the demeaning image that the white majority has created for blacks.

Although readers will be generally sympathetic to Dave's situation and understand the source of his low self-esteem, Wright makes it clear that Dave is unprepared for the responsibilities of manhood and that his decision to gain respect and maturity by owning a gun is naive and misguided. Dave lies to his mother, pays too much money for an old gun that he has only the slightest idea of how to use, and is "helpless" to deal with the violent consequences that the gun causes. Instead of giving him the respect he craves, the gun brings more humiliation and increases Dave's subservience to the white landowner. In the end, when Dave jumps a train, naively believing it will take him "somewhere where he could be a man," the reader knows that the journey to manhood will be much longer and more difficult than Dave suspects.

Possible Responses to *Questions for Discussion and Writing*

1. Dave assumes that once he's a gun owner, he'll get the respect he wants. He feels as if he's treated like a child, even though he's "almost a man." And he *is* treated like a child since his mother collects his wages, he still lives at home, his father is able to paddle him if he misbehaves, and he's called "boy" wherever he goes. He needs respect and feels a gun will provide it.
2. The accidental shooting of the mule ultimately reveals that Dave is still an adolescent, unable to deal with the consequences of his actions. His acquiring the gun may be seen as an act of rebellion, but his frenzied efforts to save the mule suggest that he didn't deliberately kill it, not even subconsciously. His hostility seems directed not at his family but at his fellow field workers who fail to pay him the respect he thinks he deserves because he's "almost a man."
3. Dave lives in a shack with no electricity or running water, eating black-eyed peas and fatback for dinner, and his working conditions are dawn to dusk at hard labor, plowing all day behind a mule. The white storekeeper is presumably better off since he runs a store and owns a catalog. Dave's father still is the authority figure in the family, but Dave clearly can manipulate his tenderhearted mother with ease.

4. Ken Kesey's *One Flew Over the Cuckoo's Nest* has a similar ending, with the character called Chief fleeing into the night, perhaps to find a better life, perhaps not. We never know, just as we never know how Dave's life will turn out. He may become just another angry young man with a gun, or he may find a better life than the one he's leaving behind. That result doesn't appear extremely likely, though, since he has no money—only a gun. The open ending seems a perfect conclusion for this story.
5. Certainly Dave's decision to leave town will result in completely changing his life. He has no money, no job, and no skills, so earning a living could be difficult. But he has gained his freedom. Sammy's decision to walk out of the A & P ends only his job, but his parents, with whom he still lives, will be unhappy to hear the news, and at the end of the story, even Sammy is feeling "how hard the world is going to be to me hereafter."

Additional Questions for Discussion and Writing
1. Examine the sentences in the first paragraph. Which are statements from the objective narrator, and which ones are thoughts going through Dave's mind? Why does the author use a third-person narrator? Is this narrator omniscient?
2. Dave had a desire to be respected and treated like a man. Is that desire in itself a worthwhile goal? Is owning and being able to use a gun a positive way to establish and demonstrate one's manhood? What alternatives, if any, did Dave have? Will Dave find the respect he is searching for?

Making Connections
→What statement about men and guns can you derive from reading Richard Wright's "The Man Who Was Almost a Man" and Tobias Wolff's "Hunters in the Snow"?

Video
→"Almos' a Man." 39 minutes, color, 1977. Film adaptation with LaVar Burton; directed by Stan Lathan. Available from Filmic Archives and Perspective Films.

WHY I LIVE AT THE P. O. by Eudora Welty [pp. 261–70]
This delightful story, which was Welty's first published work, first appeared in the *Atlantic Monthly* in April of 1941. The plot consists largely of a battle of words related by a first-person narrator in the humorous hyperbole of the Southern idiom. Welty reproduces this colorful language with consummate skill. Critics have written about the story basically from two perspectives, both focusing on Sister, the narrator. One group thinks Sister truly is unfairly treated, "the only sane person in a childish, neurotic, bizarre family," one who shows "unerring good sense and admirable mastery over the reality in which she finds herself." She is honest about her dislike for Stella-Rondo, who often seems to be a troublemaker. She lies about Sister's behavior with Uncle Rondo and eventually turns the family against her. The family does treat Sister badly (Mama even slaps her), even though she's the only one in the house doing any work. Uncle Rondo sets off firecrackers in her bedroom and finally prompts her to move out of the house.

51

Other critics, however, see Sister as primarily at fault for the rift in the family. These writers point out her exaggerated self-pity and "ironic self-exposure as a petty and jealous sibling." She leaves the family to save her pride, spitefully taking with her a number of items that the others will miss: the electric fan, the pillow (right from behind Papa-Daddy), the radio, the sewing machine motor, the thermometer, and the "great big piano lamp." The last sentence in the story makes clear her unwillingness to compromise or even to listen to other viewpoints.

Welty herself has commented on the story, suggesting that Sister will move back home once she gets over being mad. "I was trying to show how," she says, "in these tiny little places such as where they come from, the only entertainment that people have is dramatizing the family situation, which they do fully knowing what they are doing. They're having a good time. . . . It's a Southern kind of exaggeration."

Possible Responses to *Questions for Discussion and Writing*

1. Sister's bids for sympathy are so exaggerated that we laugh: she makes green-tomato pickle because "Somebody had to do it"; "Stella-Rondo hadn't done a thing but turn her against me . . . while I stood there helpless over the hot stove." Among our favorite expressions are "she like to made her drop dead for a second"; "Do you think it wise to disport with ketchup in Stella-Rondo's flesh-colored kimono?"; Uncle Rondo "piecing on the ham"; Stella-Rondo "had a conniption fit"; "kiss my foot"; and "Jaypan came within a very narrow limit of drowning."

2. The racial slur shows that Sister and probably her whole family are uneducated bigots—despite Sister's having gone to the "Normal School" and Papa-Daddy's being a leading citizen of the tiny, jerkwater town. Welty shows the racial prejudice that was endemic at that time in that place, just as Twain did in *Adventures of Huckleberry Finn*. The last sentence in the story also shows us that Sister is closed-minded, unwilling even to listen to the other side of the argument.

3. Stella-Rondo is just as snippy and rude as Sister. When Sister implies that Shirley-T is not adopted (but illegitimate), Stella-Rondo commands Sister in no uncertain terms to "make no future reference to my adopted child whatsoever." She twists Sister's words about Papa-Daddy and lies about Sister's appraisal of Uncle Rondo in the flesh-colored kimono (if we can believe Sister's report of what she had actually said). Mama takes Stella-Rondo's side in the domestic dispute because she clings to the romantic view of her family as happy and doesn't want to believe that her daughter has a child born out of wedlock, which was still very much a shameful thing at the time this story was set.

4. Sister's statement is ironic because she, too, is "cutting off her nose to spite her face" by leaving her comfortable home and moving into the small space at the back of the post office. She tells us three times how happy she is and how much she likes it there, even though there's "not much mail," so she has little to do and almost nobody to talk to. From what we've seen of Sister in the story, we can be fairly sure she wouldn't really be happy living all alone.

5. Critics have written from both of these perspectives. See discussion above.

Making Connections

→The daughter in Joyce Carol Oates' "Where Are You Going, Where Have You Been?" is also leaving home. What family dynamics are operating in each case? Are there any similarities? Any differences?

Audios

→"Eudora Welty." 1 hr. CD. The author reads six stories, including "Why I Live at the P. O." Available from Caedmon Records and Harper Audio.

→"On Story Telling." 53 minutes, 1961. Available from Audio Prose Library.

I STAND HERE IRONING by Tillie Olsen [pp. 270–75]

This story is an often bitter and despondent recounting of the trials of being poor and having children. Olsen's monologue hammers home emotionally wrenching scenes and makes the needs and wants of both mother and child painful to the reader. When the mother refuses to give a conventional "love overcomes adversity" story, the reader must live in poverty with the single mother, rather than gloss over the difficulties. Here is a long tale of missed opportunities, intimidating professionals, and the grievous insufficiency of life at the edge of poverty. It is clear that the living conditions have created spiritual and emotional deprivation as well. The mother gives up much of her life and aspirations in order to care for her children. It is no mystery to her. She tries to suppress her own feelings as she recounts the upbringing of her talented daughter, Emily, to the imaginary audience of a school counselor. The self-control is admirable, if incomplete. Olsen reflects the common experiences of millions of people, and the reverberations strengthen the tone and impact of the story.

Critic Robert Coles points out that the last words of the story "bring the reader back to the first words. . . . A working woman is making the best of *her* situation, even as she expects her daughter to do so. A mother shakes her fist at the universe, not excitedly, and with no great expectation of triumph, but out of a determination to assert her worth, her capabilities, however injured or curbed, her ability to see, to comprehend, and to imagine—and to assert too her daughter's—everyone's." And writer Amy Hempel says that "Olsen gives us the life of a family and of a generation, of the country during the Depression. . . . The story's dignity comes from the mother recounting the things she was unable to do *for her daughter* . . . What she feels is not guilt but grief."

Possible Responses to *Questions for Writing and Discussion*

1. When Emily is only 8 months old, her mother has to leave her in the care of a woman downstairs "to whom she was no miracle at all." Then the mother has to leave her with her husband's parents. At age two Emily is sent to an ill-run nursery school. When she is four or five, "she had a new daddy to learn to love." She has the red measles and doesn't recover, so has to go to a sterile and bureaucratic convalescent home for poor children and is there for eight months. She does not do well in school, she suffers from asthma, and she does not get along with her sister Susan. Her mother has four children now, besides Emily, who has to help raise the littler ones. Finally at high school age Emily displays talent as a comedian, and "Suddenly she was Somebody," who appears to have a career possibility. Her

growing up was difficult since there was never enough money, and she had to share her mother's love and attention with too many siblings, but she seems to have turned out well enough at the end, or seems to have adapted to her many disappointments by developing an at least superficially happy persona.

2. Ironing in this story seems to suggest the pressures in life that can flatten a person's attempts to succeed. It is an especially apt symbol of traditional women's work. The last line reinforces this idea as the mother seems to be hoping her daughter will cultivate her talents, will become aware "that she is more than this dress on the ironing board, helpless before the iron."

3. In that paragraph the mother recounts all the trials that Emily had to suffer in growing up and blames herself for some of those difficulties, at the same time that she makes reasonable excuses for her failings: "I was a young mother, I was a distracted mother"; "We were poor and could not afford for her the soil of easy growth." She seems to blame herself for some of those difficulties but, in fact, carefully outlines the external causes for what would appear to the social worker to be a mother's failures. The paragraph may be seen to function as expiation of the mother's guilt. If the paragraph had come earlier, it would have undercut the effectiveness of the mother's anguished accounting of all of Emily's problems.

4. The mother actually says, "Let her be," not "Let it be." She is, in effect, talking to herself, reassuring herself that Emily will be all right, even if she doesn't enjoy a stellar career: "So all that is in her will not bloom—but in how many does it? There is still enough left to live by." But she wants Emily not to be ground down by circumstances ("helpless before the iron") as she herself was while struggling to raise too many children with too little money.

Additional Questions for Writing and Discussion

1. Make a list of the major events of Emily's life. How would *you* sum up this life?
2. Ironing is emphasized in the title and mentioned several times in the story. Why?
3. What is the point of the next-to-last paragraph? Why is this paragraph needed? What would be the effect had it come earlier in the story?
4. Why does the mother say, "Let it be"? Do you think she is right to say this?

Making Connections

→Examine the varieties of mother–daughter relationships in Tillie Olsen's "I Stand Here Ironing," Flannery O'Connor's "Good Country People," Hisaye Yamamoto's "Seventeen Syllables," and Alice Walker's "Everyday Use." What connections can you see among the relationships and the settings of the stories?

Audio

→"I Stand Here Ironing." 77 minutes, 1 cassette. Includes several selections. Available from American Audio Prose Library.

SEVENTEEN SYLLABLES by Hisaye Yamamoto [pp. 276–85]
From the beginning of "Seventeen Syllables," we are aware of a cultural conflict between Tome Hayashi and her teenaged daughter (who has such an American name), Rosie.

Rosie pretends to admire her mother's haiku because she doesn't want to admit that she has not mastered Japanese, while "English lay ready on the tongue." She also does not admit that the haiku she likes is a humorous, colloquial one. In the end, Tome realizes that Rosie's promise never to marry is just a dodge like these.

Parallel plots concern the two females moving steadily away from the father's control. As Ume Hanazono (her pen name), Tome creates a strong intellectual life and companions, excluding the conventional, inartistic husband. Rosie discovers her sexuality and thinks much more of Jesus Carrasco than of her father. Both women are veering toward danger.

Ume Hanazono's life ends when her husband destroys her haiku prize. In her unhappiness, Tome tells Rosie about her sad past and how her hormones landed her in America indebted to a slow-witted husband. Rosie, enrapt with sexual feelings herself, is not ready to learn from her mother's example. Her mother, no doubt envisioning her daughter's dreadful future, finds it difficult to comfort her.

Possible Responses to *Questions for Discussion and Writing*

1. Rosie's mother would like to interest her daughter in *haiku,* but Rosie has no interest in language or poetry, only in a new boyfriend, Jesus, of whom her mother would not approve since she wants to protect her daughter from any premature sexual entanglements. The reason Rosie's mother is so concerned is made apparent at the conclusion of the story, giving it a nice unity.
2. Ume's (Tome's) literary success annoys her plodding, anti-intellectual husband by making him feel inferior. He expresses his anger by destroying her "best poem" prize right in front of the magazine editor who has delivered it, thus bringing her brief writing career to a shattering, abrupt end.
3. Rosie's feelings for Jesus are decidedly sexual: "Thus, kissed by Jesus, Rosie for the first time fell entirely victim to a helplessness delectable beyond speech." At first they have a friendly bantering relationship that soon turns flirtatious, culminating in her sneaking out to meet him after dark and receiving a kiss. Her feelings for him are important since the sexual awakening Rosie experiences with the kiss is the same hormonal surge that led her mother to ruin her life with a pregnancy by a man from a higher social class who could not marry her.
4. The episodes about Rosie and the ones about her mother focus on their relationships with men: with Jesus, in Rosie's case; with her husband and Mr. Kuroda, in her mother's case.
5. During the visit to the Hayanos, we see the tension between Rosie's intellectual mother and her dull father, as he drags the family home while all but him are having a delightful time. We can also tell that he is jealous of his wife's ability to converse with Mr. Hayanos about *haiku,* a topic about which her husband is necessarily silent and resentful. Rosie is aware of the problem in her parents' marriage but decides to ignore it.
6. Rosie's mother knows full well the power of sexual desire and the enormous price young women often pay when they respond to it. Since she herself has paid a terrible price, she tries to warn her daughter, hoping to spare her a similar fate, but Rosie's "Yes, yes, I promise" comes too quickly, too glibly. It takes Tome a few moments before she can collect herself and comfort her daughter, fearing as she does that

Rosie will most likely fall prey to the same compelling hormonal danger that Tome did at her daughter's age.

Additional Questions for Discussion and Writing

1. What does Rosie mean when she says that she "lived for awhile with two women"? Have you ever felt like this about a parent or relative? Might anyone see *you* as two people at some point in your life?
2. In what ways is *haiku* the central metaphor of the story? What does it suggest about the difficulty of communicating in two different languages, and how does it comment on the role of women in a traditional society such as Japan's?
3. Who is the main character in the story—Rosie or her mother? Compare the story to Tillie Olsen's "I Stand Here Ironing" regarding this same point.

Making Connections

→What are the young women attempting to escape in Yamamoto's "Seventeen Syllables" and Oates's "Where Are You Going, Where Have You Been?"
→Compare the sexual response and involvement of Rosie with the sexual indiscretion and punishment of Babli in "The Father." What factors save Rosie from Balbi's fate?

Video

→"Hot Summer Winds." Written and directed by Emiko Omori. Based on "Seventeen Syllables" and "Yoneko's Earthquake." 1991. PBS American Playhouse series.

A & P by John Updike [pp. 285–90]
"A & P" is a frequently anthologized story, perhaps because of the strong first-person point of view. The narrator, a 19-year-old male, lets us in on his stream of thoughts unabashedly. Students may see how this point of view is different from an objective one. The mixed tenses (past and present) reflect the way someone might really tell a story out loud.

The narrator is certainly a disaffected youth, with something negative to say about everything from pineapple juice to Tony Martin. He obviously thinks his job, the people he works with, and the shoppers are beneath him. The fact that he's stuck in a dead-end job, taking orders from a boss he doesn't respect and being careful not to upset his parents, may contribute to his snide attitude. Thus, when he quits, he is not leaving behind a beloved career.

Women in particular come under Sammy's critical scrutiny, and the only female that seems to pass is Queenie (though parts of the other girls with her are magnanimously okayed). The fact that she ignores his dubious heroism, perhaps, is what pushes him to insist on quitting. It is interesting to ponder whether Updike was creating a chauvinist monster on purpose or whether he thought Sammy really was a small-town hero. Your students may be divided on the issue.

Adventurous students might also be interested in reading "A & P Revisited" by Greg Johnson, a contemporary retelling of Updike's story that hilariously transforms Queenie and her companions into UZI-toting, leather-jacketed terrorists. It's included in a collection of Johnson's stories *A Friendly Deceit* (John Hopkins UP, 1992).

Possible Responses to *Questions for Discussion and Writing*

1. Sammy exhibits a nonchalant attitude toward his job. The ease with which he quits it certainly shows this, along with his disdain for the usual customers, whom he describes as bums, "sheep pushing their carts down the aisle," "houseslaves in pin curlers," "scared pigs in a chute." He has little affinity, either, for his co-workers. Stoksie, a young man about Sammy's age, already has "two babies chalked up on his fuselage" (a reference to the practice of fighter pilots in World War II, who would proudly affix images of enemy planes they had shot down in air battles on the fuselages of their planes). Sammy observes in what sounds a bit like a sneer, "I forgot to say he thinks he's going to be manager some sunny day." He employs a clever bit of wordplay when he says that the lecherous butcher, while watching the young women go by, is "sizing up their joints." Lengel, the manager, who doesn't even rate a "Mr." before his name, is described as "pretty dreary," with "that sad Sunday-school-superintendent stare." At the end after Sammy quits, his attitude changes. Now dejected, Lengel "begins to look very patient and old and gray."

2. Sammy quits his job as a protest against his boss's rebuke of the three young women in their skimpy bathing suits: "so I say 'I quit' to Lengel quick enough for them to hear, hoping they'll stop and watch me, their unsuspected hero." Sammy sees his gesture as an act of heroism on his part, but since it's evident that he's bored with his job and wants out of it anyway, he has made no sacrifice. The young women simply hurry out without giving him a second look, eager to get away from the embarrassing situation. He walks out, looking for "my girls," but they are long gone.

3. We have no way of knowing whether the world will be hard on Sammy hereafter. We do know that his parents will be disappointed, perhaps angry, that he has quit his job for little or no reason. His "stomach kind of fell," so perhaps he's having second thoughts already and thinking the job maybe wasn't so bad after all. But he's young and has a supportive family (his mom irons his shirts and his parents are friends of his ex-boss; perhaps they'll help him find another job). But he's definitely feeling let down because he thought he was making a gallant gesture and nobody even noticed.

4. There's no doubt that Sammy, the first-person narrator, is sexist. He objectifies the young women, focusing in detail on their bodies as they walk through the store. But the real clincher is his observation that, "You never know for sure how girls' minds work (do you really think it's a mind in there or just a little buzz like a bee in a glass jar?)." And his observation about "the plump one in plaid, that I liked better from the back—a really sweet can" is majorly offensive, as is his referring to one of the three as "Big Tall Goony-Goony." But the story itself is not sexist. The story clearly reveals Sammy's sexist behavior as adolescent and even laughable.

5. This writing assignment will help students to grasp the importance of point of view in fiction, as well as in understanding how human beings respond to social interactions in real life, depending upon their own attitudes and position in a social setting.

Additional Questions for Discussion and Writing

1. Why do you think the story is written in mixed past and present tense?
2. Can Sammy's decision to quit be seen as a positive one? Explain how it might be

interpreted as a gesture to break with conformity, to be independent, and to do the right thing.
3. What do you think of Sammy's use of detail, especially in describing people? What do the figures of speech he uses indicate about his character?

Making Connections
→Compare Sammy to Jake in Dagoberto Gilb's "Love in L.A." What do these characters have in common?

Audio
→"John Updike." The author reads six stories. 169 minutes. Available from American Audio Prose Library.

WHERE ARE YOU GOING, WHERE HAVE YOU BEEN? [pp. 290–302]
Like "The Ransom of Red Chief" by O. Henry, this kidnap story has a disturbing twist: in this case, the victim halfway (or three-quarters?) wants to go. Connie's life at home is a fairly normal, middle-class white one. However, in her view it is insufferably boring and the people in it dullsville. Fueled by the pop music that infuses the story and her life, Connie has vague dreams of escape to a more exciting world. She escapes to tawdry teenaged hangouts and liaisons and invests them with romance through a transformation assisted by song lyrics. The thin line between reality and fantasy supports the motif of deceptions and illusions in the story.

After refusing to go to a terminally dull family picnic, Connie sits in the heat in a stupefied daydream and then listens for a hypnotic hour and a half to the Bobby King XYZ Sunday Jamboree. Then the bizarrely named Arnold Friend and Ellie Oscar fatefully drive up the lane. Connie's interaction with Friend is a drama of lies, hints, deceptions, suspicions, and finally threats. It has a shimmering air of unreality most of the time, with a repeated image of distracting reflections that fool the eye. Connie's state of mind is such that even though by the end of the story she knows that Friend is not one, that he has planned her abduction and will likely carry out his threats upon her family if she does not cooperate, the unknown looks better than the known. She voluntarily walks out to him.

In one sense, Connie acts heroically, saving her family by sacrificing herself. The heroism is tainted by the fact that she actually wants to leave her family, and her future looks bleak anyway. At least, with Arnold, she is going to "so much land that [she] had never seen before." He confuses her and seduces her with images from the popular songs that seem to be her sole connection to a better life, and she succumbs.

Additional Questions for Discussion and Writing
1. How is this story different from what you'd expect from a kidnap story? What is the victim's attitude toward being abducted?
2. What role does popular teen music play in the story? Go back through the story and make a list of the places it comes up. How does it affect Connie?
3. What kind of life does Connie have at the beginning of the story? What makes her happy and unhappy? Would you call her a normal middle-class teenager?

4. Could you interpret one theme of this story to be reality versus illusion? What different parts of the story fit the theme?

Video

→"Smooth Talk." A dramatization of the story; with Treat Williams and Laura Dern. 92 minutes, color, 1985. Available from Vestron Video.

→"Joyce Carol Oates: American Appetites." 30 minutes, color, 1990. Available from Filmic Archives.

Audio

→"Joyce Carol Oates." The author reads "Marya" and "Where Are You Going, Where Have You Been?" Available from American Audio Prose Library.

Web Sites

→*Celestial Timepiece: A Joyce Carol Oates Home Page*. Offers extensive information and resources as well as a discussion forum. **http://jco.usfca.edu/**

→*Oates, Joyce Carol Forum Frigate*. A forum for discussing Oates and her works.
http://carolinanavy.com/fleet2/f2/zauthors/Oates,JoyceCarolhall/shakespeare1.html

WHAT WE TALK ABOUT WHEN WE TALK ABOUT LOVE by Raymond Carver
[pp. 302–10]

Though some readers find no fascination in listening to rich people get drunk and babble, Carver must be admired for reproducing so accurately the timbre of the event (or non-event). As promised in the opening sentence, Mel does most of the talking in the story. Though he first asserts that spiritual love is the only real love (having been in the seminary but quit for medical school), he very soon abandons that stance. The violence and suicide of Ed, Terri's old boyfriend, provoke Mel, and he says that those acts were not driven by love. Terri uselessly insists, with Mel calling her "a romantic," further confusing the scene, while Laura and the narrator are so relativistic that they won't even condemn abusive relationships.

The narrator has some kind of definition of love, made obvious when he says of Laura, "In addition to being in love, we like each other and enjoy one another's company," as though the last two items were not included in the definition of love. The idea that love does not last tangles the issue further, with Terri claiming that Laura and the narrator are too newly wed to be experts and Mel being amazed that he used to love his first wife and now does not, but loves Terri instead. The ideal of courtly love is suggested by Mel's ramble about knights—but so is the idea of not being injured. The tale of the old people who remain in love floats in and out.

As the story progresses, the effects of drunkenness come more and more into play, with the structure of the conversation becoming ever looser. At signs of sadness or conflict, the characters claim their love for each other, confounding the definition yet again. Toward the end, Mel segues into paternal love and is derailed by hatred for his ex-wife. Finally, the conversation, like the evening, fades into silence and darkness. The story delivers exactly what the title promises.

Possible Responses to *Questions for Discussion and Writing*

1. The definitions and descriptions of love begin with spiritual love, move on to possessive or violent love; then love as an absolute gets mentioned but not defined or explored; next, the narrator, Nick, describes his friendship/love relationship with Laura, and she says she knows what love is; but Terry points out that they haven't been together very long; Mel declares that "real love" is "physical love, carnal love, sentimental love" but admits that it doesn't necessarily last. The characters never really arrive at a definition of love, perhaps because midway through the story they are well into their second bottle of gin.
2. This story can be distinguished from most short stories because it has no plot. Carver's stories are recognizable for their focus on conversation, often meandering and fairly pointless conversation.
3. The narrator is saying that their love is not simply carnal but based on friendship.
4. We are introduced to the four characters in the story and know that one of them, Mel, is a cardiologist; we are given the setting—Mel's sunny kitchen in which the four are sitting around a table drinking gin; and we know they all have come from other places to live in this locale—wherever that is.
5. This assignment should inspire any creative writers in your classes.

Additional Questions for Discussion and Writing

1. Do the characters really talk about love? Or are they talking about jealousy, misunderstanding, and pain?
2. How does each couple represent a different stage of love?

Making Connections

→What type of love is described in Donne's poem "A Valediction: Forbidding Mourning" or Marvell's "To His Coy Mistress" or Lovelace's "To Lucasta, on Going to the Wars"? Do these kinds of love fit any of the categories discussed in Carver's story?

THE LESSON by Toni Cade Bambara [pp. 311–17]

Bambara's "The Lesson" aptly teaches a lesson of its own: the unfairness of the distribution of wealth in a rich capitalist society—a society "in which some people can spend on a toy what it would cost to feed a family of six or seven" for a year. Sylvia, the feisty, street-smart narrator, knows all the rules of survival in her impoverished environment, but she doesn't quite grasp the lesson in socialist economics that Miss Moore is trying to teach the children by showing them the sailboat in F.A.O. Schwartz. The academically gifted Sugar gets the point at once, but Sylvia at the end of the story is only on the verge of understanding. Intuitively, she's angry; she just hasn't figured out yet who or what is making her furious. Her final line, "Ain't nobody gonna beat me at nuthin," suggests that she soon will get the message and direct her energy and ingenuity toward beating the system.

The story is saved from being overtly didactic by the colorful language and the astute portrayals of the youngsters, with their humorous nicknames and raucous banter. Sylvia, a smart kid with attitude, is the leader of the pack. Yet bright though she is, she misses the point of the lesson because her perceptions are colored by her antagonism toward all authority figures—especially the well-meaning Miss Moore, who represents the establishment only in Sylvia's mind. This antagonism makes Sylvia a somewhat unreliable narrator, especially concerning the right-minded Miss Moore and the other adults. Sylvia starts out intending not to let Miss Moore get through to her. But there are places in the story where Sylvia is affected. One such moment occurs when she notices her own reaction: " 'Unbelievable,' I hear myself say and am really stunned." After that, she talks to Miss Moore, hesitates before entering the store, and feels anger and irritation. Since the lesson Miss Moore is teaching is the lesson Bambara wants the readers to learn, Miss Moore is surely a more admirable person than Sylvia makes her out to be.

Possible Responses to *Questions for Discussion and Writing*

1. Sylvia is a spirited survivor of the racism and poverty that define her community, a bright, verbal, and creative teenager who has learned to reject before she can be rejected and to mock before she can be mocked. Take, for example, her first reactions to Fifth Avenue: "Everybody dressed up in stockings. One lady in a fur coat, hot as it is. White folks crazy." This resourcefulness and potential make her the perfect narrator for the story because she is Miss Moore's perfect student for the lesson. She is a reliable but also entertaining narrator in her honest reporting of her strong thoughts and words. After all, this language and those views are her weapons of self-defense. She is not, however, reliable in revealing those things she cannot yet understand—that is, those things that Miss Moore is trying to get her to see about herself and her potential.

2. Miss Moore is first revealed through Sylvia's eyes as a troublesome outsider, a woman who had been to college, the woman who plots "boring-ass things" for the children. Readers who accept Sylvia's stereotypical view of this "lady" with "nappy hair and proper speech and no makeup" might expect her to be simply a teacher of the kind of cultural lessons that lead to black accommodation or acculturation, lessons about the things to be gained by aspiring to white norms. This is a conformity that the rebellious young Sylvia is not at all interested in pursuing. The adults, on the other hand, are suspicious of Miss Moore, even condescending, but they also sense some promise of opportunity in her influence. Sugar, who hasn't yet developed Sylvia's resistant stance, is more open to Miss Moore's persuasion.

3. While visiting the toy store, Sylvia experiences the familiar emotions of desire and shame, emotions that trigger her resistant pride. In her confused adolescence, this pride leads to a desire to act out, to "punch somebody in the mouth." Eventually, though, left by Miss Moore to discover the lesson for herself, Sylvia begins to articulate a more conscious if not fully understood resentment of her exclusion: "Who are these people that spend that much for performing clowns. . . . What kinda work they do and how they live and how come we ain't in on it?" As the group leaves the store, the hard work of Miss Moore's lesson leaves Sylvia with "a headache for thinkin so hard."

4. The last line of the story, "But ain't nobody gonna beat me at nuthin," captures the hope that Miss Moore has succeeded in her lesson, that the spirited, clever girl she sees when she looks at Sylvia has begun to re-see her community and her place in the larger world and that Sylvia will bring her spunk and energy to bear on changing her life, a promise that is underscored by her shift from focusing on the money as the

61

source of some immediate desire (the path taken by Sugar at the end of the story) to a focus on her mind as a place for deeper satisfaction (a need to "think this day through").

5. If students write this essay, you will want to concentrate a significant part of class discussion on question number 1, especially on Sylvia as the naïve but clever narrator of the story.

Additional Questions for Discussion and Writing

1. Briefly describe each of Sylvia's friends. How do nicknames help characterize the ones who have them?
2. In what ways is this a story about borders, both literal and figurative? Pick out examples and explain them.

Making Connections

→Explain the views about money of the child narrators in this story and Lawrence's "The Rocking-Horse Winner." Where do the children get their viewpoints? Who is able to influence them?

Audio

→"An Interview with Toni Cade Bambara and Kay Bonetti." 90 minutes. The author discusses her writing style. Available from Audio Prose Library.

A FATHER by Bharati Mukherjee [pp. 317–24]

While the Bhowmicks' marriage is troubled from the start, the tensions are heightened by the culture clash between India and America. The father is presented as an aloof, meticulous, religious person who is (in his opinion) saddled with a restive, agnostic, controlling wife, and an "untender, unloving," liberated daughter. His worship of the fearsome Kali, "goddess of wrath and vengeance," is important in understanding his irrational behavior at the end of the story. He prays to Kali, even though the goddess is a torment in his life, inspiring fear, not love or compassion. He observes "how scarlet and saucy was the tongue that Kali-Mata stuck out at the world." Just after he hears of his daughter's artificial insemination, he sees her "tongue, thick and red, squirming," and the association triggers uncontrollable rage.

The violence of that horrifying conclusion stems directly from the clash of cultural attitudes toward the daughter's out-of-wedlock pregnancy. Babli, entirely in tune with American values, chooses pregnancy through artificial insemination without even consulting her parents. The mother, who seems quite Americanized but still has Indian friends, clings to at least one aspect of her old-country morality and is furious at the prospect of shame brought upon the family by an illegitimate birth. The father, still closely aligned to the superstitious religion of his childhood, is surprisingly not outraged by the illegitimacy (because he fancies a grandchild) but goes ballistic at what he sees as the monstrosity of artificial insemination.

62

Possible Reponses to *Questions for Discussion and Writing*

1. The father in this story is an aloof, meticulous, religious person, who wakes two minutes before his alarm goes off in the morning. He spends a lot of time in prayer at his household shrine to Kali, fearsome goddess of wrath and vengeance, whose image he made himself. He is also superstitious: his neighbor's sneeze signals bad luck to him, so he goes back into the house to start his trip to work all over again. His wife and daughter, those "bright mocking women," browbeat him constantly. His religion causes trouble in the family because both women have no use for religion. For his wife it poses something of an impediment, since he devotes himself to morning prayers for so long that she must nag at him to hurry to breakfast before the French toast gets cold and rubbery, and since she also has a job to get to on time.

2. The somewhat restive mother is an agnostic, "a believer in ambition, not grace," who has taken to reading pop psychology books and nagging her husband about a multitude of things (his endless prayers, his inept bridge playing, his hiding his feelings, his unwillingness to discuss their "relationship"). Since the story is told through a limited omniscient point of view, the characterizations of both women are reflected through the father's consciousness and are thus perhaps not entirely reliable. The mother has apparently gotten the upper hand in the marriage. Her husband says she "forced" him to bring the family to "sex-crazy" Detroit, so he blames her for their daughter's illegitimate pregnancy. In the father's regretful estimation, she has changed from "a pliant wife to an ambitious woman."

3. The brittle, abrasive adult daughter, who still lives with her parents, is brilliant and works as an engineer, but she is not "womanly or tender" enough to suit her father. She is a thoroughly liberated young woman, who drives a "fiery red Mitsubishi" and does pretty much as she pleases without consulting her parents, which discourages her conventional, exceedingly proper father.

4. Mr. Bhowmick does not love his wife, did not love her, we are told, even when he married her, but took her because she came with a dowry of a two-year education for him at Carnegie Tech. Nor is his daughter "the child he would have chosen as his only heir." He would have liked her to be more tender and womanly. Since Babli shows no affection, scorns his religion, and is intolerant of his deeply held cultural values, it's not surprising that he feels ambivalent about her.

5. If the family had remained in India, the daughter would perhaps not have been exposed to the idea of single motherhood through artificial insemination as being acceptable behavior. The father is not outraged by the illegitimacy (because he fancies a grandchild) but is seized by uncontrollable rage at what he sees as the monstrosity of artificial insemination, prompting the horrifying conclusion.

Making Connections

→Compare the cultural clashes in this story with the ones in "Seventeen Syllables" by Hisaye Yamamoto. Consider how the old-world values embraced by the two fathers cause conflict with the women in their families.

Video

→"Bharati Mukherjee: Conquering America." A conversation with Bill Moyers. 30 minutes, 1994. Available from Films for the Humanities.

THE RED CONVERTIBLE by Louise Erdrich [pp. 325–31]

This story is one of fourteen related stories that make up Erdrich's first novel, *Love Medicine* (1984), which chronicles the lives of two families on a North Dakota reservation between 1934 and 1984. "The Red Convertible" takes place in 1974, when Henry Junior comes back to the Chippewa Indian reservation after more than three years in Vietnam. The first-person narrator—Henry's youngest brother, Lyman—uses past tense to describe the finality of what happened to his brother and the red Oldsmobile convertible they once shared.

After an opening frame of four paragraphs, the story is told as a flashback, beginning with background on the two brothers and their pleasure in the car and then moving to Henry's return from Vietnam and his disorientation. When Henry fixes the convertible, he momentarily regains some of his former spirit, and the brothers get behind the wheel again, trying to recapture the carefree innocence of their youth. But Henry's inner turmoil, like that of the flooded river they park alongside, drives him to self-destruction. In the last paragraph, Lyman describes how he drove the car into the river after he couldn't rescue Henry, and the terrible irony of his opening remarks—"Now Henry owns the whole car, and . . . Lyman walks everywhere he goes"—is finally made clear.

Erdrich's use of symbolism (the convertible, the open highway, the river) is natural and unobtrusive. The story's episodic structure is loose and comfortable, like the relationship between the brothers; and the laconic, understated presentation of the narrator makes his emotional loss even more poignant and credible.

Possible Responses to *Questions for Discussion and Writing*

1. The red convertible stands as a symbol of the relationship between the two brothers, reflecting their individual and collective moments of "repose" and struggle. The car runs flawlessly through the months the pair travel the country; Lyman puts the car "up on blocks" while Henry is away at war; when Henry returns with post-traumatic stress, Lyman batters the car to match the frail brother's psychic state; Henry repairs it in a gesture of love for his brother; in their final drive, Henry realizes the impossibility of returning to his pre-war self and Lyman sends the car into the water in recognition of the end of their shared lives.

2. The picture, taken during a fleeting post-war moment of peace and brotherly connection, becomes too painful for Lyman to live with day to day, reminding him of the cost of the war to Henry and to him. Thus it stands as a symbol of the loss outlined by the story as a whole. Lyman seems hopeful at the moment the picture was taken ("Just the way he said it made me think he could be coming around"). This suggests the picture becomes painful only later, when he rediscovers it and finds he cannot even find joy in remembering this rare moment of calm.

3. Lyman runs the car into the river to return it to his brother, as he has tried to do in the past, and to bring light and understanding to his terrible loss.

4. The discussion of questions 1–4 will provide a number of ideas for this essay.

5. Students might use the condition of the convertible (question 1) as a guide to outlining their response to this prompt.

64

Additional Questions for Writing and Discussion

1. What do you think happened to Henry in Vietnam that changed him?
2. Describe the effect of the first paragraph when it is reread after finishing the story.
3. What do the episodes of travel (the place under the willows where they rested, taking Suzy home to Alaska) add to the story?

Making Connections

→Analyze the narrator of this story. Is he reliable? Compare him to other first-person narrators (Sammy in "A & P," Sylvia in "The Lesson," or the mother in "I Stand Here Ironing").

Audio

→Interview with Erdrich and her husband, Michael Dorris, about the centrality of a Native American identity to their work. 1 cassette, 50 minutes. Available from American Audio Prose Library.

PART III WRITING ABOUT POETRY

Chapter 12 How Do I Read Poetry? [pp. 335–38]

This brief chapter is a general presentation, an overview of terminology so that your students will have a base to work from. These concepts will all be more fully explained in the chapters following. Be sure to call to the attention of your students the useful list of "Critical Questions for Reading Poetry" at the end of this chapter.

One excellent way to introduce your students to the study of poetry is to dazzle them with its sound. If you read poetry well (or if you know someone who does), a prepared reading can help students hear the pleasures of the form. Another excellent choice is to play recorded poetry for the same purpose. Or, if you write poetry or have colleagues who do, you can arrange for a live poetry reading and, possibly, a discussion of why people write poetry and why it's important and valuable in our technological world.

Activities for Creative and Critical Thinking
You can help your students to enhance their appreciation for poetry and integrate their reading and writing skills by using some of the following projects:
- Find a song lyric that you think deserves to be called poetry. Write a short essay about this lyric that explains its poetic merits.
- Listen to some recent examples of rap and compose a short rap lyric of your own, one that tells a story.
- Record several different people reading the same poem aloud. Then write an analysis of these oral readings, focusing on the different interpretations that various readers give to the poem.
- Write a parody of any poem in this book. Do it in either prose or verse, but make it follow the structure of the original as closely as possible.
- Rewrite a lyric poem as an essay or a story. Assume the point of view of the persona in the poem; try to express the persona's feelings and ideas in prose. Don't just transcribe the poem into prose; try to capture the tone and message in your own words.
- Write a background commentary on the situation and emotions of the speaker in a poem. What circumstances and/or motives led this person to say what he or she says in the poem?
- Write an imaginary journal entry for the speaker of a particular poem.
- Write a letter to a poet, telling the author what you think of his/her poetry. Or ask questions about a specific poem. If the poet is still alive, send your letter to her/him.

Chapter 13 Writing About Persona and Tone [pp. 339–56]

Encourage students to use the term *persona* or *the speaker* (instead of, "the poet says") for the sake of accuracy. Sometimes poets do speak in their own voices, but often they do not. And when they do not, the persona frequently is voicing ideas and attitudes that are the opposite of those espoused by the poet. Tone is sometimes of little importance in a poem, but when tone is important, it can be crucial. To miss an ironic tone is to miss the meaning of the poem.

Who Is Speaking? [p. 339]

As an introductory writing experiment, ask students to adopt a persona and write in the "voice" of that persona. For instance, have them write as a parent to a son or daughter at college who keeps asking for more money (or who wants to drop out of school or has gotten in trouble with campus security). You can make the writing prompt as detailed or as general as you think it needs to be. You can also direct the writers not to identify their personas explicitly in the text, and then have other students (in small groups or pairs) try to figure out who is writing. Ask them how they determined the identity of the writer (persona)—i.e., what clues were provided in the text?

What Is Tone? [p. 340]

In this chapter we focus on verbal irony, since it's the main form of irony appearing in poetry. Because students frequently fail to pick up on irony, you may want to direct their attention to the other kinds—situational irony and dramatic irony.

To get at tone in written discourse, you can vary the above writing activity and direct your students to write more than one version of the same text—i.e., a letter from an angry, frustrated parent and one from an easy-going or permissive parent. Ask your students to discuss what changes in word choice and sentence structure occur as the tone changes.

A brief experiment involves asking your students to rewrite just a few lines of a poem to alter the tone. How many words have to be changed? Can one alteration change the tone? Insist that students find precise adjectives to describe the different tones they have created. Or ask your students to rewrite the titles of poems to suggest a different tone. What happens when we change "My Papa's Waltz" to "My Daddy's Dance" or "The Old Man's Rock 'n' Roll"? Can "The Ruined Maid" be retitled "The Fallen Woman"? Why didn't Hardy call his poem that?

Describing Tone [p. 340]

You might want to add these to the list of adjectives that can describe tone: angry, austere, bombastic, breezy, colloquial, comic, confessional, dreamlike, earthy, erudite, facetious, irreverent, nostalgic, ominous, pompous, prurient, sardonic, sensuous.

Asking Questions About the Speaker in "My Papa's Waltz" [pp. 345–46]

There is a good deal of disagreement about the tone of this poem. Individual responses to these questions will vary a lot, depending on personal experience and taste. Encourage students to be honest, and allow for a variety of opinions.

Describing the Tone in "The Ruined Maid" [p. 347]

Responses to these questions will vary, of course.

1. An innocent young woman from rural England (probably Hardy's home of Dorset) encounters a friend ('Melia) who has run away to London. The unnamed young woman questions 'Melia about her fancy clothes and citified ways.

2. "Maid" means an unmarried young woman, a virgin. This last meaning is crucial to the ironic tone and the idea of lost innocence. Hardy does not mean a female servant.
3. One definition for the noun *ruin* is "physical, moral, economic, or social collapse." The poet's almost cynical point turns on the fact that 'Melia's supposed moral collapse is accompanied by physical, economic, and social improvement.
4. 'Melia is probably a well-paid prostitute or a "kept woman." The bracelets, feathers, gown, and painted face (lines 13–14) suggest her occupation, as does her "lively" lifestyle (line 20) and her tendency to "strut" (line 22). In current American slang we might call her a "party girl" or a "call girl."
5. The opening tone of the questioner's lines is one of amazement and disbelief; by the end of the poem she is speaking with admiration and envy.
6. 'Melia seems proud, proper, cool, and even condescending. One critic has said she speaks with "cheerful irony" about her "ruin." Certainly she does not act ashamed.
7. The use of "ain't" in the final line might be taken as a slip into her former vernacular speech, suggesting that her urban polish does not run deep. But it is also possible to see 'Melia reverting to the ungrammatical language intentionally, with obvious relish, to emphasize the difference between herself and her former friend. This interpretation reads the last line as a final mocking jab at her friend's excessive naiveté.
8. Hardy's tone is ironic, mocking, even sarcastic and cynical. The still innocent maid is poor, gullible, and confused; the ruined maid is self-possessed, attractive, and well fixed. This ironic reversal denies the traditional wisdom about the "wages of sin."

Stanley Renner provides some interesting social background and commentary on this poem in his article "William Acton, the Truth about Prostitution, and Hardy's Not-So-Ruined Maid," *Victorian Poetry* 30.1 (Spring 1992): 19–28.

Describing the Tone in "The Unknown Citizen" [p. 348]
1. Writing prompt.
2. He is identified by number—no name is given.
3. The speaker (persona) is a representative of the state, some bureaucrat who helps to keep track of the masses. The persona uses the plural to identify with the state that he or she works for, and to cover any personal responsibility for the opinions and conditions expressed or implied.
4. The name is comical, as is the rhyme.
5. The capitalization suggests that these concepts have become personified and are paramount in the society portrayed in the poem; they are impersonal entities that have become much more important than individual persons, who remain numbers.
6. The persona praises the Unknown Citizen for his conformity. Auden himself is critical of the Unknown Citizen and would surely deplore the ideas expressed by the speaker in the poem.
7. The poem is satirical. The tone of the satire is sometimes humorous, but overall, Auden takes a relentlessly critical approach in exposing the conformist, dehumanized society that the speaker represents and supports.

Discovering Tone in "Go, Lovely Rose" [pp. 348–49]

1. It appears that the woman has rebuffed the speaker in some way, refuses to see him or receive his attention.
2. The rose is a traditional symbol of romantic love, as well as of beauty that does not last long.
3. "Uncommended" means, literally, unsung; thus she is unnoticed and hence unpraised.
4. "Wastes" in line 2 strikes a slightly harsh note, with overtones of pining away in love sickness. Both lines have an edge to them. Is it too much reality to suggest that she is wasting her life while her body is wasting away, anticipating the "die" of line 16? The "shuns" in line 7 suggests a deliberate, almost obstinate avoidance of life's pleasures.
5. The last imperative in the sequence of polite commands—go, tell, bid, *die*—startles us a little. But in the time period when the poem was written, the word *die* carried a double entendre: it also meant "to experience sexual orgasm."
6. No, poems at this time were usually sung.
7. Cajoling, charming, graceful, but quietly insistent, perhaps. There also seems to be just a touch of hostility or resentment lurking beneath the effortless charm of the speaker's words. The "then die" shocks us into focusing on the specter of age and death that *carpe diem* (seize the day) poems usually raise in their arguments for sexual pleasure. Contrast the tone of the speaker of this "invitation to love" lyric with that of the speaker of Andrew Marvell's "To His Coy Mistress" [p. 399], who seems more passionate and urgent in his entreaties.

Discovering Tone in "One Perfect Rose" [p. 349]

1. They both use the rose as a symbol of love, and they both employ a twist or turn in tone to make their points.
2. Parker's poem exploits the tonal shift to create a humorous, down-to-earth comment on romantic love (and romantic love poems).
3. The apostrophe changes the two-syllable word to a one-syllable word that fits the iambic meter of the line. But the poet may also be mocking the artificial language of many love lyrics, which seem to resort frequently to this linguistic device—thus giving her own poem a quaint, old-fashioned touch.
4. An amulet is a magical charm, ornament, or signifier.
5. It changes from traditionally romantic to openly materialistic. The single word "limousine" upsets all our expectations—in both rhythm and diction—and throws the whole stanza into another gear.
6. The total effect is parody. The tone is humorous and iconoclastic, as the writer slyly undercuts the established tradition of romantic idealism in poetry.

Analyzing the Student Response [p. 356]

We have deliberately included a sample student paper that argues for a questionable interpretation in order to allow your students to exercise their critical thinking skills.

1. The student states what he takes to be Housman's theme in the final paragraph of the essay. But surely Housman intended the poem to convey a broader meaning than the student settles for.

2. The student identifies Housman as the speaker in the poem in the fourth paragraph ("Housman tries to convince us . . ."). The speaker seems to be a detached (but not necessarily impartial) observer who could indeed be the poet.
3. The student fails to identify tone in the poem, which makes the analysis go off the track. Most readers think the speaker's tone is ironic. Who in his or her right mind would want to die young just in order to avoid seeing sports records broken? Although the student's opening sentence seems to use the same irony, he somehow misses the irony in the poem itself.
4. The student says that Housman "tries to convince us that it is best to die young," but he has missed the gentle irony of the line, "Smart lad to slip betimes away." Yes, those "Eyes the shady night has shut / Cannot see the record cut," but who would willingly choose to have that happen? To say, as the student does, that the poet thus "applauds the athlete's death" is to take seriously a message that—at best—might be intended to offer some comfort, to find some positive note in the tragedy.
5. The student allows his own experience as an athlete to color his understanding of the poem. He clearly agrees with the poet that sports records are not worth dying for, but he fails to see that Housman was being ironic. In the last paragraph, the student says that the poet "seems to think that setting records and living in the limelight are all that athletes are looking for in their lives." Not so. The poet, if able to respond, would probably say that the student makes some perceptive comments about the poem but unfortunately misses the point.

Chapter 14 Writing About Poetic Language [pp. 357–74]

Cultivating in your students a sensitivity to the literal and connotative meanings of words is crucial to their understanding and appreciation of poetry. We believe that the best way to go about making them responsive to the language of poetry is through close examination of numerous poems in class. Requiring students to learn definitions of the standard terms that are used in discussing poetry (metaphor, personification, paradox, etc.) may be counterproductive if your students already harbor negative feelings toward poetry. The important thing is for them to be able to *recognize* a metaphor and to grasp its meaning, not necessarily to be able to *define* one.

Examining Poetic Language [pp. 364–65]
1. The poem establishes its comparison by contrasting the temperate loveliness of the beloved with the "rough winds," the too-hot sun, the fading sun, and the shadow of death. The poem is a tribute that immortalizes "thy eternal summer," i.e., the unfading loveliness of the beloved.
2. Students should have fun with this assignment as they learn a great deal from it about the importance of rhyme and meter, as well as word choice. If any group feels intimidated by trying to write a serious poem as good as Shakespeare's, allow them to write a humorous version. Read the completed poems aloud to the class and ask them to discuss the effectiveness of the word choice and imagery. If some have attempted parodies, you might want to ask them to read Shakespeare's own parody, "My Mistress' Eyes Are Nothing Like the Sun" [p. 396 in the anthology].

3. The poem compares the soul's quest for meaning with the patient construction of a spider's web. The soul is personified. When your students substitute synonyms, they will become aware of the perfection of Whitman's word choice. You may want to put them in groups after they have written their versions in order to discuss how changing the words distorts the meaning, alters the images, and destroys the meter. Encourage them especially to see that "ductile" ("till the ductile anchor hold") is a key word in understanding Whitman's search for a belief that is flexible, not a rule-bound creed.

4. *Metaphors*: The turtle is identified with or described in terms of several different objects, without the use of *like* or *as*. The images used to convey the point or subject of the implied comparison are often quite striking. It might be worth the time to explore the visual pictures these images put across.

>line 2: "a barely mobile hard roll" and "a four-oared helmet"
>line 4: "rowing toward the grasses. . . ." (the turtle's locomotion = rowing)
>line 8: "stuck up to the axle" (identified as a car or truck, linking back to "mobile" and "dragging a packing case" in previous lines)
>lines 10–11: "convert / Her shell into a serving dish"
>line 13: "change her load of pottery [echoing "serving dish"] to wings"

Simile: ". . .like dragging / a packing-case places" (lines 5–6)

Personification: use of personal pronouns *she* and *her*; "her modest hopes" (line 7), "never imagining some lottery" (line 13); "Her only levity is patience / The sport of truly chastened things" (lines 14–15)

Assonance:
>lines 2–3: barely . . . hard, mobile . . . roll . . . four-oared, afford
>line 4: rowing . . . toward
>lines 5–6: track. . . graceless . . . dragging . . . packing-case places
>line 6: almost . . . slope
>line 7: modest hopes
>line 11: dish . . .lives

Alliteration:
>line 6: packing-case places
>lines 11–14: luck-level . . . lottery, load, levity
>line 10-11: She skirts . . . shell . . .serving. . . She

Internal rhyme: four-oared, afford (lines 2–3); ditch, which (line 10); lottery, pottery (lines 12–13); wings, things (lines 12,15)

5. In a general sense, the extended metaphor compares life to weaving a tapestry. A more particular meaning comes to light when students consider the nature of a tapestry, which frequently has a detailed, coherent pattern and may also tell a story. The persona in the poem tries to weave lasting meaning and pattern into his life span, only to find this task impossible. He takes several tactics, such as not looking behind him and tying new knots as they unravel, unsuccessfully. These tactics represent different ways of living—being future oriented and present oriented, respectively. His efforts to make a sensible narrative of both the past and the future are futile and, as we see in the last lines, these efforts also ruin present experience. The extended metaphor suggests that trying to control our lives so that they acquire lasting meaningfulness is ill fated.

71

6. The central paradox in "My Son My Executioner" was nicely stated in a popular Bob Dylan song: "He not busy being born is busy dying." The new child promises an immortality of sorts (since he will probably live longer than his parents and hold them in his memory) while at the same time reminding his parents that they are themselves getting older, moving toward death.

Choosing Vivid, Descriptive Terms [p. 367]

After students complete the exercise on improving sentences from their earlier papers, you might put them in groups to discuss each other's word changes. Ask them to consider whether the changed or added words constitute an improvement or not. If not, ask them to think of another wording that would be better.

Sample Student Paper [pp. 368–74]

The second draft of the sample student paper was marked (as shown in the text) by the instructor. The final draft includes the changes the student, Sonya Weaver, made in response to those comments, plus some of her own revisions and corrections.

After spending a few minutes reading and discussing Donne's poem [p. 398 in the Anthology of Poetry], you might want to read Sonya's second draft aloud (as the class follows in their books). Ask them how they would have revised the marked passages. Then let them compare their changes with those Sonya made in the final draft. Discuss which revisions are better and why. Be sure that your students have pen and paper when they work on their suggested revisions. And try to allow time for them to devise good sentences.

Chapter 15 Writing About Poetic Form [pp. 375–94]

Some readers are not much interested in the mechanics of poetry; they may even think that looking at the details of form will rob a poem of its beauty and mystery. Although this attitude can be a rationalization for wanting to avoid the hard work of reading poetry, it's true that form is most meaningful when related to content and discussed in context. Having students memorize the structure and rhyme scheme of a Shakespearean sonnet doesn't work as well as asking them to explain how the form of a particular sonnet contributes to its overall impression.

Exercise on Poetic Form [p. 377]

In this exercise, students are asked to arrange the lyrics of a song in lines on a page. If you use this as an individual exercise, you may ask students to write answers to the questions in the assignment. As a small group activity, the exercise could be completed by four or five students listening to a tape or CD and deciding on the arrangement together. In this way, the questions will be answered in the course of the group's discussion. If more than one group works on the same song, it would be profitable to compare the two arrangements and ask each group to justify its decisions.

Experimenting with Poetic Forms [pp. 385–86]

1. "We Real Cool" has a jazzy, syncopated rhythm created by the placement of the subject, "We," at the end of the lines and by the shortness of the words and sentences. These two factors encourage a reading with unusual pauses, as in musical syncopation. The placement of "We" also functions to emphasize the word, perhaps stressing the egotism of the persona.
2. The alliteration of *s* sounds in "Eight O'Clock" suggests the evil hiss of a snake or the discouraging hiss of air going out of a balloon or tire, both negative in effect. The variety of *o* and *ou* sounds (assonance) produces an ominous resonance, like the tolling of the bell which will mean the prisoner's doom. The repeated *k* sound in the second stanza is sharp and harsh, like the prisoner's fate and the sound of the gallows as the trap falls. Objectively, the poem tells the brief story of a prisoner who is listening to the town's church clock strike the hours until eight, which will be the time of his hanging. An objective account, of course, leaves out the subjective elements—the poetic effects and appeals created by alliteration, personification (the steeple in stanza 1 and the clock in stanza 2), and other devices.
3. This is a very demanding exercise, and some students will not see the differences in stanza use. In general the quatrains are coterminous with sentence units; the stanzas point out these syntactic structures. Some authors, like Donne and Cummings, play against the traditional expectations in surprising, even devilish, ways.
4. Tell students that they may add words as they rewrite the lines. There are no exact right answers, but here are our rewrites:
   a. Because he served the greater community in everything he did.
   b. He worked in a factory until the day he retired, except when he was in the war.
   c. How pretty a town anyone lived in, with the sound of bells floating up and down.
   d. The little men and small women didn't care for anyone at all.

Ideas for Writing [pp. 387–89]

The Ideas for Expressive Writing involve creative composition. They can replace or supplement a critical paper on poetic form.

Topics 1 and 4 under Ideas for Critical Writing combine analytical writing with a comparison and contrast format, while topics 2 and 5 are typical analyses, requiring the writer to separate the elements of the poem and, ideally, to argue how they work together to support or create the poem's meaning. Topic 3 calls for applying the principles of deconstruction—or, rather, to consider how the poet deconstructs the sonnet form for his own purposes; it's a speculative topic that should appeal to students who prefer a less conventional topic.

Exercise 1: Distinguishing among synonyms [p. 389]

a. *Renowned* and *famous* both mean widely known and honored; *famous* is used in reference to all pursuits, while *renowned* usually refers to intellectual or artistic fame. *Notorious* also means widely known, but the reputation is likely to be a negative one.

b. An *indifferent* parent is neither especially good nor especially bad; a *detached* parent is objective, not ruled by emotions; and an *unconcerned* parent is free of worry.

c. To *condone* an action is to overlook the degree of wrongness or inappropriateness. *Excuse* is most often used to mean pardon for social errors, like sneezing or being late. To *forgive* involves letting go any bad feelings or resentment one may have about a wrong action.

d. *Steal* is the most general word, meaning to take someone else's property without permission. *Pilfer* means to steal in small quantities and repeatedly, as, for example, your roommate might pilfer your beer supply. In the context of stealing, *robbery* usually means directly stealing from a person by using threats of violence or actual violence, whereas *burglary* involves breaking into a place intending to take something unlawfully, and *ransacking* involves a search for things to steal. *Looting* is stealing on a bigger scale, like plunder that takes place in war or a riot.

e. An *apparent* error seems to be real, but may or may not be. A *visible* error may be perceived by the eye. An *egregious* error is obviously bad.

Exercise 2: Words with similar sound or spelling [pp. 389–90]
a. apprise—to inform; appraise—to evaluate
b. anecdote—a little story; antidote—a remedy
c. elicit—bring out; illicit—not legitimate
d. martial—pertaining to war; marital—pertaining to marriage
e. statue—sculpture; statute—rule or law
f. human—a person; humane—kind, merciful, compassionate
g. lose—misplace, fail to win (verb); loose—not tight or dense (adjective)
h. idol—a worshipped symbol; idle—inactive, without a job
i. accept—approve, receive, take in; except—exclude, omit
j. simple—easy, uncomplicated; simplistic—ignoring complications or complexities, over-simplified
k. beside—next to; besides—in addition to, except
l. weather—atmospheric conditions; whether—if
m. incidence—rate of occurrence; incident—event or happening
n. angle—a figure in geometry, a position or vantage point; angel—a celestial being

Exercise 3: Precise adjective form [p. 390]
a. An intelligible essay is merely understandable; an intelligent one is logical and thoughtful.
b. A hateful sibling is malicious; a hated sibling is intensely disliked, deserving or not.
c. A likely roommate is probable or promising; a likable roommate is pleasant.
d. An informed speaker knows the subject well; an informative speaker is enlightening.
e. A workable thesis is practical; a working thesis is temporarily adopted until it proves practical or impractical.

Exercise 4: Malapropisms [p. 390]

a. superficial
b. pinnacle
c. refuse
d. examinations
e. rude

Exercise 5: Words that fit context [pp. 390–91]

a. *Stubbornness* has a negative connotation of being unreasonable or bullheaded; replace with *tenacity* or *steadfastness.*
b. *Poignantly* suggests something moving or touching; replace with *obviously.* *Sympathize with* implies compassion or understanding; replace with *support.*
c. *Displeasure* is not strong enough for shouting; a better choice would be *rage* or *frustration.*

Sample Student Paper on Poetic Form [pp. 391–94]

This student paper, about 500 words long, is a good example of how poetic form can be discussed along with a poem's meaning. It's rare to see an analysis of poetic form without any interpretation of the work's meaning. Curvey's essay relates the attitude of the speaker to the images in the poem and then to its form. The last sentences sum up the relationship nicely: "The continuity and inner logic of the sonnet reflect the speaker's appraisal of the woman, as being both conventional and unique, a person with a wholeness and unity all her own. Though influenced by the demands of custom, she remains splendidly herself." In other words, the poem both follows traditional sonnet form and also violates it to maintain its meaning.

One device that may not be obvious to your students is the use of repetition to maintain the focus of the paper. The first paragraph says that the speaker *admires* the woman, and the first sentences of paragraphs 2 and 3 also use the words *admire* and *admiration*, while paragraph 4 begins with a cognate, *compliment*. In this way, the reader is reminded in each paragraph to focus on the positive characteristics suggested by images in the poem: flexibility, strength, integrity, self-esteem, generosity, and love.

You might point out that whenever students encounter a poem with a familiar or common form, such as this sonnet of fourteen lines, they need to examine it to see whether it follows the conventions of that form and if not, which conventions are broken. This analysis may help illuminate the poem's meaning, as we see in the Curvey essay.

ANTHOLOGY OF POETRY

WHEN IN DISGRACE WITH FORTUNE AND MEN'S EYES (Sonnet 29) by William Shakespeare [p. 395]

This sonnet departs from the usual Shakespearean structure of three quatrains and a couplet: the last 6 lines form a unit (a sestet). In the first 8 lines the speaker cites circumstances when self-doubts overwhelm him; in the next 4 lines the speaker observes that the remembrance of the loved one ("thee"), which seems to occur at random ("haply" means "by chance"), lifts the speaker's spirits. The famous simile that ends the poem indicates that the speaker's joy is like the return of the lark's song at the beginning of the day. The lark's burst of joy suggests that heaven—called "deaf" in line 3—has suddenly become keener of hearing. The last two lines, comprising a separate sentence, sum up the ideas expressed in the lark simile (lines 9–12), suggesting that the speaker's spirit is genuinely restored by the memory of "thy love."

Students might profit from paraphrasing the poem, as several words that sound familiar had different meanings than they have today. "Featured," for instance, meaning "alike in features," would be paraphrased as "looking like." And "scope" could mean either accomplishments or breadth of understanding or knowledge.

Possible Responses to *Questions for Discussion and Writing*

1. In the highly romantic and idealized world of Renaissance love poetry, the sentiment that "love conquers all" is readily accepted. The central contrast (or tension) in this poem is between the speaker's public misfortunes and his personal treasures, and there is simply no contest: "sweet love" wins every time, at least in poetry.
2. The speaker posits a time when he will be down on his luck: alone, despondent, frustrated, envious of those around him, even suicidal (line 9).
3. It would change an erotic love poem into a religious statement about the insufficiency of material wealth. This interpretation does not fit in easily with the rest of the 154 poems in Shakespeare's sonnet cycle, which focus on human love and passion.

Making Connections

→Compare this sonnet's portrayal of love as a solace against the harshness of the world with Matthew Arnold's explication of that same idea in "Dover Beach."

THAT TIME OF YEAR THOU MAYST IN ME BEHOLD (Sonnet 73) by William
    Shakespeare [p. 396]
This sonnet explores the connections between mortality, death, and love. The time frame becomes increasingly shorter, moving (in the three quatrains) from a season to a part of one day to a moment of recognition. The bold and complicated metaphors picture the aging speaker as a winter-ravaged tree, the twilight moving into night, and a feeble fire choking on the ashes of its own expended fuel. The common link to the three quatrains (autumn, sunset, a dying fire) is diminution or dying. The couplet may need explication.

Possible Responses to *Questions for Discussion and Writing*

1. The speaker presents himself as getting older: he's in the autumn of life and moving into the cold and dark of winter.
2. The first quatrain describes the approach of winter as the dying leaves drift to the ground. The second quatrain presents images of falling night, and the third quatrain develops an image of a dying fire whose embers are being extinguished by its own ashes. They all suggest loss of light and heat (and waning life).
3. The last two lines might be difficult to explain, but the idea is that the speaker's lover (the "thou" of the poem) realizes that the time for love (and sex) is growing shorter

and that it would be a good idea to take advantage of the time that's left. The cliché, "make hay while the sun shines," is not a bad summary of the idea expressed in the final couplet.

Additional Questions for Discussion and Writing
1. How is a body like boughs, and how are bare boughs like a ruined choir loft?
2. Does love always grow stronger between people as they get older? Write a brief response to this sonnet, exploring the relationship between love and aging.

Making Connections
→How do this poem's thoughts and feelings about love and aging compare with those expressed in "Sailing to Byzantium" by William Butler Yeats?
→Compare the attitude toward aging and death expressed in Shakespeare's sonnet with Hayden Carruth's speculations on his own mortality in "In the Long Hall."

MY MISTRESS' EYES ARE NOTHING LIKE THE SUN (Sonnet 130) by William Shakespeare [p. 396]
In Shakespeare's day it was fashionable for poets to imitate the sonnets of Petrarch, the Italian poet whose praise of his beloved Laura started the rage for sonnet writing. The result of all the imitation was a surplus of Petrarchan conceits (or elaborate comparisons). In Sonnet 130, Shakespeare, who often drew on Petrarchan conventions himself, pokes fun at poets who thoughtlessly use the exaggerated figures of speech. Shakespeare is confident that his readers have read numerous imitations of Petrarch, and he turns their clichés to his own uses. The last line is a bit difficult because the words *she* and *compare* are both nominals. It might be paraphrased this way: I think my love is as rare as any woman ("she") who is misrepresented ("belied") through false comparisons ("false compare").

It may be helpful to point out that in Shakespeare's time the term *mistress* meant "beloved" or "chosen one" and had not yet acquired the connotations of illicit lover or kept woman that contemporary usage has.

Possible Responses *to Questions for Discussion and Writing*
1. The poet is showing that he's aware of the stale similes and excessive metaphors that other poets use to try to outdo reality. He is rejecting them in favor of a description that is more honest but just as complimentary.
2. He asserts that her beauty doesn't need to be exaggerated; she is just as attractive as any woman who has been falsely represented by conventional poetic descriptions.
3. See the discussion above.
4. The focus of this exercise is on language and its abuses. Commercials would be another good target for parody, especially those ads for medications that have a long list of dreadful side effects.

Additional Questions for Discussion and Writing
1. How do the negative connotations of the words *false* and *belied* help you to figure out that the last two lines contain a true appraisal of the speaker's mistress?

2. How does the poem's argument divide up among the three quatrains and the couplet?

Making Connections
→What different attitudes toward the beloved are expressed in Shakespeare's sonnets "Shall I Compare Thee to a Summer's Day?" and "My Mistress' Eyes Are Nothing Like the Sun"?

DEATH, BE NOT PROUD by John Donne [p. 397]
This sonnet is an intense and mocking (though not humorous) apostrophe (or address) to Death. Its central theme is based on the Christian belief in resurrection. The expression is paradoxical throughout. The speaker says Death should not be arrogant: Death is not final; neither is it "mighty" or "dreadful"; it's not even competent. Actually, Death is pitiful ("poor Death"); far from being terrifying, it really should be welcomed like "rest" and "sleep." And there are other reasons to deprecate Death: it's a slave to human will and depends on poison, war, and sickness. Sedatives are even more effective in producing sleep, so why is Death so swelled with pride? As the final couplet makes clear, we can transcend Death by robbing it of its dominion.

Donne wanted control of his own dying. He wrote a treatise in defense of suicide in which he claimed that Jesus committed suicide. To a friend he wrote: "I would not that death should take me asleep. I would not have him merely seize me, and only declare me to be dead, but win me, and overcome me."

Possible Responses to *Questions for Discussion and Writing*
1. He dismisses Death as an overrated, ineffectual fraud.
2. The paradox is that Death will die (line 14). By personifying death, the speaker can assign human characteristics and fallibilities: Death becomes a "servant" and can be dismissed as "poor Death," weak and powerless.
3. The speaker advances three claims to argue against Death's power: that people don't really die (lines 1–4); that death is really just a pleasant sleep, a rest and delivery from life (lines 5–8); that Death must depend on murder, war, poison, sickness, etc. (lines 9–12).
4. One must share the speaker's unqualified belief in an afterlife for the arguments to be valid and meaningful.

Making Connections
→Compare Donne's attitude toward death with Dylan Thomas's in "Do Not Go Gentle into That Good Night."

A VALEDICTION: FORBIDDING MOURNING by John Donne [pp. 398–99]
In his biography of Donne, Izak Walton claims that the poet wrote this poem for his wife in 1611, when he was about to depart on a diplomatic mission to France. In the course of the poem, the speaker uses five conceits or metaphors to define the calm and quiet that he thinks should characterize his departure: 1) the death of virtuous men, 2) movement of the celestial spheres, 3) the assurance of spiritual love (as opposed to physical love), 4)

the expansion of gold beaten into foil, 5) the conjoined legs of a drawing compass.

The simile of the first two stanzas must be linked to the title. The point is that the parting lovers should be like virtuous people who accept death easily because they are assured of being in paradise. The contrast between earthquakes (which can be accounted for) and the "trepidation of the spheres" (which is more significant but less destructive) sets up the contrast between the love of earthbound ("sublunary") lovers and the spiritual love of the speaker and his beloved. Their love does not depend on physical contact; it is as refined as gold, which can be expanded into gold foil without any break or separation. The final three stanzas develop the famous conceit in which the souls of the lovers are compared to a drawing compass (some students may visualize a directional compass). The best way to illustrate this famous conceit is to bring in a draftsman's compass (even a dime store variety) to demonstrate the movements described in the poem.

The student paper, "Images of Love," which is at the end of Chapter 14 in the text, analyzes these metaphors and their progression through the poem.

Possible Responses to *Questions for Discussion and Writing*
1. "Valediction" is a Latinate term for saying goodbye. The speaker forbids mourning because it would be inappropriate, unseemly, and unnecessary to cry and carry on.
2. Virtuous men have nothing to fear or worry about when they leave this life, since they're sure they're going to paradise. The speaker says the lovers should face their separation with the same grace and confidence.
3. The "dull sublunary" (earthbound) lovers need physical presence to sustain their relationship. The speaker and his beloved represent something more refined; their love transcends the sensual. They have attained the Platonic ideal.
4. His beloved, like the stationary foot of the compass, gives him strength and support, and inexorably draws him back to where he started (with her). Because the compass is used to draw circles, it is a most apt simile to describe the unity and perfection that the speaker claims for his love.

Additional Questions for Discussion and Writing
1. Explain the reference to astronomy in stanza 3. (In the medieval cosmos, the heavenly bodies were thought to be fixed, while everything under the moon was subject to change.)
2. What qualities of beaten gold make it an appropriate metaphor for the love that the speaker is describing? (Gold is refined, precious, durable, and capable of being expanded greatly without breaking apart.)

Making Connections
→Compare the vision of physical and spiritual love that Donne projects to the one presented in Sharon Olds's "Sex Without Love" or to the version expressed by Theodore Roethke in "I Knew a Woman."

To His Coy Mistress by Andrew Marvell [pp. 399–400]
This is one of the most famous *carpe diem*, persuasion-to-love poems ever written. It incorporates a distinct syllogistic form (an if-but-therefore argument) that distinguishes it

from other *carpe diem* poems. The title identifies the characters: the speaker is a would-be lover; he is addressing his "coy" (reluctant) lady. His argument is: if there were time, I'd woo you properly, but life is short and we'll be dead soon; therefore we'd better become lovers now.

The first section sets up a hypothetical situation in which there is vast space and time. The Ganges and Humber rivers are approximately on opposite sides of the globe. The allusions to Noah's flood and the conversion of the Jews evoke a span from Genesis to the Last Judgment. The speaker's "vegetable" (as opposed to rational) love will grow "vaster than empires but more slow."

The next section, beginning with "but," refutes the hypothesis of the first section. There is a note of urgency in the image of time's chariot pursuing them like an enemy, and the vastness of time is changed to deserts of eternity. The lines are full of images of death, dust, dryness, and isolation. The speaker also bawdily sketches the consequences of too much coyness: no one makes love in the grave. In the last section, the speaker's logic (or pseudo-logic) requires that the lovers behave differently. The images change from slowness, distance, and great size to excitement and vitality: "fire," "sport," "devour," "roll," "tear," "rough strife," "run." Time becomes a slow-jawed, devouring beast that will itself be devoured by the vigorous lovers.

Possible Responses to *Questions for Discussion and Writing*
1. The speaker acts the patient courtly lover in the opening stanza, content to wait and to love and appreciate from afar.
2. In the second stanza the lover reminds his lady of their mortality, the fleeting passing of time (life) and their approaching death (eternity).
3. The speaker changes from patient, to concerned, to seductive ("Now let us sport")— and aggressive ("like amorous birds of prey, / Rather at once our time to devour"). Other key words include "fires," "sport," "tear," and "rough strife."
4. The metaphor stands for the sexual consummation the lover envisions, a victory over his lover's "fortified" resistance.
5. The poem is a classic representation of the *carpe diem* theme of the period. Students will likely enter into lively debate about the various motivations of the two lovers.

Additional Questions for Discussion and Writing
1. Why does the speaker use "amorous birds of prey" instead of more conventional love birds (like doves or larks)?
2. What words and phrases have sexual connotations?
3. Write an answer to the argument in Marvell's poem, either in poetry or in prose.

Making Connections
→Edmund Waller's "Go, Lovely Rose" is another *carpe diem* poem with a sexual proposition similar to Marvell's. Do the pleadings in these two poems differ? Which do you think would be more likely to overcome a young maiden's resistance?

ODE ON A GRECIAN URN by John Keats [pp. 401–02]
This poem is structured as a reading of the urn. It also brings up the contrast between timeless art and human mortality. The speaker muses on the unchanging beauty of the urn and his own suffering mortality. Grecian urns were vessels for the ashes of the dead; their carved or painted figures depicted a joyous afterlife in the Elysian Fields. The design on the circular urn appears to continue forever (an image of eternity or the seamless perfection of art).

In the first stanza, the urn is addressed as a "bride," a "foster child," a "sylvan historian," and the poet sketches a montage of the pictures that cover it. In stanza 2, he moves closer and considers a piper and a lover, figures that animate the poem's central idea: some ideal, unheard music is more beautiful than that which can be heard. This idea is further illustrated in stanza 3 by a series of poetic observations. In stanza 4, the speaker imagines what is not represented on the urn and, in the final stanza, reflects on the conclusions to be drawn from the graceful ancient shape.

Possible Responses to *Questions for Discussion and Writing*
1. Like all of the sense experiences described in the poem, the sweetness of the painted melody is eternal, experienced by each viewer throughout time.
2. The urn's figures will live, will be youthful and beautiful, eternally, never experiencing human frailty, frustration, loss, illness.
3. The paradox of the "Cold Pastoral" imparts a mildly ironic reading to the poem, creating a tension between the cold surface of the urn and the romantic, warm pastoral images painted upon it. The promise of eternal beauty offers condolences to humans facing their own mortality, thus the urn acts as "friend to man."
4. Keats's aesthetic theory, "Beauty is truth, truth beauty," should generate lively and useful debate among your students.4

Additional Questions for Discussion and Writing
1. The urn is called "sylvan" probably because it displays woodland scenes, but in what sense is it an "historian"?
2. What disadvantages do living lovers experience (lines 28–30)?

Making Connections
→How might the speaker in Rita Dove's "Daystar" respond to John Keats's lines about beauty and truth (lines 49-50).
→Compare Keats's expression of his relationship to art with that of Billy Collins in his "Introduction to Poetry." Or, explore the relation of the narrator to the art in "My Last Duchess." Or compare the static image of Keats's urn with the vital image of Aunt Jennifer's prancing tigers in Adrienne Rich's poem.

SONG OF MYSELF (SECTION 11) by Walt Whitman [p. 403]
Whitman's very long poem, "Song of Myself," is a hymn to America, to democracy, and to human sexuality. Contemporary readers, including Ralph Waldo Emerson, were shocked by the eroticism of the work but praised it nonetheless for its power and probity.

Lines like "The scent of armpits, finer than prayer" must have given Mr. Emerson quite a turn; yet he still welcomed Whitman as the outstanding new poet of his day.

"Section 11" presents a kind of parable of loneliness and desire. Some students today may still be taken aback by its boldness. Most of the imagery in "Song of Myself" is homoerotic, but these verses are couched, at the beginning, at least, in heterosexual terms as the lady in her imagination goes "Dancing and laughing along the beach" for "she saw them and loved them." We envision her as a rich, lonely, and repressed woman, perhaps middle-aged, who is aroused at the sight of the presumably naked young men cavorting in the water near her "fine house." The images of the young men are pure Whitman—intensely erotic regardless of gender orientation: "The beards of the young men glisten'd with wet, it ran from their long hair, / Little streams pass'd all over their bodies." And the lady's "unseen hand also pass'd over their bodies, / It descended tremblingly from their temple and ribs." She is overcome by desire, as she "puffs and declines with pendant and bending arch," in what is surely a delicate description of a sexual climax. One critic also notes homoerotic arousal among the young men who "float on their backs," as "their bellies bulge to the sun," with the final "souse with spray" suggesting male ejaculation. In his essay on Whitman, Havelock Ellis, a pioneering early twentieth-century sex researcher, paid tribute to the "Homeric simplicity and grandeur" of the poet's expression in this episode. There may be some significance in the number twenty-eight, which is the length of a lunar cycle.

Possible Responses to *Questions for Discussion and Writing*

1. The woman is hiding behind the window blinds because she does not wish to be seen ogling a bunch of young men swimming in the nude. She is rich ("owns the fine house by the rise of the bank") and lonely ("Twenty-eight years of womanly life and all so lonesome") and apparently sexually attracted to the male nudity.
2. The woman can stay "stock still" in her room while splashing with the young men in her imagination.
3. The phrase "souse with spray" could describe male ejaculation, given the sexually charged language that permeates the poem: "she saw them and loved them," "glistening with wet," "little streams pass'd all over their bodies," "unseen hand also pass'd over their bodies," "descended tremblingly," "their white bellies bulge to the sun," "puffs and declines with pendant and declining arch."
4. Whitman seems way ahead of his times in presenting a woman with a lusty sexual interest. In his day, women were thought to be far less responsive to sexual urges than men. Consider the old joke about Queen Victoria, whose daughter complained that she didn't want to have sex. The queen supposedly responded, "My dear, it is your duty: just lie there and think of England!" But Whitman declared that he wanted his poetry to celebrate everything human: "sex, womanhood, maternity, lusty animations, organs, acts." Your students today may find nothing unusual about the lonely twenty-eight year old woman lusting after the twenty-eight skinny-dipping young men.
4. The deliberate repetition of words and phrases at the beginning and end of the poem are characteristic of Whitman's freewheeling style and lends emphasis and cadence to the lines. The occasional unusually long lines of verse give an impression of breathless, unbroken speech, reflecting the excitement of the secret watcher. But

82

consider, too, that since short lines give a choppy, abrupt feeling, the long lines give a fluent, flowing effect, as in lines 10 and 11 with water running down the hair and its little streams passing all over their bodies. Also in the long line 16, all the actions are run together—all three sentences—to keep the movement going. 4

Making Connections
→How does this poem compare to other poems about sex and love, such as Marvell's "To His Coy Mistress," Dickinson's "Wild Nights—Wild Nights!" or Olds's "Sex Without Love"?

DOVER BEACH by Matthew Arnold [p. 404]
The persona in the poem is standing at a window with his beloved looking from the white cliffs of England across the moonlit channel toward France. (Since the poet is male, it seems reasonable to assume that the persona is also.) He calls his love to the window and muses on the beauty of the landscape and the "eternal note of sadness" in the sound of the sea. The tide is in, and he remarks that the "Sea of Faith" (religious belief) was once "at the full" but now has retreated (under the onslaught of scientific discoveries of Darwin and others that contradicted the biblical account of creation). The solution posed in the poem for the resulting uncertainty is to have faith in each other, because the poet envisions a world without religious faith as being a place of darkness and strife. ("Shingles" are gravel beaches.)

Most of Arnold's poetry was written by the age of 45 and examined the theme of human alienation and disconnection from the changing world of the nineteenth century. He continued to write as a literary critic until the end of his life, believing it was the best vehicle for social reform.

Possible Responses to *Questions for Discussion and Writing*
1. The setting seems to be a drawing room at night ("the moon lies fair") with a couple standing at a long window, looking out over the English Channel toward the French coast. The persona is presumably male, speaking to a woman ("Ah, love, let us be true / To one another!"), who is perhaps the Marguerite to whom Arnold dedicated a poem in 1857.
2. The "Sea of Faith" is retreating following the stir caused by Darwin's *Origin of Species* in 1859, his earthshaking book promulgating the idea of evolution.
3. The persona proposes the strength of human love with faith in each other as a solution to the loss of religious faith.
4. Images of sight and sound abound in the poem; the "lack of sight" image would be the "darkling plain . . . / Where ignorant armies clash by night." Your students could argue that these images contribute to the effectiveness of the poem by providing concrete evidence to illustrate Arnold's abstract ideas.

Additional Question for Discussion and Writing
What is the cause of the "sadness" in line 14? What is the speaker's response to the ebbing "Sea of Faith"?

Making Connections

→Explain how Updike's story "A & P" is also about a loss of faith. How does it compare to Arnold's conception? Similarly, explain the young boy's loss of faith in Countee Cullen's "Incident" in terms that Arnold would understand and accept.

MUCH MADNESS IS DIVINEST SENSE by Emily Dickinson [p. 405]

Dickinson states quite succinctly in this little poem one of the important truths of human survival: it's dangerous to be a nonconformist—even, or especially, if you're right. She begins by pointing out that many things condemned as crazy by society actually make good sense. We think at once of Galileo and Darwin and others who discovered truths that society didn't want to hear about. She then says that much of what people accept as sensible is patent madness. Consider the nuclear arms race, for example. Her final line, asserting that dissenters will be "handled with a Chain," probably reflects the treatment in her day of chaining asylum inmates to the wall. Today, students are more likely to think of handcuffed protesters.

Possible Responses *to Questions for Discussion and Writing*

1. As examples of something, perhaps historical, that was thought to be madness but turned out to be sensible, you might bring up the ideas of Darwin and Galileo to get your students started. They, then, may bring up the idea of travel in vehicles like cars, trains, airplanes, or even spaceships—all of which seemed wildly fanciful, dangerous, deafeningly noisy, and (in the case of space travel) prohibitively expensive to many people when the concepts were first introduced.
2. Asking for something that is accepted by most people in society that you personally consider "madness," may bring responses ranging from nuclear proliferation, war, and the defense budget, to personal peccadilloes like motorcycles, all terrain vehicles, jumping out of airplanes for fun, the cost of the space program, and so on.
3. By "handled with a Chain," Dickinson could mean that dissenters will be treated the way mad people were handled in asylums in her day—by being chained to the wall.

Additional Questions for Discussion and Writing

1. What does it mean that "the Majority / In this, as All, prevail"?
2. Discuss the conflict between the individual and society expressed in this poem.

Making Connections

→Compare this poem's theme of appearance vs. reality with Stevie Smith's expression of a similar idea in "Not Waving but Drowning."

BECAUSE I COULD NOT STOP FOR DEATH by Emily Dickinson [p. 406]

This poem reveals Dickinson's calm acceptance of death. She presents the experience as being no more frightening than receiving an unexpected gentleman caller. Stanza 3 presents stages that the persona reviews during this journey to the grave—childhood (the recess scene), maturity (the ripe, hence, "gazing" grain), and death (the setting sun)—as she passes to the other side, where she experiences a chill since she is not warmly dressed. In fact, her garments are more appropriate for a wedding—a new beginning—than for a funeral, which we tend to think of as an ending. Her description of the grave as her "House" indicates how naturally she depicts this new state. The eternity she spends there seems timeless to her. If the poem has a theme, it is a transcendental one—that death is not to be feared since it is a natural part of the endless cycle of nature.

Possible Responses to *Questions for Discussion and Writing*

1. The action depicted in the poem is the traveling of a soul from death to whatever lies beyond ("the Horses' Heads / Were toward Eternity"). The action described in stanza 3 is a review of the journey to the grave: childhood (the recess scene), maturity (the ripe, hence "gazing" grain), and death (the setting sun). The "House," of course, is the grave.
2. Death is personified as if he were a gentleman caller: he is kind, polite, unhurried, and civil.
3. The persona's attitude toward death is completely accepting. She has, apparently of her own volition, "Put away / My labor and my leisure too"; she says, "He kindly stopped for me"; she describes the grave in a comforting image as a "House" and reassuringly says that eternity for her is timeless.
4. The theme is transcendental: that death is not to be feared since it is a natural part of the endless cycles of nature. That attitude is very similar to Whitman's calm, welcoming acceptance of death at the conclusion of "Song of Myself": "I bequeath myself to the dirt to grow from the grass I love, / If you want me again look for me under your boot soles."

Additional Questions for Discussion and Writing

1. Do the clothes the speaker is wearing suggest typical burial garments? If not, what do they suggest?
2. Why couldn't the speaker stop for death?

Making Connections

→Contrast the personification of death in this poem with that of John Donne in "Death Be Not Proud." How do they differ? Which do you find more appealing?

WILD NIGHTS—WILD NIGHTS! by Emily Dickinson [pp. 406–07]

Emily Dickinson was famously celibate, but she is known to have fallen in love with a married Boston minister. This poem may express her unrequited desire for the man she called her "master" in several poems. Notice that the poem is couched in the conditional ("should be," "might I"), so the passion expressed is a longing, not a fulfillment. The word "luxury" (line 4) formerly meant "excess," suggesting wild abandon—a surfeit of sensual delights. Stanza 2 (elliptical, with "are" understood in line 5) presents the image of a heart (source of love) as a vessel safely in port (no longer needing the compass or chart), united with the lover after weathering any storms that might have separated them. "Rowing in Eden" in the final stanza suggests the epitome of bliss, as the speaker longs to "moor" (to be held safely and securely) in the arms of the beloved. Probably the poem has no theme. It's a lyric poem expressing subjective emotion.

85

Possible Responses to *Questions for Discussion and Writing*

1. The speaker is looking forward to being united with her lover for a night of ecstasy.
2. The word "luxury" in Dickinson's day meant "excess"—in this case the excess of wild sexual abandon that the speaker is hoping for.
3. A paraphrase of the second stanza might go this way:
   > Undamaging are the winds—
   > To a lover sheltered in port—
   > There is no longer need for a compass—
   > There is no longer need for a chart!
4. In stanza 2, Dickinson presents the image of a heart (the traditional source of love) as a ship safely in port, united with the lover after weathering any storms that might have separated them.
5. In the last two lines, the speaker longs to "moor" (to be held safely and securely, like a ship is in port) "in Thee" (in the arms of the beloved).

Making Connections

→How is this poem different from or similar to other poems about sex and love, such as Whitman's "Song of Myself (Section 11)" or Olds's "Sex Without Love"?

TO AN ATHLETE DYING YOUNG by A. E. Housman [pp. 407–08]

In this poem Housman appears to be congratulating a young athlete for having died in his prime, since his glory would have faded quickly as he aged. Presumably he is not serious in recommending early death as a remedy for loss of fame but is commenting on the way we tend to remember the best of those who die before their laurels (in the poem, wreaths of laurel bestowed on early gladiators to be worn as a crown of triumph) have faded. President Kennedy is one good example; Amelia Earhart is another; perhaps even Elvis Presley, although his laurels were beginning to go a trifle limp. You may need to explain the image in the first stanza of the athlete being carried in a chair through the town as a celebration of his prowess; he would, of course, be once more "carried shoulder-high" in his coffin. Note, too, the first stanza is in past tense, the rest of the poem in present.

See the student response to this poem, which misses the irony. It is presented for analysis and discussion at the end of Chapter 13.

Possible Response to *Questions for Discussion and Writing*

1. The "road" down which "all runners come" is the road to the grave, that "stiller town," where the quiet dead are laid to rest. The laurel is an evergreen tree with leaves that, woven into a crown, bestowed honor on winners of ancient Greek athletic contests held at Delphi every four years (the early forerunners of our present-day Olympic games). We learn in line 11 that the "laurel" (the honor won in the race) will fade all too quickly. The poetic voice continues his wry suggestion that the youth, "Smart lad," was fortunate to die before someone else broke his record, and his fame wore out, "And the name died before the man."
2. The final stanza suggests that actually the garland is not worth much at all since, even though "unwithered," it is "briefer than a girl's." (Garlands for girls, of flowers

instead of laurel, encircle their heads, while those for males leave an opening above the brow—think of pictures of Julius Caesar.) But the greatest sadness is that the young athlete's garland, signifying his honor, will be acknowledged only by those silent "strengthless dead" in that silent "stiller town"—no cheering or waving flags. Most of us would not consider approbation by the dead worth dying for. But, on the other hand, we can all think of examples of famous people, gone to an early death, whose failings are now forgiven and forgotten as they live on in our collective memories—President John Kennedy, Amelia Earhart, Janis Joplin, Elvis Presley, John Lennon, Michael Jackson, and so on.

4. Housman in this poem is undermining the widely accepted belief that athletic success is glorious.4

Additional Questions for Discussion and Writing

1. Why is it important that the young athlete be a runner (rather than a football player or a tennis champ)? What archetype does running a race suggest?
2. How does the poem undermine the belief that athletic success is glorious?
3. One reader has suggested that the speaker is almost envious of the young athlete because he (the speaker) has experienced the fate of watching his own glories fade and die. Can you find evidence in the poem to support this interpretation?

Making Connections

→Compare this poem with Emily Dickinson's "Because I Could Not Stop for Death" or with John Updike's "Ex-Basketball Player."

THE SECOND COMING by William Butler Yeats [pp. 408–09]

Yeats developed a complex personal mythology, which sheds light on this poem, but it can be understood without special knowledge. He believed that civilizations moved in cycles of 2,000 years; the passing of one and the rising of the next would be accomplished in great upheaval. Although the poem makes use of Christian imagery (appropriate to the ending of the era following the birth of Christ), the "Second Coming" anticipated in the poem sounds anything but Christlike.

The first stanza depicts a world out of control, perfectly conveyed in the image of the falcon beyond hearing its handler. The "ceremony of innocence" (baptism) has been drowned in the "blood-dimmed tide." The lines, "The best lack all conviction, while the worst / Are full of passionate intensity," are prescient in their apt description of what happened in Nazi Germany as Hitler rose to power. The huge beast that "slouches toward Bethlehem" can be seen as fascism, which drenched much of the world in blood during World War II. Yeats, of course, in 1921, simply saw it as the coming civilization—as violent and pitiless as the one that is passing. The phrase "twenty centuries of stony sleep" refers to the pre-Christian era, which was "vexed to nightmare by a rocking cradle"—by the birth of Christ, who did not, after all, prove to be the Prince of Peace.

Possible Responses to Questions for Discussion and Writing

1. The world described by the speaker in the first stanza is in utter chaos, as if following some cataclysmic natural disaster or a bloody, destructive world war.

2. In the poem, the "ceremony of innocence" (perhaps baptism) is drowned in "the blood-dimmed tide." Yeats believed that ceremony was the civilizing principle that could save humanity from being engulfed in turbulence. In another poem he writes, "How but in custom and in ceremony / Are innocence and beauty born?"
3. Just as water, used in baptismal ceremonies, symbolizes sacredness and spirituality, a desert, devoid of life-giving water, symbolizes a total lack of spirituality. So it is entirely fitting that the "rough beast" appears from the "sands of the desert."
4. Yeats believed that history moved in 2,000-year cycles, with each cycle ending in upheaval and catastrophe. So the "twenty centuries of stony sleep" would be the pre-Christian era that was "vexed to nightmare by a rocking cradle," meaning by the birth of Jesus in that cradle in the manger.
5. Some early critics thought that the "rough beast" represents the 1917 Russian Revolution, but others later proposed that the image represents the rise of Adolph Hitler and fascism. Yeats accepted that interpretation as possibly being what his unconscious mind had fashioned into the imagery in this poem. In *A Vision,* Yeats wrote that he felt "we may be about to accept the most implacable authority the world has known." He got that right.

Additional Questions for Discussion and Writing
1. What image does the description of the beast—with the body of a lion and the head of a man—conjure up? (The Sphinx.) Why is this an appropriate form for the beast?
2. Write a paper discussing the bird imagery in the poem. Consider why the falcon/falconer image is particularly appropriate. Why is the beast accompanied by the reeling shadows of "indignant desert birds"?

Making Connections
→Compare this poem to "Fire and Ice" by Robert Frost.
→Compare the image of god portrayed in Yeats's poem with the image of the deity presented in the setting of Judith Cofer's "Latin Women Pray."

RICHARD CORY by Edwin Arlington Robinson [p. 410]
Part of the success of this poem lies in the way it builds to an unexpected climax. But certainly the simplicity of the speaker's diction contributes to its effectiveness, as does the spare imagery ("he glittered when he walked"), and the rhyme and rhythm. The theme addresses the problem of illusion versus reality. We are often deceived by the surface of things. Young people, for instance, often long for the life of a rock star—to be an Elvis Presley or a Janice Joplin—but when that idol dies of a drug overdose, the glittering life looks considerably tarnished. Students may state the theme as "It's better to be poor than to be rich and miserable," which is an acceptable response, but encourage them to learn to state themes in more sophisticated language. The theme may involve the idea that people who seem totally privileged can harbor inner tortures, unguessed by their fellow citizens. For instance, it could be that Richard Cory was horribly lonely in his singularity among the townspeople.

Possible Responses to *Questions for Discussion and Writing*

1. The speaker is a working class citizen of the town where Richard Cory lives, but seems to be speaking for the town. Ask what the use of "we" suggests.
2. Richard Cory is a rich, well-educated, gracious person. A gentleman is considered a person who is polite and careful of others' feelings, knowing how to behave properly in all situations.
3. Images of royalty include "from sole to crown," "imperially slim," and "richer than a king," among more subtle suggestions in lines like, "We people on the pavement looked at him." The onlookers of lower classes seem not to resent Richard Cory's status, only wishing that they had been born to a similar situation.

Making Connections

→Compare the ironic twist in this poem to the irony in Stevie Smith's "Not Waving but Drowning."

MENDING WALL by Robert Frost [pp. 410–11]

This poem may or may not be about walls. Certainly the lines, "Before I built a wall I'd ask to know / What I was walling in or walling out / And to whom I was like to give offense," call to mind several famous walls, like the Iron Curtain, the Bamboo Wall, the Great Wall of China, and the Berlin Wall, not to mention metaphorical walls that separate people who fail to communicate or who hold opposing positions. Frost portrays the neighbor (who finds walls necessary for no good reason) in such an unflattering light that most readers fail to notice that the speaker (who wryly questions the need for walls) is not exactly rational about them himself, and also that he is the one who lets the neighbor know when it's time to repair the wall in the poem. One critic has suggested that the poem is about two kinds of people: conservatives and liberals; in which case, we can perhaps safely say that the poet favors a liberal bent.

Possible Responses to *Questions for Discussion and Writing*

1. The speaker in the poem is a farmer, or at least the keeper of an orchard, who has a sense of humor (he wryly teases his neighbor about repairing this wall that they do not need in the first place) and seems a friendly, reasonable person who would prefer to get along without a wall. The neighbor, though, "moves in darkness" (meaning, in the speaker's opinion, in ignorance) and is deaf to the speaker's reasoned arguments—he just keeps repeating an adage that he learned at his father's knee: "Good fences make good neighbors."
2. The line "Something there is that doesn't love a wall" appears twice in the poem, but so too does the line "Good fences make good neighbors." Both express key concepts in the poem, which probably accounts for their appearing twice, but they also express opposing ideas. "Something there is that doesn't love a wall" suggests that perhaps walls cause animosity. And, indeed, that will serve as the theme of the poem, since the speaker supports it with good evidence, and the neighbor who wants the wall is described as looking "like an old-stone savage, armed." Quite a few people quote that line—"Good fences make good neighbors"—as if the advice makes good sense. So maybe ironically, in the real world, the "old-stone-savage" has the last word.

89

3. The speaker is not in favor of walls. He keeps pressing his neighbor for reasons to think walls in general are good, and reasons against them: "Before I built a wall I'd ask to know / What I was walling in or walling out, / And to whom I was like to give offense." But neither does he like hunters, who damage walls like his, just to "have the rabbit out of hiding, / To please the yelping dogs." Maybe he just gets tired of mending the troublesome wall.

4. Ask your students to declare whether they are pro-walls or against-walls, and put them into groups to brainstorm for a paper supporting their position. Then ask each group to write a claim in support of the opposite position. Finally, assign the class to write individual essays arguing for the position of his or her choice using personal experience as evidence.4

Additional Questions for Discussion and Writing
1. Why is the wall in the poem made of stones? (It's located in Frost's native, rocky New England.)
2. Is "mending" a gerund that denotes what the men are doing (mending the wall) or is it a participle that describes the wall? What kind of wall would a "mending wall" be?

Making Connections
→How do you think the neighbor in this poem might respond to the attitude toward nature expressed in Whitman's "When I Heard the Learn'd Astronomer" or in Thomas's "The Force That Through the Green Fuse Drives the Flower"?
→Compare the symbolic meanings of walls in this poem with the symbolism of fences in August Wilson's play *Fences.*

DESIGN by Robert Frost [p. 412]
Frost's description of the spider in this sonnet presents the perfect image of innocence as plump and dimpled, like a baby, and white besides. As critic Randall Jarrell notes, the spider holds the moth up, like a priest presenting a "sacrificial victim" at a Devil's Mass, and the moth is "full of the stilling rigor of death." The line "Mixed ready to begin the morning right" makes this "witches' broth" sound like a nourishing breakfast cereal. And the flower that should have been blue has been turned to white—a white suggestive of Melville's whale. The speaker's questions in the sestet lead us to speculate on who or what controls the universe. The "design" of the death described seems so deliberate as to suggest some malevolent force "of darkness to appall" (the spider was "brought," the moth was "steered"). But perhaps even more chilling is the implication in the final line that nothing controls our fate, that there is no god, that all is pure chance.

Possible Responses to *Questions for Discussion and Writing*
1. The title relates directly to imagery throughout the poem, which conveys the theme, i.e., the "design" revealed in the death of the moth is not the divine providence promised by Christian doctrine, guiding and protecting the faithful, but rather a malevolent and treacherous luring of the innocent ("white") moth to its death; surely it is a "design of darkness to appall," a creation worthy of Satan, the Prince of Darkness.

2. The spider is described in pleasant words usually bestowed on cute, plump babies—
"dimpled" and "fat"; "white," of course, is the color of innocence. This "snow-drop
spider" is a far cry from the usual image that the word *spider* calls up of a scary
creature at Halloween, often black, and potentially poisonous.
3. The speaker's questions lead us to query the deceptively innocent appearance of the
spider and how it came to be lurking on a white flower (providing perfect
camouflage) when the flower should have been blue, and also the speaker wonders
what "steered" the white moth to its hideous fate. The answer could be simply fate,
but the poem points instead to a "design of darkness to appall." Although that answer
is undercut by the final line, "If design govern in a thing so small," (meaning, "Oh
well, maybe not to worry"), we are not much comforted by the suggestion that
perhaps no one is in charge.
4. Frost's use of white, the color of innocence and purity, to label all that is treacherous
and deceptive in the poem invests the color with the horror of nothingness that chills
to the bone.

Additional Questions for Discussion and Writing
1. What is the tone of "Mixed ready to begin the morning right"?
2. This poem is a sonnet. What kind is it? How does the sonnet's limited rhyme scheme
help to emphasize the interlocking of ideas and the impact of the last two lines?
3. Analyze the use of white and whiteness in this poem. How does the word *appall*
contribute to this motif?

Making Connections
→Contrast the chilling image of the spider in Frost's poem with the positive spider image
presented in Whitman's "A Noiseless Patient Spider."

PIANO by D. H. Lawrence [p. 413]
The persona recalls a childhood emotion from the vantage point of an adult's perspective.
The poem hovers on the verge of sentimentality but is saved from it by the specific
images that re-create for readers what he felt as a child—the joy and warmth and security
associated with his loving mother. The soft singing of the woman in the first line triggers
these memories of his mother. He manfully struggles to resist "the insidious mastery of
song" but the sound "betrays [him] back." Eventually—despite the singer's change from
a soft song to a loud lively one, played with feeling—the speaker can't keep from
dissolving in tears. Even though he is aware that his recollections are nostalgic and
heightened by memory ("the glamour of childish days is upon me"), he nonetheless cries
"like a child for the past."

Possible Responses to *Questions for Discussion and Writing*
1. In the first line of the poem the speaker is in the present with a woman who is
singing to him; in the third line, he has gone back in memory to his childhood when
he was sitting beneath a grand piano while his mother was playing.
2. We don't know who the woman is in the first line, but her singing stirs in him
memories (in line 4) of his mother's singing.

3. Perhaps the speaker prefers not to dwell on the past because it was a much happier time for him and is now gone; perhaps also his mother is now gone.

Additional Questions for Discussion and Writing
1. Why does the speaker say the music "betrays" him back to his childhood?
2. Is this poem sentimental? If not, why not?

Making Connections
→Contrast the warm nostalgia of the grown son in "Piano" with the more troubling memories of the grown son in "Like Riding a Bicycle."

THE LOVE SONG OF J. ALFRED PRUFROCK by T. S. Eliot [pp. 413–17]
The persona is walking through a rather rundown section of London to a highly fashionable, late afternoon tea at which he arrives just as the poem ends. Once students discover that the speaker is talking to himself, that he is both the "you" and the "I," the poem becomes manageable. They may also need help in seeing the "love song" of the title as ironic, since it is clearly not a love song at all, but a wimpy debate about whether he dares to ask the lady an "overwhelming question"—probably whether he might sit beside her or take her to dine or some such inconsequential thing. Since the whole comic but somehow touching scene depends upon Prufrock's self-centeredness, coupled with his exaggerated fears of inadequacy, you might start with a thorough discussion of his character, beginning with his name (a "prude" in a frock coat, which happens to be what he is wearing). The poem doesn't reveal much about the lady he wishes to approach, but the response expected from her (in lines 96–99) suggests she has a demeanor of bored sophistication (which is reinforced by the refrain, ". . . the women come and go / Talking of Michelangelo"). So, poor Prufrock talks himself out of even asking her and resigns himself to walking alone on the beach, convinced that he will never hear the mermaid's sexy song. The "human voices" of the last line are the voices he hears upon arriving at the party, waking him from his reverie to "drown" in the sea of people among whom he feels so inadequate. Despite the comic tone, Eliot is seriously criticizing the triviality and sterility of the society presented here.

Possible Responses to Questions for Discussion and Writing
1. The speaker of this interior monologue is the J. Alfred Prufrock of the title, who is speaking to himself.
2. He is walking through a rather rundown section of London to a highly fashionable, late afternoon tea at which he arrives just as the poem ends. He is both the *you* and the *I* in this ironic "love song."
3. J. Alfred Prufrock's name says a lot about the kind of person he is—pretentious, stiff, and wearing a frock coat. But he clearly lacks self-assurance in his wimpy debate about whether to ask the lady an "overwhelming question"—probably whether he might sit beside her or take her out to dine or some such inconsequential thing. The whole comic but somehow touching scene depends upon Prufrock's self-centeredness, coupled with his exaggerated fears of inadequacy, which make him wary about attending this party. He considers "parting his hair behind" in order to

92

pull it forward to cover his bald spot. His life is no more than a series of these social occasions where coffee and tea are served; so he measures "out his life in coffee spoons"—a perfect metaphor to capture the insignificance and sameness of it all. The women make him nervous because he expects them to be haughty and reject whatever he says: "That is not what I meant at all; / That is not it at all." He thinks he ought to be a crab, "scuttling across the floors of silent seas," where he would not be expected to converse and interact with others. His exaggeration is an attempt to cover his basic fear of being a social failure. He is like both Polonius and Hamlet since he shares Hamlet's hesitation to act, but he is far more like Polonius because he thinks of himself as a tragic figure, while he is actually somewhat pathetic. He wonders if he dares to eat a peach because he fears he would look foolish if the juice should drip down his chin, or perhaps he worries about his delicate digestion. He does not think the mermaids will sing to him because mermaids are all about sexual enticement, and he dares not even hope. By the end of the poem, Prufrock resigns himself to walking alone on the beach. The human voices of the last line are the voices he hears upon arriving at the party, waking him from his reverie to "drown" in the sea of people among whom he feels so inadequate. Despite the comic tone, Eliot is seriously criticizing the triviality and sterility of the society presented here.

Additional Questions for Discussion and Writing
1. Why is this poem called a love song?
2. Consider what the sea might symbolize and how Prufrock is involved with it— especially in the last nine lines. Write an essay arguing that the sea (oyster shells, ragged claws, mermaids, walking on the beach) functions as a controlling image.

Making Connections
→What does J. Alfred Prufrock, the speaker in Eliot's "love song," have in common with the woman described in Walt Whitman's much shorter poem, Section 11 of "Song of Myself"?

AMERICA by Claude McKay [p. 417]
McKay is another black writer, like Paul Laurence Dunbar, who was expressing his resentment at the treatment of blacks in America long before the Civil Rights movement. In this sonnet the feelings of the persona are ambivalent: he loves the land that oppresses him and will not cry out against it. Instead, he delivers a warning: he sees the strength of America being undermined, worn down, by racial injustice (as a granite monument is eroded by the winds of time) and warns that the country cannot survive it. He predicts that her "granite wonders" (those splendid monuments, especially the Lincoln Memorial, which signify the ideals embraced by the country in theory but not in practice—liberty, equality, justice for all), those "priceless treasures," are crumbling and will end up "sinking in the sand." His tone is fervent but rational—and remarkably unresentful.

Possible Responses to Questions for Discussion and Writing
1. The speaker in the poem is a person of color, probably black since McKay was black.

2. In the first three lines, the speaker is being fed "bread of bitterness" (racial hatred) by a figure (representing white racism) whose attacks inflict pain like a "tiger's tooth," slashing his throat so cruelly that he is losing his "breath of life." Racial hatred, he is saying, can and does kill both the spirit and the body. [Both the figure and the country are presented as female since America is customarily personified that way (perhaps because of the Statue of Liberty?). Germans, on the other hand, think of their country as male, the Fatherland.]
3. The speaker loves America for the same reason Carl Sandburg loves Chicago—"her vigor" and "her bigness." Implicit in the last four lines of the poem is the fear that America may lose her strength and greatness because of ingrained racial prejudice.

Additional Questions for Discussion and Writing
1. What are the "granite wonders" of line 10? What do they signify?
2. Can you describe the tone of this work?
3. Why is it surprising that this poem is a Shakespearean sonnet?

Making Connections
→Compare McKay's feelings about living in a racist country to those expressed by Langston Hughes in "Harlem (A Dream Deferred)" and Countee Cullen in "Incident."

REAPERS by Jean Toomer [p. 418]
"Reapers," with its steady rhythm and onomatopoetic *s* and *c* sounds, drives home the inexorable process of the world's work. Students may need to look up reapers, scythes, and hones to visualize the poem's images. The slaughter of the field rat makes the work seem heartless, as do the silence and the color black. The fact that death is called the "Grim Reaper" must come into play here. The poem is an excellent example of crystallized imagery.

Possible Reponses to Questions for Discussion and Writing
1. The steady rhythm of the poem perfectly fits the activity described—the sharpening of the scythes and the rhythmic swishing of the cutting swings. The mowing in the second stanza with the horses slowly and steadily stepping follows a similar steady rhythm of the working animal.
2. Far from being a "joyful romp," the plodding rhythm, combined with the description of the repetitive action of mowing, suggests a dreary boredom. The silence of the workers (line 4) also suggests their draining tiredness.
3. The bloody slicing of the innocent field rat introduces the Grim Reaper. There is an undercurrent of seething anger in the poem, and the whetting of steel on whetstone suggests that the farm implement could easily become an instrument of death to others, not just field rats. If the black reapers are slaves, they might be envisioning in the scene the possibility of insurrection followed by freedom.

94

→ Account for the difference in tone concerning the work being done in "Reapers" and the work being done in Haney's "Digging." Also compare to the tone of "My Mother Sews Blouses" by Valdés.

NOT WAVING BUT DROWNING by Stevie Smith [p. 419]

This poem concerns the difference between public image and inner reality. On a literal level, the drowned man (who, given poetic license, may speak for himself) was misinterpreted in his death throes; other people thought that he was cheerily waving. Even when these people find that he's dead, they misinterpret the cause of death. The dead man takes his insistence to a metaphorical level, saying that he was alienated and misunderstood all his life.

Possible Responses to *Questions for Discussion and Writing*

1. The two speakers are the persona (presumably standing on the shore, addressing the dead man) and the dead man (presumably lying on shore, having just drowned). The persona misunderstood the man's gestures as he was drowning, thinking he was just giving a friendly wave, as a lark, to someone on shore, which was in keeping with the demeanor he had always exhibited and which led people to think he was carefree and happy.
2. The lines tell us that the dead man was, as he says, "much too far out all my life"— i.e., he was in over his head, drowning in troubles. His perpetual coldness stemmed from his alienation: nobody noticed or acknowledged that he was in trouble. Instead, everyone thought he was always "larking," horsing around and enjoying himself, when actually he was lonely and desperately in need of companionship and understanding.
3. Suggest that students use the poem as a starting point—as a way to get into the topic—for this essay.

Making Connections

→Contrast the way this poem treats death and dying to the way these same topics are approached in "To An Athlete Dying Young" by A. E. Housman.
→Compare the meaning of death of the drowning man in this poem with the suicide in Robinson's "Richard Cory."

HARLEM (A DREAM DEFERRED) by Langston Hughes [p. 420]

The "dream deferred" in the poem is, of course, the same dream that the Rev. Martin Luther King later made the centerpiece of his famous "I Have a Dream" speech: the dream of equality in American society. The poem suggests through metaphor the psychological damage of unrealized hopes—of promises given to African Americans and not fulfilled, going all the way back to the forty acres and a mule promised to each black family following the Civil War. The simple structure, the spare diction, the scabrous similes, the stunning last line, all mesh perfectly to produce a poem of remarkable power and portent. Read it aloud for full effect. Lorraine Hansberry used a phrase from this poem for the title of her play "A Raisin in the Sun."

1. What is the "dream deferred" mentioned in the opening line?
2. What effect do all the visual images describe?
3. How do these consequences culminate in the meaning of the final line?
4. Examine the similes Hughes employs to evoke the effects of the deferred dream, and write an essay discussing the social implications these images convey.

Making Connections
→Compare Hughes's feelings about living in a racist country to those expressed by Claude McKay in "America" and Countee Cullen in "Incident."

THEME FOR ENGLISH B by Langston Hughes [pp. 421–22]
Students enjoy this poem because they've probably received an assignment like the one the English teacher gives here. The contrast between the English teacher's assumptions and the student writer's is clear. In his theme, the student experiments with different ways to describe himself: the details of his physical situation, his likes and dislikes, the difference in race between him and his classmates and teacher, his citizenship, and so on. It seems that he stops in relief when he reaches the bottom of the page.

Questions for Discussion and Writing
1. What would you write if you had the assignment that the speaker's teacher gives the class? How would you decide what to include?
2. What is the student's attitude toward the assignment? How can you tell?
3. The teacher says, "And let that page come out of you—then, it will be true." What do you think she means by this? What ideas about writing does she probably hold?
4. Do you think the racial difference is an important part of this poem? Or do you think the main point is about how the teacher and the student look at things differently?

Making Connections
→Compare the speaker in this poem with the speaker in "America" by Claude McKay. Can you see any similarities in their attitudes?

INCIDENT by Countee Cullen [p. 422]
This simple lilting poem conveys a grim experience: a young boy's introduction to mindless racism. Although he is unfamiliar with the other boy's ugly reaction, somewhere deep within he understands how devastating and pervasive it is. It blots out nine months of experience in Baltimore. Of course, racist attitudes will shadow the speaker's life forever.

Possible Responses to Questions for Discussion and Writing
1. The theme: This poem conveys the cruel, wounding unfairness of mindless racism.

2. The author chose the simple form and simple language to convey verisimilitude because the speaker is an eight-year-old boy.
3. Suggest that students begin their essays with a reference to this poem, using its theme as a jumping-off point for relating their own experience.

Additional Questions for Discussion and Writing
1. Look carefully at the stanza division in the poem. Can you explain why the stanzas are separated the way they are? (Each stanza is a sentence: the second and third stanzas are compound sentences. The third one acts as a summing up for the whole poem.)
2. How do the lilting meter and happy rhymes belie the ugliness of the incident? Why do you suppose the poet chose to present the brief story in this way? (The speaker seems to have made a kind of peace, or truce, with the incident, although he hasn't forgotten it completely.)

Making Connections
→Compare the speaker in this poem with the speakers in Gwendolyn Brooks's "We Real Cool."

I KNEW A WOMAN by Theodore Roethke [pp. 423–24]
This poem draws its strength from its many evocative comparisons. The woman is compared to a goddess, a bird fancier, a dancing teacher, a sickle, a goose, and a musician, to name a few. The speaker is obviously obsessively in love with her, but at least sees the humor in his own obsession. Notice that we almost always see the woman in motion; Roethke thus avoids the traditional objectification of the beloved woman.

Possible Responses to Questions for Discussion and Writing
1. The woman in the poem is compared to a goddess, a birdsong, a sickle, a goose, and a musician; however, the emphasis on her charming movements makes the dominant image one of dancing. The comparisons to a sickle and a goose are unusual but serve to convey the lovesick silliness of the narrator's point of view—everything the woman does is entrancing, even the most mundane.
2. In stanza 2, "She was the sickle; I, poor I, the rake," requires a bit of farming knowledge. The sickle dramatically whacks down the crop with its razor-sharp edge; the rake comes behind it, methodically stacking what's left behind. Thus, the rake can never come before (or even alongside) the sickle but must slavishly follow it and pick up the leavings, as the smitten narrator is happy to do. Extra humor comes from contrast with the old definition of "rake" as a rather promiscuous ladies' man, which this devoted admirer certainly is not.
3. The joy of the poem is in the lover's conveyed understanding that he is foolishly in love—he is meek, a martyr, a gander, a compliant dancing student, so crazy about the woman that, glad to be a slave, he asks, "What's freedom for?"

→Compare Roethke's idealization of female beauty with Frost's admiration of female virtues in "A Silken Tent."

ONE ART by Elizabeth Bishop [pp. 424–25]

This poem is a tightly crafted villanelle. Bishop manages to say something worthwhile while adhering to the tricky rules of this form, which require using only two rhymes and repeating two of the lines according to a set pattern. Line 1 is repeated as lines 6, 12, and 18; line 3 as lines 9, 15, and 19. The first and third lines return as a rhymed couplet at the end. The rhyme scheme is aba (abaa for the last stanza). Bishop varies line 3 as she repeats it; she also uses ingenious rhymes ("last, or" in l.10) and off rhymes ("fluster" and "gesture") to meet the demands of the very limited rhyme scheme.

The poem's meaning is also somewhat tricky. On the literal level, the speaker seems to say that it's easy to lose things (it's something you can "master"—or learn to deal with) and that loss is not "disaster." But as the poem progresses and the losses move from the trivial (keys) to more significant things (time, beloved places, a loved one), we realize the speaker is being ironic, that losing is difficult and not something one can "master" (except to ignore or accept the losses). The parenthetical imperative in the last line suggests that the speaker is forcing herself to admit that some losses are indeed disastrous.

The references to a lost "continent" and a lost love may be personal: Bishop lived for many years with a lover in Brazil and wrote this poem after she returned to America. Bishop's father died when she was 8 months old, and she never saw her mother again once the latter was confined to a mental hospital. The draft of the poem was titled "How to Lose Things" and probably referred to her companion at the time.

Possible Responses to *Questions for Discussion and Writing*

1. The poem is a villanelle. The repetition makes the theme seem light and emphasizes the dailiness of "losing," setting the reader up for the more serious closing twist and reversal.
2. The central experience of the poem is the narrator convincing herself that she can survive the loss of love as she has been able to deal with the many other changes in her life, from the insignificant ("lost door keys") to the life changing (moves from city to city, continent to continent).
3. The everyday losses include things that may or may not be able to be replaced (keys, a mother's watch); time ill spent; memory and the control of the details of our lives (names and places); homes and even countries. Most importantly, however, she explores the loss of a loved one.
4. Coming to terms with the idea of loss (and not the lost items themselves) is the art the narrator outlines. The emphatic and parenthetical "*Write it!*" reveals the truth of the difficulty of mastering the art.

Making Connections

→Compare this poem to Dylan Thomas's "Do Not Go Gentle into That Good Night," another villanelle.

AIDS by May Sarton [pp. 425–26]

Sarton explores the ways in which AIDS affects everyone. (At the time Sarton wrote this poem, AIDS was almost always fatal.) The "we" of the poem clearly includes AIDS victims and their friends and lovers; your students may also point out that society in general has been challenged by the epidemic. The seeming oxymoron of "reckless design" is reflected in the subtle and irregular rhyme scheme of the poem. The speaker grapples with the strange mixture of "despair and hope" that the disease evokes and actually manages to end on a positive note, suggesting the renewal of love.

Possible Responses to *Questions for Discussion and Writing*

1. The "we" of the poem is the collective of people who, unprepared, must find a way to respond to the AIDS crisis, especially as friends and lovers.
2. Used to turning for pleasure and "hope" to lovers and friends as part of an active present and an expected future, the friend must now act for these same lovers and friends in the face of death, loss, and "despair." His acceptance of this brings him the "discipline" and "grace" that lead to a new kind of expanded "love" that counters "fear."
3. They are "blest" in the sense of "grace" by being given the tragic but important opportunity to experience a deeper, more complex love.

Additional Questions for Discussion and Writing

1. "AIDS" includes two unusual one-line stanzas. What is the effect of these stanzas? Why are they set off from the other lines?
2. This poem is more than 20 years old. Is its perspective on AIDS outdated?

Making Connections

→Compare Sarton's exploration of attitudes toward death among the living to Dickinson's view of the dying in "Because I Could Not Stop for Death" or to Donne's conception of death in "Death, Be Not Proud."

THE STREET by Octavio Paz [p. 427]

Four lines into this poem the reader has entered the sensory experience of the persona. The scene seems familiar, dreamlike, and cinematic. Stumbling blindly down a long, dark street is a bleak image of life's journey. Things don't improve, either. The persona is frightened by his own shadow (in Jungian terms) following him, and in the last four lines of the poem he becomes the shadow pursuing himself in the same nightmarish maze of streets, in which neither figure is quite real: both are "nobody." The poem can be read as a portrayal of anxiety or of identity dissolution.

Possible Responses to *Questions for Discussion and Writing*

1. The first four lines of the poem are like a familiar nightmare, with its ominous and menacing tone. The poem drops the reader directly into the eerie scene with no explanation or orientation, much as a bad dream does. The first lines practically force

the reader into an uncomfortable identification with the "I" of the poem.

2. The main sensory appeals are sound and silence; kinetic references such as stumbling, stepping, slowing, and running; and only a few visual images, usually of darkness and blindness. These combine to convey fright and confusion, with blindness not only literal but also in the sense of not understanding what is happening. Further dreamlike, the main character is himself pursued by his own shadow, and then becomes the shadow pursuing himself, who then is named as "nobody." The poem seems to be an extended metaphor for life's journey, or at least a particularly grim part of it. Some readers may have a psychological interpretation, in which the narrator is experiencing acute anxiety or losing his sense of self.

3. The image of the dry leaves suggests death and desiccation, while the doorless buildings that loom along the street suggest that there is no escape to a welcoming or rescuing household within. The doorlessness literally shuts the narrator out of ordinary social life.

Additional Questions for Discussion and Writing

1. The persona is simultaneously being followed and following himself, never being caught or catching up, and always identifying himself as "nobody." This is obviously an extended metaphor, but a metaphor for what?

2. The street clearly stands for something. Is it a metaphor or a symbol or metonymy? What's the difference? Explain your choice.

Making Connections

→Consider the extended metaphors in this poem and in Hayden Carruth's "In the Long Hall." What do the poems suggest about the meaning of life?

TO THE MERCY KILLERS by Dudley Randall [p. 428]

This powerful rejection of euthanasia is a Shakespearean sonnet. The strong language, as well as the concise form, lends the poem its vigor. The speaker clearly feels that despite the outward appearance of suffering and the experience of pain, there is something still valuable in life, which should not be cut short.

Possible Responses to *Questions for Discussion and Writing*

1. "Mercy" is not a word usually coupled with "murder," and "kindly killers" would—without the irony—be an oxymoron.

2. For people who believe euthanasia should be allowed to end the suffering of the terminally ill, the speaker's attitude is difficult to understand. Although some people object to mercy killing on religious grounds (that only God should decide when someone dies), the speaker in this poem doesn't seem to be taking that position. He (or she) seems determined to hang on to life as long as possible, even if it's painful—perhaps because the speaker feels that this life is all we have.

3. In the last line the speaker's life is compared to a light bulb: it could be "put out," but the speaker wants it left on, to "still glow."

4. A writer agreeing with the speaker's position might respond with the argument that only God can justifiably end a human life, or that life is precious and should be clung

100

to at all costs. Those choosing to argue against the speaker's position could point out the loaded language used in the poem: *murder, traitor, accomplice*, and especially *glow,* a word with pleasant, positive associations that are usually belied by the physical state of a dying person.

Making Connections
→In what ways is the theme of this poem similar to the one expressed in "Do Not Go Gentle into That Good Night" by Dylan Thomas?

Do Not Go Gentle into That Good Night by Dylan Thomas [p. 428]
This poem was addressed to Thomas's agnostic father, who had cancer of the throat. One interesting thing about it is its complex form; it's a villanelle, which you may want to define for your class. The poem basically exhorts the father not to accept death passively. Stanzas 2 through 5 give examples of people who admirably fight death: wise men (writers, philosophers), good men (philanthropists, social reformers), wild men (poets, artists), and grave men (scholars, perhaps religious philosophers).

Possible Responses to *Questions for Discussion and Writing*
1. The image of "that good night" represents death itself, while the "dying of the light" suggests the loss of health or gradual debilitation that often precedes death.
2. The repeated pattern in those stanzas describes the different ways in which people ("men" in the poem) face death. The "wise" are not ready to die (and hence, "Rage, rage against the dying of the light") because they had not yet been able to inspire others with their ideas ("their words had forked no lightning"); the "good" are not ready to die because they have not yet been acknowledged for their modest ("frail") accomplishments; the "wild" ones, who partied hard and lived dangerously, are not ready to die because they mourn the coming loss of zestful delight; the "grave" ones, "near death," who see metaphysically through "blind eyes," seem ready to die because they envision a scene of blazing light and joy; finally, the speaker addresses his father, near death ("there on that sad height") and begs him not to "go gentle into that good night," but "Rage, rage against the dying of the light."
3. In line 17, addressed to his father—"Curse, bless me now with your fierce tears, I pray"—the speaker begs to be cursed for his past misdeeds and then absolved with a blessing so that father and son can bid a final farewell on friendly terms.

Additional Questions for Discussion and Writing
1. Do you think the speaker's reaction is normal? How would you react in a similar situation?
2. Examine the use of paradox in this poem ("blinding sight," "sad height," "fierce tears," "Curse, bless, me now"). How does paradox fit the tone and message?

Making Connections
→Compare the attitude toward death in this poem to the one expressed in Housman's "To an Athlete Dying Young" or Randall's "To the Mercy Killers."

SADIE AND MAUD by Gwendolyn Brooks [pp. 429–30]
This poem is dated in an interesting way. Clearly, the speaker thinks Sadie, who "stayed at home" and bore two out-of-wedlock children, had a better life than Maud, who "went to college." That "Ma and Papa / Nearly died of shame" seems quaint, even hard to believe today. But at the time Brooks wrote this poem, she felt the proprieties governing the lives of young women were too restrictive—as they were. Today, many people think we have moved too far in the other direction, since the cost of caring for literally thousands of out-of-wedlock children has become a heavy social burden.

Stanza 4 implies that Sadie's girls will follow their mother's lifestyle, not their aunt's, since Sadie "left as heritage / Her fine-tooth comb" (lines 15–16). That comb is the emblem of Sadie's irrepressible (irresponsible?) lifestyle, as "one of the livingest chits / In all the land" (lines 7–8). *Chit* means an immature young girl.

Possible Responses to *Questions for Discussion and Writing*
1. The bare events of Sadie's life suggest a tragic arc: she stays at homes and has two children—but never marries and dies young. Her short life is full, however, and her character is lively and strong. She passes this legacy along to two independent daughters. By contrast, Maud, who would seem to have had the greater advantage by going to college and living up to the cultural mores, lives an isolated, barren life.
2. Sadie is resourceful, ferreting out and taking advantage of every possibility.
3. By reversing narrative expectations, Brooks refocuses the reader's attention on character. It's not the events of life that matter but what one does with those events.
4. The discussion of this poem might focus on the contrasting choices the students' high school classmates made, or perhaps the lives led by their parents and grandparents.

Making Connections
→Contrast points of view on what young black women should do: in this poem and in Toni Cade Bambara's story "The Lesson."

THE BEAN EATERS by Gwendolyn Brooks [p. 430]
Perhaps inspired by Picasso's "The Frugal Repast," this poem also paints a picture of a poverty-stricken couple who continue to live after life has lost its zest. Reminders of their past surround them in their "rented back room." Although the overall tone remains grim, the word choice makes the description tender, respectful, and deeply human.

Possible Responses to *Questions for Discussion and Writing*
1. The aging couple eats beans because they lack money—and choices. Their frayed surroundings reinforce this image.
2. The beads and other objects are the remains of their past lives, suggesting beauty (the beads, cloth) and perhaps children (dolls), but also a frugally lived life (receipts).
3. "Mostly good" makes the couple human, subject to our common weaknesses and thus more easily identified with by the reader. Further, with this modification, Brooks resists romanticizing the poverty she examines through the poem.

4. The daily life of the elderly, especially of the poor, is reduced to a smaller stage, with fewer events and choices. Eating, dressing, and cleaning become the major events of the day.

Additional Questions for Discussion and Writing
1. What is the effect of describing the couple as "yellow"?
2. What does the line "Dinner is a casual affair" suggest?
3. Why is the word "remembering" repeated, and why is the couple remembering "with twinklings and twinges"?
4. Write an essay on the use of concrete details in this poem, focusing on how they contribute to tone.

Making Connections
→Compare Brooks's exploration of the relationship between poverty and memory to Tillie Olsen's exploration of that same concept in "I Stand Here Ironing."
→Contrast the circumscribed existence of the old couple in this poem with the fullness of the life cycle experienced by the couple in Cummings's "anyone lived in a pretty how town."

YOU ALL KNOW THE STORY OF THE OTHER WOMAN by Anne Sexton [p. 431]
"She" in the poem is the other woman, the mistress of a married man. And the story, of course, is that she is a convenience, bound to ignominious secrecy and ultimate disappointment. "A little Walden" compares the love nest to Thoreau's idyllic retreat from civilization, but, as we find out in line 5, "it's a bad translation," not quite idyllic. All the comparisons emphasize the brevity and fleeting nature of the lovers' encounter, as well as the objectification of the woman, which is crystallized in the final simile.

Possible Responses to Questions for Writing and Discussion
1. The story of the other woman may have changed since Sexton wrote this poem in 1967. The story in those days was that the unfaithful husband would tire of the other woman sooner or later, dump her, and continue in his marriage. The divorce statistics today suggest that perhaps in many cases the husband now dumps his wife and carries on with the other woman—or some brand new other woman. (Also fairly common today is the dumping of husbands by wives who think they've found a more suitable mate, but the poem does not touch on this version of the marriage-go-round.)
2. Metaphors: "She is private in her breathbed"—Sexton coins a new term by combining the heavy breathing of sexual intercourse with the bed on which it occurs; "as his body takes off and flies"—not literally, but the rapid action and soaring feeling of the sex act is equated with flying; "God comes in like a landlord / and flashes on his brassy lamp"—the coming of daylight (God's "brassy lamp") ends the sexual idyll; "He puts his bones back on"—no longer the enfolding lover, the man, resuming his upright stature, puts his suit and tie back on; "when it is over he places her, / like a phone, back on the hook"—she's feeling at this point as if she's just been used and then discarded. The last metaphor is unmistakable because when a phone is placed back on the hook, the connection ends.

3. The man behaves as if he was only using the woman as a sex object. To paraphrase line 6 through 14: Daylight is no friend to lovers; God, like a landlord, sends in the morning light to evict them; now she is no longer ecstatic; he is no longer cuddly and pliant, as he acts as if nothing has happened between them ("turns the clock back an hour"); lines 12–14 are difficult, but it helps to know that at the time the poem was written in 1967, many women still wore hats and girdles, which might explain the "boards" (perhaps the corset enclosing and binding her body) and the "roof, the removable roof" (perhaps the hat topping her head).

Additional Questions for Discussion and Writing
1. Explain the house imagery in the poem. Is the speaker comparing herself to a house (rented and used by the landlord)? Look closely at lines 12–14.
2. What is the pun in the word "breathbed"? Why is daylight "nobody's friend"?

Making Connections
→Explain how Gabriel Spera gets humor out of a similar situation in "My Ex-Husband."

AUNT JENNIFER'S TIGERS by Adrienne Rich [p. 432]
The controlling image of the prancing tigers serves both to unify the poem and to amplify Aunt Jennifer's plight in her oppressive marriage. The gorgeous tigers, "proud and unafraid," provide a sharp contrast with the woman who created them with her "terrified hands." Unlike the tigers, who "pace in sleek chivalric certainty," Aunt Jennifer "flutters" under the domination of her husband. Although absent from the poem, the husband's domineering presence is felt in "The massive weight" of the wedding band that "sits heavily" on her hand. Unlike the tigers, which "do not fear the men beneath the tree," Aunt Jennifer was "terrified" into submission by unnamed "ordeals she was mastered by." In the last stanza we see that Aunt Jennifer will escape her confined, fearful existence only in death, but her spirited tigers "Will go on prancing, proud and unafraid."

Possible Responses to Questions for Discussion and Writing
1. The tigers share the human traits of pride, bravery, stateliness, and self-assurance ("certainty"). They lead a life in which they are both feared and admired, and their "prancing" suggests that they very much enjoy that life.
2. Aunt Jennifer's life, on the other hand, is fearful ("her terrified hands"), oppressed ("ringed with ordeals"), and restricted ("mastered by"). The tigers possess the freedom, strength, and bravery to live in freedom—a complete contrast with Aunt Jennifer's narrow existence. She probably chose the tigers for her tapestry because she admires them and longs to be like them.
3. The "massive weight" of her wedding band symbolizes the weight of her oppressive marriage. Historically wedding rings were symbols of ownership of the wife by the husband, but today wedding rings are supposed to symbolize eternal love.
4. Responses will vary, but certainly a strong case can be argued for reading the poem as sympathetic to Aunt Jennifer's plight and revealing as its theme that marriage can be bondage as easily as it can be bliss.

Additional Questions for Discussion and Writing

1. Although her husband never appears in the poem, what can you tell about him from the poem?
2. Why does the poet use the word "mastered" instead of "defeated" or "beaten down"?
3. Write a paper analyzing your response to the tigers in the last stanza, still "prancing, proud and unafraid." Are you comforted that Aunt Jennifer's artistic creation will live after her? Or are you sad that she was so unlike her tigers?

Making Connections

→How does Aunt Jennifer's marital situation compare to that of Nora in *A Doll's House*? What would Nora think about Aunt Jennifer, and what advice might she give her?

MIRROR by Sylvia Plath [p. 433]

The mirror in this poem is personified, given a human voice to express its point of view on its important role in the woman's life. In the first stanza the mirror acts as a truthful "little god," and in the second stanza it acts as a reflecting lake which contains both the past and the future. Both the god and the lake images connote power, which mirrors certainly have over people, especially women. The poem is basically free verse, but all lines contain five stressed syllables in a kind of sprung rhythm.

Possible Responses to *Questions for Discussion and Writing*

1. The voice of the mirror is unusual and meaningful in this poem. The mirror has a point of view that no other observer has, because it sees the woman at her most self-critical yet accurate state. She sees herself as she believes others see her, in the mirror.
2. The stanzas are divided by the mirror's point of view. In the first stanza, the mirror is truthful and reports only what it reflects. In the second stanza, the mirror is more sensitive to the woman's feelings as she looks at herself.
3. Candles and the moon both give forgiving light to the faces of older women; in this sense, they are "liars."

Additional Question for Discussion and Writing

Write a poem or essay from the point of view of some nonhuman object that has importance in your life. Use personification to give the object its own voice. (It may be interesting to hear your students talk or write from the voice of other inanimate objects in their lives, such as easy chairs, backpacks, and computers.)

Making Connections

→Compare the reflecting abilities of the mirror in Plath's poem with the function of the wall in Frost's "Mending Wall."

EX-BASKETBALL PLAYER by John Updike [pp. 434–35]

Though aging ex-cheerleaders are a common target of sympathy, ex-basketball players rarely get much. This poem chronicles in rich detail the dead-end life of a man whose only golden moments were as a sports star—and that, only in a small-town high school. Your students may know such a person. The details, which give the poem its authentic flavor, also date the poem, and your students may want to look at the picture of the old-fashioned gas pump on page 435 to appreciate the personification in stanza 2. You may also need to explain what Necco Wafers, Nibs, and Juju Beads are.

Possible Responses to *Questions for Discussion and Writing*

1. Flick Webb had all his moments of glory as a high school basketball player, and drifted into the life of a mundane worker as an adult. His name reflects his past—in that he could *flick* the ball and handle it as though he had *webbed* hands—as well as his present—in that his heyday was over in a *flicker* and he's now caught in a *web* of ordinariness and boredom. We have no clue that he has a rich inner life to supplement his tiresome existence.
2. The "I" of the poem is a citizen of the same town as Berth's Garage. He knows the streets, people, stores, and sports lore of the town well. The speaker seems to be the same age or a bit older than Flick—at least, he was of an age to go to games Flick played in high school.
3. Each line has five stressed syllables (pentameter), more or less. The stanzas are like paragraphs in a prose essay. Each one takes up a new topic developing the overall theme: the town, Berth's garage, Flick's basketball feats, his current work, his current leisure. The thesis is implied.
4. The poem is full of description, yet we have little insight into Flick's point of view. The idea that he never learned a trade, is "kind of coiled," and doesn't make eye contact with Mae might suggest that he's somehow trapped in his life, unable to expand into a fully adult human being. Whether he's aware of this is not clear.

Additional Questions for Discussion and Writing

1. Note that Pearl Avenue runs past the high school, stops, and is "cut off / Before it has a chance to go two blocks." How does this relate to Flick Webb?
2. Explain the extended personification in the second stanza. What does "Five on a side" refer to? What do "rubber elbows hanging loose and low" suggest? What is the personification in lines 29–30, and how does it relate to the second stanza?
3. Try writing a description of some familiar part of your hometown with as much detail as Updike gives in this poem. You might add a town character if you want.

Making Connections

→Compare this poem to A. E. Housman's "To an Athlete Dying Young" or Edward Hirsch's "Execution."

BARBIE DOLL by Marge Piercy [p. 436]

Though this condemnation of sex role expectations may seem heavy-handed to older students, younger ones usually appreciate it. The Barbie Doll is a perfect symbol of utterly unobtainable female appearance: if you have such a doll, you might measure the body parts and note the odd proportions of torso to leg, leg to neck and head, waist to bust, and so on. The girlchild in the poem is well socialized into her role, and the discovery that intelligence, strength, personality, and charm-school self-improvement cannot redeem her "big nose and fat legs" drives her to suicide—or perhaps plastic surgery, a metaphoric death which "cuts off" the ugly parts and destroys her original looks (and her identity?). She looks perfect in her casket (her new self?), though, dressed in a nose and nightie like Barbie's.

Possible Responses to *Questions for Discussion and Writing*
1. The young woman who finds herself unable to reconstruct her natural body to conform to social standards of beauty is, ironically, able to be made beautiful in death, in her casket.
2. Most often seen as an iconic figure of fashionable beauty, meant to teach young girls to aspire to standardized adult feminine beauty norms and behavior (set hair, appropriate make-up, high heels—as well as performing domestic tasks and projecting a feminine, passive affect), Barbie is the embodiment of what Piercy suggests is a plastic and dangerous kind of social enculturation.
3. While the poem perfectly captures Piercy's 1970s feminism, students are likely to enter into lively debate about its relevance to current beauty standards. A quick review of the covers of a few teen magazines would be an interesting addition to the conversation or useful evidence for student essays.

Additional Questions for Discussion and Writing
1. Do you think the "girlchild" is literally dead at the end of this poem?
2. How might a male respond differently to this poem differ than a female would?

Making Connections
→Compare the issues about beauty and identify raised in this poem with those that Jane Martin explores in the play *Beauty*.

HOMAGE TO MY HIPS by Lucille Clifton [p. 437]
Clifton's piece depends on its unusual topic for praise, poetry, and power. Notice that throughout the description, the hips are depicted in images that connote freedom and self-determination. Considering that the poet is an African American woman, the images are no doubt purposeful, suggesting that her spirit has "never been enslaved" (line 8).

Possible Responses to *Questions for Discussion and Writing*
1. The unexpected element is the object of the homage. Have your students look up *homage* in the dictionary. What are some typical targets of homage? The hips are an unusual choice, being an ordinary body part and often unwanted at a certain size. Thus, Clifton is celebrating something that is usually mundane or even ridiculed in our society.
2. There are a number of racist remarks and jokes about black women with large hips; however, within the black community, differing beauty aesthetics make large, strong bodies both positive for the woman and attractive to others. Clifton mirrors her community's rejection of normative beauty standards and turns the racist attitudes upside down in writing an homage instead.

3. In the last three lines Clifton also turns the power relationship between the sexes upside down, as she glories in the mysterious effects her hips can have over men.
4. Answers will vary, but you may need to start a discussion to capture students' imaginations. For example, being an intellectual or a nerd can be negative at certain ages, yet turn out to be a major advantage. Furthermore, some physical problems can work for, as well as against, people: for example, controlling diabetes or allergies can be important practice in self-regulation, a true strength.

Making Connections
→Compare the persona in this poem to the speaker in "Daystar" by Rita Dove.

DIGGING by Seamus Heaney [pp. 438–39]
The speaker in this poem admires the work done by his forefathers, who were potato farmers. Their strength and skill and their connection to the earth make him nostalgic. Male virtues are venerated in the competition of cutting turf and in the way the grandfather tosses off his milk and returns to work without missing a beat. The speaker, a writer, has a pen instead of a spade to assert his manhood; the opening image of the pen as a gun supports this line of interpretation in an unsettling way.

Possible Responses to Questions for Discussion and Writing
1. The speaker reveres strength, stamina, skill, and dedication in his forefathers.
2. Many students remember their grandparents as hardworking; maybe they even remember or hear tales of their great-grandparents' efforts. Second- or third-generation citizens whose forefathers immigrated to the United States may well remember the strengths of their parents and grandparents as they struggled to make their lives in a new country.
3. Writing poetry might be seen as nourishing the spirits of readers the way that potatoes nourish the body. Furthermore, the peat warms the household as poetry might warm the heart of a reader. The highly developed skill and exactness shown in the father's labor is also required of a good poet. *Digging* also has a double meaning—both digging into the ground, but also digging into the consciousness and history of human beings. The last image contrasts with the very first image, when the pen is "snug as a gun," that is, an instrument of destruction. Instead, the poet turns to the craft as an instrument for life, not death.

Additional Questions for Discussion and Writing
1. How can you fit in the disturbing image in the first two lines with the rest of the poem?
2. Do you think the speaker regrets that he's not doing the same kind of physical work as his father did?

Making Connections
→Compare this poem with these other poems about writing: "Sonnet" by Collins and "Theme for English B" by Hughes.

→Compare "Digging" with other poems written by sons about their fathers: "Those Winter Sundays" by Robert Hayden, "My Papa's Waltz" by Theodore Roethke, "Like Riding a Bicycle" by George Bilgere.

INTRODUCTION TO POETRY by Billy Collins [pp. 439–40]

Why is "Introduction to Poetry" humorous? Perhaps it reverberates with many students' experience in a required literature course, where the secret meaning of a work seems to be something extricated by barbaric means, and then inflicted upon bewildered students. The first five metaphors for approaching a poem are what a professor would wish from his or her students, but the sixth one, torture, is the one they perceive as potentially effective. Asking your students what their experience with Intro to Lit classes was like will help most of them understand the point of view.

Possible Responses to *Questions for Discussion and Writing*
1. It's crucial to understand that "I" is the instructor of poetry and "they" are the students in class. The title is a common name for a college course, and it also describes the experience of students who are forcibly introduced to poetry as a genre.
2. The five metaphors provided by the speaker evoke exploratory methods that are experimental and active: looking at it as a picture, listening to its sound, watching an animal navigate the piece as though it were water, illuminating the poem by turning on a light switch, and even skimming over the surface. These methods are quite different from most people's classroom experiences with learning to appreciate poetry. Thus, the metaphor that describes the students' approach is one of torture, suggesting that the poem will only give up its real meaning through violent methods. Students will vary in describing their processes of understanding an unfamiliar poem; perhaps they can choose from one of the six metaphors in the poem and expand upon it.
3. The torture approach is humorous because it appears at odds with the goals of poetry, such as expressing emotions and providing enjoyment to the reader. It also is a bad approach because it suggests that each poem has one secret interpretation that it purposely attempts to hide from the reader, like a spy with a clandestine plot.

Making Connections
→Compare the tone of this poem to "Sonnet" (in Chapter 15), also by Billy Collins. What do these two poems suggest about Collins's attitude toward literature and how to read it?

SEX WITHOUT LOVE by Sharon Olds [pp. 440–41]

The main difficulty in reading this poem is construing the tone or attitude of the speaker. Our own preconceptions about sex without love get in the way of clearly perceiving what the speaker's point is. Some of the images have a positive bent—the ice skaters, dancers, great runners, and true religious. There is also an attractive realism to those who have sex without love. Other images, though, are negative, like "fingers hooked / inside each other's bodies." Perhaps the speaker herself is struggling with mixed feelings on the issue. Some readers believe that the poem takes place during a sex act, citing lines 8–10 as the point of orgasm.

Possible Responses to *Questions for Discussion and Writing*

1. The people are compared to dancers, ice-skaters, unwanted babies, religious purists, and runners. These comparisons are mixed in connotation. However, they are all alone in an existential sense, as the closing of the poem confirms.
2. The speaker believes that people who have sex without love are realistic: "They do not / mistake the lover for their own pleasure." The theme of being ultimately alone is presented dispassionately.
3. Students may see a suggestion that people who believe that sex and love are intertwined are fooling themselves, escaping from the existential loneliness that is our true state. Love is presented as an illusion.

Additional Questions for Discussion and Writing

1. Note how often the speaker uses the word *not*, ending with "not the truth." What is the truth? Why doesn't the speaker ever state her idea of truth directly?
2. Discuss the mix of religious and athletic metaphors. Do they work together or cancel one another out?

Making Connections

→Compare the treatment of sex and love in this poem with that in John Donne's "A Valediction: Forbidding Mourning." How does Donne's distinction between earthly and spiritual love parallel Olds's views?

INVENTING MY PARENTS by Susan Ludvigson [pp. 441–42]
As the title suggests, Ludvigson's poem imagines her parents as the couple depicted at the counter in Hopper's painting. Instead of an alienated pair in a stark, bleak setting (which is the way many viewers of the painting see them), Ludvigson envisions her charming, sophisticated parents drinking coffee in a "bright café" (line1). This poet's positive impression of the setting invites us to view the scene in the painting as warm, almost homey. The details she gives us about her parents' conversation tell us a great deal about the two of them and their relationship. We can safely assume, for instance, that they are young. They have a five-month-old daughter, and they contemplate how the Second World War "will change them" (line 3); perhaps he could even be drafted (the painting is dated 1942). They are also quite literary and well educated. They discuss modernist writers of the 1930s: Ernest Hemingway, who wrote about war; Sinclair Lewis, who wrote about small town USA; Kay Boyle, who wrote pacifist fiction; F. Scott Fitzgerald, who wrote about the American Dream (about which the couple disagree in l.6). At the end of the poem, the husband recites a line from John Donne's "The Canonization." We see the mother as highly imaginative in her fanciful vision of the American Dream (lines 7–11) and intellectual, as "her face is lit by ideas" (line 13). The father is clearly animated, genial, and agreeable: his gestures "are a Frenchman's. When he concedes / a point, he shrugs, an elaborate lift / of the shoulders, his hands and smile / declaring an open mind" (lines14–17). He genuinely listens to his wife and near the end recites the line from Donne to make her laugh, "light / as summer rain when it begins"

110

(lines 27–28). Ludvigson envisions a meaningful sexual bond for her parents, suggested only by their pleasure in "being alone together" (line 23) while "savoring / the fragrant night" (lines 22–23), and in the father's humorous injunction from Donne, "For God's sake / hold your tongue, and let me love" (lines 25–26).

Possible Responses to *Questions for Discussion and Writing* [p. 558]
1. Ludvigson's view of *Nighthawks* creates a tone of love and also includes a child's existence in stanza 2.
2. The couples are having a smart, literary conversation, implying that they are educated.
3. The mother seems engaged in life and sensitive, while the father is shown as expressive and enthusiastic. Their conversation and actions support these ideas.
4. The sexual relationship of the couple is light, fun, and intimate, as we see from their decision to walk out the door to go home and make love in stanza 2.

Making Connections
→How does Ludvigson's use of her parents differ from the way that other poets treat their parents, such as Roethke in "My Papa's Waltz," Gina Valdés in "My Mother Sews Blouses," George Bilgere in "Like Riding a Bicycle," Robert Hayden in "Those Winter Sundays," Seamus Heaney in "Digging."

MY MOTHER SEWS BLOUSES by Gina Valdés [pp. 442–43]
Students need to understand the garment industry in order to appreciate this poem. Along the U.S.–Mexican border, clothing factories are set up, and piecework is sent to the Mexican side to be done without union pay and U.S. safety controls (in other words, very cheaply). Final steps are taken on the U.S. side so that the garments can be considered U.S.-made. In the poem, the speaker's mother risks her vision for one dollar a blouse while thinking about going to night school, no doubt to upgrade her job. The hope seems pitifully futile, given her circumstances.

Possible Responses to *Questions for Discussion and Writing*
1. The mother is poorly paid because she works in a sweatshop—a place where undocumented immigrants to the U.S. or unprotected workers in other countries make goods, usually for U.S. markets. Much of the clothing we buy at least partly originates in such sweatshops (if it is finished in legally protected U.S. sites, it can be labeled "Made in the U.S.A."). You might ask your students to do some research on brand names and sweatshops.
2. The loss of sight is definitely a loss of power, which the mother experiences. Blindness is also symbolically associated with lack of knowledge, wisdom, or insight; perhaps the mother has little knowledge of her alternatives. The black lint symbolizes the evil effects of sweatshop work, using the conventional association of black with evil, as well as its gradual incursion into the workers' lives.
3. The mother is "thinking about night school" because more education would qualify her for a better job. Students who work in sweatshop conditions often serve more than eight hours a day and often work nights, conditions that will interfere with going to night school and doing the necessary studying. Also, being near-blinded

111

every six months will impair her studying. Nonetheless, she is at least thinking about school, which could be interpreted optimistically.

Making Connections
→Compare this description of a parent's work with the one presented in "Digging" by Seamus Heaney.

EXECUTION by Edward Hirsch [pp. 444–45]
The poem is a tribute to the speaker's former football coach, a man who loved football and loved winning even more but who is now dying of cancer, "wobbly and stunned by illness" (line 28). His "favorite word, Execution" (line 9), is capitalized on the chalkboard by the coach and serves ironically as the title of the poem. The "awkward adolescent bodies" (line 16) of his high school players could never execute his clever plays well enough to achieve "the ideal game he imagined" (line 19). But the cancer is clearly going to perform its *execution* of the coach "with a vengeance" (line 32), like the team did from downstate, who "battered [them] all afternoon" (line 31) with "machine-like fury" and defeated them with "perfect execution" (line 34).

Possible Responses to *Questions for Discussion and Writing*
1. The coach is dedicated to football with "perfect unquestioning faith," as if to a new religion (line 11). The plays he outlines on the chalkboard are compared to a spiderweb, sprinkled with players like a "constellation" of stars (lines 7–8), "shining" under his motto "Execution" (line 9). The game is also compared to warfare and to the harmonious movement of the planets (lines 13, 15). In line 22, the young players are "challenged to hammer" the coach in practice sessions.
2. The downstate team played with the "perfect execution" that the coach tried but failed to achieve with his own team. The speaker remembers the long-ago game because he sees in the "wobbly and stunned" (line 28) demeanor of the coach a crushing loss in his battle with cancer like the defeat suffered by their team on the gridiron that day.
3. The coach's love of winning "more than his own body, maybe even / More than himself" (lines 25–26) accentuates his devotion as a religious experience, since the saints often mortified the flesh and gave their lives for the faith. The speaker is implying that the coach is an acolyte in the service of Football.
4. Students could argue this one either way, possibly influenced by their own experiences with coaches. But the evidence in the poem presents the coach as a man who reveres the game and works hard (too hard?) to field a good team, including the "punishing drills" and doubled practice times (lines 20–21). His "elaborate, last-second plays" usually work, so he is good at what he does. He may be a sympathetic figure because he seems to be dying a long, agonizing death.
5. The irony of the title lies in the two meanings of "execution." As the coach's favorite word (lines 9–10), it means a skilled, near-perfect performance, but the term can also mean the taking of a life, as in the coach's slow "execution" by cancer. It is also ironic that the coach's players, who are diligently schooled but imperfect in executing plays, are defeated by a downstate team which has achieved "perfect

112

execution" (line 34). Similarly ironic is the coach's "perfect unquestioning faith in . . . the idea of warfare" (lines 13–14), an idea that proves correct, but unfortunately not for him. When tested in action against the team from downstate who attack with "Machine-like fury" and the "deadly, impersonal authority" of war (lines 34, 33), the coach's less war-like team goes down in defeat.

Making Connections
→Compare the situation of the coach in this poem with that of the dispirited young man in Updike's "Ex-Basketball Player."

DAYSTAR by Rita Dove [pp. 445–46]
A question about who in the class identified with the woman in the poem may start an interesting discussion. Many of us wish for a solitary time in which we do not have to fulfill any of our roles, even freely chosen ones. Notice that the things the woman watches are utterly undemanding. The last stanza suggests that she does not welcome sex with her husband. Perhaps she feels that she is not real to him at the time ("nothing"), or perhaps she is avoiding the thought of conceiving another child. Though the night is usually associated with solitude, in this case the noon hour is associated with it. This irony may be the source of the title (the "daystar" is the sun).

Possible Responses to *Questions for Discussion and Writing*
1. The sun is the daystar. Instead of doing her daydreaming under the romantic night stars, the woman in the poem dreams under the daystar, behind the garage, in a decidedly contrasting setting.
2. Perhaps older students will identify with the woman in the poem because they have experienced times when they feel that the demands of their roles overburden them and obliterate their individual identities. Students of any age may also relate to the stress of daily activities that are contradictory to their ideas of self, and to the lack of time to relax and daydream. In your class discussion, these may be times when students mention needing solitude. The persona wants "a little time for thinking," implying that the rest of the day is taken up with unthinking activities.
3. Liza is the toddler daughter, and Thomas is the husband. They are important characters because their demands run the woman's life. The writer refrains from identifying them because the point of view is interior to the woman, who knows who Liza and Thomas are. It would break the point of view to inwardly ponder "Liza, her toddler," or "Thomas, her husband." Students may think of several reasons why the woman herself has no name. The lack of a name may emphasize that she represents a whole class of woman and not just an individual; she may have no identity other than her role as wife and mother and thus no name; and again, in interior monologue, one rarely thinks of oneself by name.
4. In the last stanza, Thomas and the woman have sex, though obviously the woman is detached from the act. She disappears from the encounter and becomes "pure nothing" instead of a dutiful wife submitting to her husband. This is the way she escapes her roles.

Making Connections

→Compare the coping mechanisms of Rita Dove's tired housewife/mother with those of the three women worshipping their unresponsive male god in Judith Cofer's "Latin Women Pray."

IN SECOND GRADE MISS LEE I PROMISED NEVER TO FORGET YOU AND I NEVER DID by Alberto Ríos [p. 447]

Most of us can remember a teacher or other adult who did not conform to our childhood expectations of what grownups were like. The second graders' opinion of Miss Lee was markedly different from that of their parents, who most likely disapproved of her unkempt blonde hair and sexiness. Even the lack of punctuation in the poem's title emphasizes that we hear a child's voice as the narrator.

Possible Responses to *Questions for Discussion and Writing*

1. Miss Lee broke the mold of a stereotypical grade school teacher: she was too sexy and exotic, too cosmopolitan. Even the first line of the poem describes a "letting-go moment," something a second-grade teacher is not supposed to have in front of her class (or in some communities, even outside of class). She was probably fired when students carried stories from her classroom home to their parents, and the parents complained to the principal.

2. Second-grade students are around seven years old. The apple story no doubt impressed the narrator and other students because they were totally unused to being told about French lovers and kissing. Generally, children remember incidents having to do with sex and bodily elimination, as well as surprising things that adults and other children did. They also remember people who were very different from their parents, who so far constituted their world of adults. Students may bring up anecdotes on these themes in your class discussion of childhood memories.

3. The child obviously has a crush on Miss Lee and sees nothing inappropriate about her appearance or behavior. In fact, he finds her "Like a real movie star," an image of the ideal woman that reinforces his naïve point of view. He even believes that Miss Lee returns his feelings (lines 16–17). In contrast, from the parents' point of view, she is threateningly single and sexy, and unfit for grade school teaching. The fact that the narrator has no insight into how parents might feel about Miss Lee sustains the childish point of view. He also seems to have no insight into the severe demotion from teaching to selling encyclopedias door to door!

Additional Questions for Discussion and Writing

1. What is a "letting-go moment"?
2. If you were a parent, what would you think of a teacher telling second graders about the habits of French lovers?

Making Connections

→Toni Cade Bambara's story "The Lesson" also considers a teacher from a child's point of view. In both "The Lesson" and "Miss Lee," explain how an adult point of view would change the narrative.

THERE ARE BLACK by Jimmy Santiago Baca [pp. 448–49]

The realities of prison life are expressed in this poem by an ex-convict. He focuses on the fact that both inmates and guards come from all races; the fact that the guards will keep their own people imprisoned and subject them to cruelty is especially brutal. The speaker understands the urge for power that makes a man a prison guard—the money and command that the same men could probably never find in other jobs open to them. He believes that they must harden their hearts, water down their blood, and turn off their minds in order to "seclud[e] themselves from their people."

Possible Responses to *Questions for Discussion and Writing*

1. The horrifying element about the prison guards (and some of the prisoners) is their dehumanization. Eventually most fail to identify with their brethren.
2. The guards keep their jobs because probably these are much better jobs than they could get otherwise: their abilities to buy things and to become powerful are specifically mentioned. The poem also suggests that the power goes to their heads after some time in the job. You might discuss what other jobs dehumanize workers through money or power or both.
3. The two types of convicts are those that are nasty and brutal and those that are passive and daydreaming.
4. Most poetry lovers would say that all subject matter is appropriate for the genre. Material that is emotional, moving, and revealing about the human condition is traditional for poetry, and "There Are Black" certainly exemplifies this material. However, some readers may prefer poetry that emphasizes the beautiful, noble side of love, life, and nature, such as Carl Sandburg's "Fog" and John Donne's "Death, Be Not Proud." We notice the dearth of such poems in our anthology: this lack may be an interesting topic for class discussion.

Additional Questions for Discussion and Writing

1. Why are the lines indented and arranged as they are? (The long lines build intensity and create a sense of the persistent noise and chaos of prison life.) What kind of verse would you call this? (Free verse.)
2. Can you explain the figure of the "ancient mummy"? (Possibly the dehumanized specters of the caring human beings the guards used to be.)

Making Connections

→Compare Baca's use of strong, vivid images to depict violence with the similar use of such imagery in "To the Mercy Killers" by Dudley Randall and "Dulce et Decorum Est" by Wilfred Owen.

LATIN WOMEN PRAY by Judith Ortiz Cofer [pp. 449–50]

The Latin women (evidently, Latin American) are viewed by an outsider who sees them as unsophisticated dupes of the Catholic Church. The persona evidently sees the ridiculous aspects of these "brown daughters" praying to a white God derived from a tradition far away from their own ("with a Jewish heritage"). Appealing to this God is apparently useless, yet the women continue to so do with zeal. Their understanding of God is placed on a practical, worldly level—they hope he is bilingual, while more thoughtful believers would say that God understands all languages. The poem's God is not a sympathetic character. The women are driven by a pitifully misguided hope.

Possible Responses to *Questions for Discussion and Writing*
1. The setting—with votive candles, kneeling, a white image of God—describes a Catholic church. Also, the idea that the women are Latina suggests that they are Catholic, Catholicism being the major religion of Latin America.
2. God is described as Anglo (with a Jewish heritage), a Great White Father, imperturbable, all seeing, unmoved. The women are described as brown, daughters, persistent, fervently hoping. The contrasts in these descriptions demonstrate the power relationship between the two, especially in terms of the detachment on God's side and the passion on the women's. They are complementary in the traditional father–daughter relationship. This view of the God–human relationship can be compared with other views; many believe in a loving, listening God who consists of a colorless force (not a white male); others define God as the energy found in the universe and in our souls, and so on.
3. The women probably pray for hope, health, money, love, happiness, a better life for their children, and an eventual home in heaven, but the society they live in almost ensures that they stay exactly where they are. They persist in their prayers because it is their only option, not seeing any realistic way their hopes will materialize. Being helpless, they hope that some father figure will intervene and save them.
4. The image of God as lustful adds an especially nasty and shocking note to the poet's description. Given the father–daughter relationship, incest is suggested, as well as the objectification of women. If any reader had a doubt about the poem's point of view toward the Catholic God, this image would make the hostility clear.

Additional Questions for Discussion and Writing
1. What is the speaker's tone? What does the speaker think of the women she's describing? How can you tell?
2. What do you think of the last line? Is it a comic (perhaps sarcastic) line?

Making Connections
→Consider the women described in this poem, who need for God to be "if not omnipotent / At least . . . bilingual" in order for their supplications to be meaningful; compare them with the mother who wants to go to night school in order to escape her debilitating job in Gina Valdés's "My Mother Sews Blouses." Does the hope of the women in either poem seem rational or helpful? Or is it delusional?

WHAT I WOULDN'T DO by Dorianne Laux [pp. 450–51]
This poem is structured by a bracket topic, the job the narrator quit: selling *TV Guide* over the telephone. This topic begins the poem intriguingly, because the reader must wonder what the other jobs were. The question is quickly answered by a sequence of

116

descriptive passages about menial jobs that many people would not like. Each job is described in highly sensory terms, and each is presented with both good and bad elements. When the narrator returns to say finally what she hated about telemarketing, we have a good idea of her character. We are prepared for her keen sensitivity to the disappointment in the strangers' voices.

Possible Responses to *Questions for Discussion and Writing*
1. The narrator has worked in a fast-food place, at a laundromat, cleaning houses, cooking at a sanatorium, and at a gas station and donut shop. All of the jobs were lowly and probably not well paid, and all included serving others in some way, though in an impersonal, structured way. She describes each job with lots of sensory details and without resentment.
2. You can tell that the narrator is sensitive to colors and sensory appeals, and that she was efficient at all of the jobs and enjoyed her own efficiency. Also, she is good-natured about them, even though many people would abhor the work.
3. In contrast with other jobs, in the *TV Guide* job the narrator was a supplicant and was supposed to use persuasion. This may be a position she was poorly suited for. She also had to deal with the disappointment of others when they found out she was a salesperson rather than a loved one calling. The nature of *TV Guide* may be that it is a text for the lonely, or that it is a fairly useless item, furthering her dislike of trying to sell it.
4. Students may share their writings about the jobs they hated or loved with classmates. Consider holding a discussion about which writings are more effective, negative or positive ones, or what other features make certain writings stand out.

Making Connections
→Compare the attitudes toward work displayed by the narrators of "What I Wouldn't Do," Seamus Heaney's "Digging," and Gina Valdes's "My Mother Sews Blouses." What principles do the narrators use in evaluating their workplaces.

BULLY by Martín Espada [p. 452]
The irony of the poem is that the Boston school in 1987 is being taken over by the descendants of natives of the Caribbean, Cuba, Hispaniola, and Puerto Rico in much the same ways as the United States defeated the Spanish in Cuba and the Philippines in the brief Spanish-American War in 1898. The Treaty of Paris, which ended this war, gave the United States Puerto Rico, Guam, and the Philippines, which the government proceeded to exploit ruthlessly and to suppress the native governments through wildly unequal power and resources. Several details in the poem are subtle parallels with events in the Spanish-American War, such as the "brown children devouring the stockpiles of the cafeteria," a reminder that starving, underprepared U.S. troops led by war hero Teddy Roosevelt devoured the food supplies of defeated Spanish troops in Cuba. Other parallels and historical references will come to light when your students research the topics in question 1, below.

Possible Responses to *Questions for Discussion and Writing*

1. You might divide the four research topics (Teddy Roosevelt, the Spanish-American War, eugenics, and Taino Puerto Rican ancestors) among four groups of students, so that each group can collect information and then discuss together how their discoveries help them understand the poem.
2. The surprising images in the poem will also be illuminated by the understanding created by the exercise in question 1. It makes sense that Teddy Roosevelt's image is nostalgic for the Spanish American War, where his bullying style made him a hero in the U. S. press; also, his fist would be lonely without a weapon or reins, because he was known for his masculine love for boxing, hunting, riding, and roping. Another telling image is in lines 23–24, "Once Marines tramped from the newsreel of his imagination," because scholars now believe that the purported justifications for the Spanish-American War were fictions developed by the U.S. news media.
3. The four stanzas relate to stages in the transition of the school. The first describes the conventional statue of Roosevelt in the school auditorium. The second depicts the invasion of the school by children (in the same way their ancestors were invaded by Roosevelt and his ilk). The third implies some symbolic revenge (being surrounded) on behalf of the peoples that Roosevelt belittled in the past. The fourth shows the conquest of the old statue, and what it stands for, by the new population.
4. The "bully" is Roosevelt, and the expansionist and racist ideals he represents. The title is appropriate in terms of the massive superior force that the U.S. used to overwhelm a much less prepared Spain, and native movements, in the Spanish-American War. The city and date allow the reader to locate when and where the transition of the school's population was occurring. Students may find more reasons for the choice of Boston and 1987, specifically, through doing some research.

Making Connections

→Compare the attitudes toward war memorials expressed in "Bully" and "Facing It" by Yusef Komunyakaa.

PAIRED POEMS FOR COMPARISON [pp. 454–63]

THE PASSIONATE SHEPHERD TO HIS LOVE by Christopher Marlowe [pp. 454–55]
Using the conventions of the pastoral (the speaker assumes the pose of a shepherd), the speaker-poet invites his loved one to join him in a carefree love. Students may not find the invitation convincing; it is too artificial and the enticements (which carefully avoid the mention of any sexual pleasures) are charming but modest. But what do contemporary swains promise their loved ones? Are the modern conventions any more persuasive? Certainly, the innocent tone will appeal to some students' romantic impulses. This poem should be studied in conjunction with Raleigh's reply.

Possible Responses to *Questions for Discussion and Writing*

1. The speaker offers the joys of nature, clothes, jewelry, and entertainment. His repetition of the "If" clauses may suggest that he is uncertain whether the woman

will accept his offers. Some readers may also think that making so many offers in a row sounds a note of desperation.

2. The speakers' promises seem lavish, though we note that most of the enticements are indeed available to a shepherd, being derived from nature. Only the gold buckles, coral clasps, and amber studs are extravagant items. However, it may seem doubtful to a modern reader that the shepherd can come through with all his promises.

3. Most modern readers would not be enticed by the appeal, unless they are attracted to rural pleasures. Also, there is no allusion, even a delicate one, to sexual or romantic attachment, which calls into question the speaker's passionate nature.

THE NYMPH'S REPLY TO THE SHEPHERD by Sir Walter Raleigh [pp. 455–56]

This is the famous critical response to Marlowe's poem. In it, the speaker (the "nymph") systematically points out the illusory nature of the world offered to her by Marlowe's shepherd: men lie, weather turns bad, flowers and young women fade and wither as do gowns, skirts, and posies. In short, the poem offers a wry comment on love and the passage of time. The speaker implies that the shepherd's carefree love could not survive the passing youthful joys and her loss of beauty. The allusion to Philomel (line 7) is heavily charged with the tragic consequences of untrammeled lust. Philomel was raped by her brother-in-law, who tore out her tongue so she couldn't accuse him; the gods later turned her into a nightingale.

Possible Responses to *Questions for Discussion and Writing*

1. The nymph points out the temporary quality of natural wonders—flowers fade, winter comes, love dwindles.

2. As noted above, the nymph's reply shows awareness of time's ravages on nature, people, and love.

3. Readers will disagree on whether they like the shepherd or the nymph's point of view better. It may depend on how many romantic ideals each reader harbors. Also, women readers may enjoy the nymph's reply because they too suspect a silver-tongued suitor. If you don't have time for each student to write an essay of comparison, you might list pros and cons on each side of the matter as a class.

4. The students' responses to either the shepherd or the nymph should be fun to exchange and read in class or electronically.

MY LAST DUCHESS by Robert Browning [pp. 456–58]

This dramatic monologue seems to allude to the life of Alfonso II, Duke of Ferrara, in northern Italy, whose first wife died three years after she was married to him. She was rumored to be a victim of poisoning. Through the offices of an agent (to whom the duke may be speaking in the poem), Alfonso married the sister of the Count of Tyrol four years later.

The Duke's cold arrogance emerges from the outset of the poem. Selfish pride controls all his relationships with people. The Duchess is not alive but the subject of a painting by a famous artist. (Wives and works of art seem identical to the Duke—both are collectibles.) In lines 21–31, the poet engages our sympathies for the Duchess, despite the

Duke's contemptuous criticism of her failings. What were the commands that ended her smiles? Browning once explained: "That she should be put to death, or he might have had her shut up in a convent."

Lines 47–53 make it clear that the Duke has been addressing the emissary of the Count whose daughter he hopes to marry. Has the Duke unwittingly revealed too much of his cruel nature, or was he just making it clear what he will expect from his new duchess? Critics have taken both sides of this question: some seeing him as calculating and in control; others suggesting that his arrogance is almost pathological and leads him to say too much (note the abrupt shift in the subject in line 47—has the Duke realized he should shut up about his last duchess?).

Possible Responses to *Questions for Discussion and Writing*

1. The Duke of Ferrara is showing a painting of his previous wife to a visiting emissary, whose visit evidently is aimed at arranging a marriage between Ferrara and a Count's daughter.
2. The last Duchess was easily pleased and amused. The Count believes that she was flirtatious in her friendliness to men from all ranks; however, we are led to think that the Count was possessive and vain and may have misinterpreted his wife's high spirits. He thinks of her as property, like his acquisitions of highbrow art objects.
3. Readers may disagree on whether the Duke is accidentally or purposely showing his nature and his attitudes. Certainly lines 35 to 46 seem like clear messages about what happens to an uppity wife in his household. However, the Duke is so arrogant that he may not be sensitive to his own threatening tone.
4. Most readers would warn the Count about what kind of marriage he may be sending his daughter into. Especially if the Count's daughter is a lively gal, her future at the Duke's looks grim. The Duke might be described as jealous, possessive, arrogant, acquisitive, shallow, and sexist.

Additional Questions for Discussion and Writing

1. How does Browning make us understand that the Duke's remarks are biased?
2. What evidence is there that hypocrisy is another aspect of the Duke's character? Why does he, three times, deprecate his ability to relate precisely what he wishes?
3. What is the effect of mentioning another work of art at the end of the monologue? What does this remark show us about the Duke? Is there any significance to the statue of Neptune taming a seahorse?
4. Although the Duke is unsympathetic, are you still fascinated by him? If so, explain why.
5. How would the Duke's refusal "to stoop" and his insistence upon the importance of his "nine-hundred-years-old name" (or comparable attitudes) be manifested today?

MY EX-HUSBAND by Gabriel Spera [pp. 458–60]
You may want to reproduce both poems on overhead transparencies and project them side by side for purposes of comparison. Spera says, "A good parody (as opposed to

satire) recognizes the merits of the original, highlights distinctive stylistic elements, accentuates the inevitable failure of imitation, and leads to a greater appreciation of the original work. I think that's what makes it fun."

Possible Responses to *Questions for Discussion and Writing*

1. Students will have fun making the exact comparisons between the two poems—the fancy painting turns into a photograph, the ex-wife chooses "never to get stuck," and now "Claus" is a sharp divorce lawyer, for example. The ex-husband turns out to be a philandering cad, something that isn't suggested about the Duke in the Browning poem.

2. Both speakers make clear decisions to get rid of spouses they believe unfaithful and undiscriminating in their affections. The speaker of "My Ex-Husband" gets a divorce rather than having her husband killed.

3. Many readers, especially women, will identify more readily with the ex-wife in "My Ex-Husband" because she found herself in a situation that is familiar to most. She does show some defensive assertiveness—"No, / We'll take my car," for instance—but this is quite understandable after a humiliating marriage. On the other hand, the Duke of Ferrara seems to have no redeeming qualities except for his wealth and power. Both speakers are preoccupied with their previous marriages and determined not to repeat their perceived mistakes. Both also have an element of snobbery—for example, the ex-wife hates to be in the same position as some "bimbo / In the steno pool." In both poems, the readers' sympathies lie with the wronged woman.

THOSE WINTER SUNDAYS by Robert Hayden [pp. 460–61]

This poem is about the expression of love, as is clear from the last line. The father's thankless and painful work to nurture his family is presented as a repeated ritual. The image is unusual, since it is conventionally mothers that do the unregarded labor that children grow up to recognize as valuable. On the other hand, the inability to communicate feelings verbally, which we see between men in this poem, is typically male.

Possible Responses to *Questions for Discussion and Writing*

1. As an adult, the speaker realizes that his father repeatedly showed his love, while the child did not perceive the demonstration.

2. The home had "chronic angers," which suggests strife within the household or problems brought home from work. The father has a hard labor job; thus, we can infer that the house is not luxurious. This idea is supported by the fact that it gets so cold during the night. The plural "angers" suggests that perhaps each member of the household harbors his or her own anger. It also suggests that more than one problem creates strife in the home.

3. Love can be expressed directly, through words, hugs, smiles, and caresses, or indirectly, through serving another person. The father's "austere and lonely" expressions of love are concrete services, such as polishing the boy's shoes and building up the fires in the cold, dark morning.

4. In religious observances, an "office" is a ceremony or ritual for a specific purpose,

121

such as Office for the Dead. The father's repeated services to show his love for his family convey a ritualistic tone and do serve a specific purpose.

Additional Questions for Discussion and Writing

1. This is a memory poem, looking back 40 years. Which details are the ones the older speaker now realizes, but which the boy wouldn't have noticed or cared about? How can a reader tell what the boy felt then and what the speaker feels now?
2. Describe the father based on the speaker's sparse description. What does the word "too," in the first line, imply about the father?
3. Can you describe the speaker? How does he contrast with his father?

LIKE RIDING A BICYCLE by George Bilgere [pp. 461–63]

This poem, like "Those Winter Sundays," describes a father as loving but troubled. The father attempts to help the child learn to ride a bike, but he is too impaired himself to perform the job he knows belongs to him. The speaker contrasts an ideal, fairy-tale situation with the reality of his father's failure. Nonetheless, this failure is linked to the child's and then the adult speaker's prized self-reliance. The forgiving and even thankful attitude toward an inadequate parent makes the poem's message unusual.

The beautiful, nostalgic opening narrative (stanza) about a boy learning to ride a bike from his supportive, effective father is tinged with sadness when the adult speaker refers to a "perilous adult launch," which appears to be his own recent divorce. Yet the emotional guidance of the father remains in this scene, helping the adult son move "forward / Into the future's blue / Equilibrium." However, the whole scene is undercut by the next stanza, a narrative that describes the real story: a fat, drunken, stinking, stumbling father who was too much of a mess to support the boy's clumsy efforts and who finally "swore and stomped off / Into the house to continue / Working with my mother / On their own divorce." The boy went on to learn to ride the bike alone, finding some bittersweet pleasure in being a "lonely western hero." The closing stanza suggests that the adult speaker nonetheless managed to get launched and can now enjoy the pleasures of life with a "soft urgency all over." Unlike other poems implying that inadequate or cruel parents ruin their children's lives, Bilgere's presents a refreshing alternative point of view: that a person can overcome abuse and disappointment and make a virtue of loneliness.

Possible Responses to *Questions for Discussion and Writing*

1. A gantry is the huge metal frame that holds a missile up at a launch site, then releases the missile and remains attached to the ground as the missile flies upwards. This image is the romantic ideal of father and son presented in the first stanza.
2. The boy's relationship with his father, as expressed in the second stanza, first seems dominated by disgust at his drunkenness, smoking, and physical clumsiness. After the father gives up, the boy appears to have some sympathy for him, suffering his own divorce, and uses the image of both parents about ready to hit the hard ground. Some students might say that the boy's disappointment with the real-life situation was probably influenced by the idealized vision he wishes for, expressed in the first stanza.

3. The first stanza describes the ideal scene of a loving father teaching his boy to ride a bike with just the right amount of support and release, while the second stanza presents the reality. The third stanza, somewhat unexpectedly, pulls the reader into the mind of the grown-up boy, who has learned not only to survive disappointment and loneliness but also to enjoy life.
4. Most students will focus on the contrast between the men who narrate the poems. Hayden's speaker, as an adult, regrets that he had so little appreciation for a devoted father, while Bilgere's speaker is able to appreciate what he learned from an incompetent and careless one. Bilgere's attitude is definitely more complex, in our view.

A PORTFOLIO OF WAR POETRY [pp. 464–73]

TO LUCASTA, ON GOING TO THE WARS by Richard Lovelace [p. 464]

This poem may be related to an actual parting: Lovelace fought in the service of Charles I during the Puritan Revolution (1642–1645). The theme, which seems to be a serious one, is that honor (duty to country and king) takes priority over duty to Lucasta. She is "chaste" and "quiet"; war is personified as a "new mistress" with greater vitality, and the speaker calls his departure an instance of "inconstancy." This comparison is in keeping with the light and witty tone (which may confuse some readers because of the seriousness of the message). The closing line makes a serious affirmation: the speaker's love for Lucasta is based on a greater love of honor, which is a driving force in the speaker's life.

Possible Responses to *Questions for Discussion and Writing*

1. The speaker appears to be a young, idealistic man who has a romantic view of fighting for his country.
2. The speaker's "new mistress" is "The first foe in the field," meaning that he will aggressively chase the first enemy he encounters.
3. The virtues of loyalty to a beloved woman versus loyalty to duty to country, or "honor," are contrasted. The speaker argues that he could not love the woman properly if he did not put honor first, implying that he would lack character strength and therefore not be capable of the love she deserves.

Additional Questions for Discussion and Writing

1. What is the tone of the poem?
2. What is the meaning of "nunnery" to the speaker?
3. Look up the term *synecdoche* in the glossary. Find several examples of the poet's use of this figure of speech. (Lucasta's "chaste breast and quiet mind" stand for her physical and mental attributes; "A sword, a horse, a shield" stand for war.)

WAR IS KIND by Stephen Crane [p. 465]

By far Crane's finest and most widely reprinted poem, "War Is Kind" presents the same strongly antiwar theme as *The Red Badge of Courage*. Stanzas 1, 3, and 5 directly address those who survive war but lose those they love, whereas stanzas 2 and 4 seem to be spoken to the military (especially in lines 20–21). Notice that the meter changes in the indented stanzas, suggesting the cadence of marching men—until the final melodious line, "A field where a thousand corpses lie." The incongruity between the sound and the meaning reinforces the already acute irony of the line. Lines 25 and 26 are admired for the moving simplicity of the image (the "bright splendid shroud" being the son's dress uniform) and the wonderfully effective use of alliteration. The short three-word lines, which serve as a refrain, are most emphatic.

Possible Responses to *Questions for Discussion and Writing*
1. Stanzas 2 and 4 act as refrains: notice the similarity between them. These stanzas take a general point of view on patriotism and war, while stanzas 1, 3, and 5 deal with specific situations (the bereaved maiden, babe, and mother).
2. The flag is called "the unexplained glory," suggesting that most citizens don't understand the policies and philosophy of their country. They are taught to respond emotionally to patriotic symbols and exhortations.
3. The tone is ironic—there is a discrepancy between the words on the page and the intended meaning. The poem's message is that war is *not* kind, but cruel and stupid.

Additional Question for Discussion and Writing
In stanzas 1, 3, and 5, who is being addressed? Why did the poet write three long lines and two short ones in those stanzas instead of four long lines?

DULCE ET DECORUM EST by Wilfred Owen [pp. 465–67]
Owen died in the trenches near the end of World War I not long after writing this powerful poem, which was published posthumously. The persona describes weary troops slogging through the mire (which often literally sucked the boots off their feet) away from the front, so exhausted that they fail to hear the "hoots" of the gas canisters dropping just behind them. These canisters have spent their fuel; thus they, like the men, are exhausted ("tired") after their journey through the air. One soldier fails to struggle into his gas mask in time, and his death throes—described in telling detail—haunt the persona. The last lines condemn the ancient practice of glorifying war (in epic poems, in popular songs, in heroic monuments, in John Wayne movies, in patriotic speeches) that for ages has served to fire the ignorant enthusiasm of young men to seek the "desperate glory" mendaciously associated with war. (Students may remember Crane's "unexplained glory" in "War Is Kind" [p. 465] and Henry Fleming in *The Red Badge of Courage*, who, at the beginning of that novella, was desperate for glory.)

The following account of the effects of mustard gas was written by a nurse in World War I:

> With mustard gas the effects did not become apparent for up to twelve hours. But then it began to rot the body, within and without. The skin blistered, the eyes became extremely painful and nausea and vomiting began. Worse, the gas attacked the bronchial tubes, stripping off the mucous membrane. The pain was almost beyond endurance, and most cases had to be strapped to their beds. Death took up to four or five weeks.

124

Possible Responses to *Questions for Discussion and Writing*

1. Five-Nines are 5.9-caliber explosive shells, in this case apparently filled with poison gas. They are "tired" because the shells are falling behind the men as they stumble away from the battle toward a place to rest. Poison gas fills the lungs with fluid, giving the effects of drowning.
2. The "you" in the third stanza is someone in civilian life who evidently has passionately defended war. Most readers will hear "My friend" as having an ironic tone—the person who defends war is not really a friend. However, it could also be that the person is a real, noncombatant friend whose ideas are uninformed.
3. The "desperate glory" would involve battlefield heroics of some kind, desperate because there are other, less suicidal ways of being a hero. Norman Mailer's *Naked and the Dead* is a famous example of desperate glory.
4. The "old Lie" is "It is sweet and fitting to die for one's country." This philosophy lies behind suicide bombers in our current age. It is also used to comfort citizens whose loved ones die in contemporary wars.

Additional Questions for Discussion and Writing

1. Why is the man in stanza 2 described as "drowning"? What is the "green sea" actually?
2. What is the source of the title of the poem? Why is it in Latin?

NEXT TO OF COURSE GOD AMERICA I by E. E. Cummings [pp. 467–68]

By the end of the poem, we realize that it is a political speech, given perhaps at a campaign rally. The high-sounding illogic of it is simply an exaggeration of the empty and frequently contradictory rhetoric found in patriotic diatribes. The lack of punctuation and meaningless line breaks emphasize the smooth flow of nonsense pouring from the speaker's lips. The last line points up the speaker's blustery style and also his comfortable position (in contrast to the young men who died in the war).

Possible Responses to *Questions for Discussion and Writing*

1. The poem begins with quotation marks to immediately indicate that it's a direct quotation from someone's speech.
2. Within the first three or four lines, the reader is aware that the patriotic phrases are jumbled together and often incomplete. This mixed-up rhetoric suggests that it is a parody of political speech.
3. Some clichés include "land of the pilgrims," "oh say can you see by the dawn's early," "my country 'tis of." The clichés don't go together sensibly. An example of a contradiction is that in one spot is the statement, "thy sons acclaim your glorious name," while at the end, the speaker asks, "then shall the voice of liberty be mute?"
4. The closing of the quotation marks before the last line of the speech shows that this line is not part of the speech. Now the position of the political speaker is clarified— he is comfortably out of the real line of fire.

125

Additional Question for Discussion and Writing

Why is this poem included in a portfolio of war poems? What is the connection to war?

SIX NATIONAL GUARDSMEN BLOWN UP TOGETHER by Peg Lauber [pp. 468–69]
Peg Lauber's poem is a requiem for six national guardsmen whose remains are being returned by the military after they were killed in the Iraq war. She tells us in the opening stanza that they "grew up together on the bayous" (probably in Louisiana), where they "hunted, fished, trapped together." But on the other side of the globe they themselves became the prey, as the enemy hunted them down for the slaughter. Setting is important in conveying the contrast between the world of nature, where the young men once held sway, and the world of war, where now their shattered bodies are delivered home. Nature is impotent in the face of war machines: the "lumbering" cargo plane carrying "what is left of the men" frightens away the "Cajun Air Force" of seventeen white pelicans. Only the screeching gulls are left to cry an "appropriate requiem." The final image shows families, "bent / weeping into their small children's hair," as those crying children realize that their fathers, in those "flag-draped" boxes, are never coming home again.

Possible Responses to *Questions for Discussion and Writing*

1. The title sounds like a newspaper headline. It provides the factual background necessary to understand the poem from the first lines.
2. The setting for the poem is the naval base airfield where the families wait for the plane to bring the remains of the six soldiers home. The natural setting of this home is emphasized, at odds with the war experience. Seven local animals are mentioned. The ones that the boys hunted are contrasted with the idea that in war, the boys themselves are the prey. The pelicans and gulls represent two natural responses to the effects of war—to flee and to mourn. In the second stanza the pelicans are frightened and scattered by a huge war machine, the "cargo plane carrying / what is left of the men" (lines 15–16). In the final stanza only the gulls have not been frightened away by the fearful plane or the flag-draped coffins. They swoop and glide, crying a mournful dirge over the weeping survivors.
3. The Jack-in-the-Box simile in the final lines reflects the bereft children's point of view—they might think in terms of a familiar toy. The realization that war is not play but a deadly pursuit changes their thinking and feeling forever.

FACING IT by Yusef Komunyakaa [pp. 470–71]
Students must understand the visual situation in order to appreciate this poem; the photo on page 470 should help. You may want to show other pictures of the Vietnam Veterans Memorial. Get people who have visited there to talk about the experience. The highly reflective surface of the Wall, on which the names of Vietnam dead are engraved, mirrors the people who are visiting the memorial as well as the scene behind them. The speaker in "Facing It" captures the odd sensory experience thus created when he says, "I'm stone. I'm flesh." He moves in and out of the Wall, becoming part of the names and also

126

merging with the other visitors (who are reflected). Metaphorically, he is part of the Vietnam tragedy (the Wall) but also he is still alive. Students might also want to explore the various meanings of the word *facing* in the title. The speaker is facing (in front of) the monument, but he's also facing (confronting with awareness) the Wall's significance and, thus, the meaning of his war experience (and perhaps the war's meaning to the country).

Possible Responses to *Questions for Discussion and Writing*

1. The "It" in the title, literally, is the Vietnam Veterans Memorial, which is made of polished stone with the names of the dead engraved into it. On another level, the speaker of the poem, a war veteran, is facing the war experience and its aftermath, as well as his own responses. The speaker's intention not to cry helps readers understand the point of view in the poem.
2. The speaker is a Vietnam veteran himself and so identifies strongly with the names on the wall, so he half-expects to see his own name there. Readers might also interpret these lines to mean that he feels half-dead himself, or that he feels survivor's guilt when confronted with the names of the dead.
3. A woman visiting the memorial is able to walk away (unlike the war dead), but first she is imprinted with the experience (the names reflected on her blouse). The red bird may represent the power of nature over human artifice. The plane in the sky is a peacetime plane, perhaps chosen in contrast to the planes over Vietnam. The white vet's image is close to the black vet's (the speaker's), and their eyes' meeting might further an interpretation that the war brought the two races together. The white vet probably has not really lost his arm, but it looks that way in the mirror of the monument. This image reminds the reader of all the vets who didn't die but lost limbs in the war. The final image is explained in the next question's response.
4. The speaker thinks for a moment that the woman is trying to erase the names of the dead—to obliterate the experience, or to bring them back, a reader may think. However, she is really brushing her son's hair. The error in perception reveals the vet's point of view, which is distorted in such a way that he instantly sees everything as pertaining to the war experience, even when it does not. The woman's act is really one of nurturance, not destruction. Many readers will also see a symbolic meaning in that the woman is literally grooming the boy, and figuratively grooming him to become a soldier like the ones in Vietnam.

IN RESPONSE TO EXECUTIVE ORDER 9066 by Dwight Okita [pp. 472–73]

Some students may need a little background beyond the head note in order to fully understand this selection. In 1942, at the beginning of WWII, President Franklin D. Roosevelt signed Executive Order 9066, forcing over 100,000 Japanese Americans then living in this country, whether citizens or not, to be sent to relocation camps in the West and the arid Southwest. Their property was confiscated, and most Americans went along with the injustice, considering it necessary for national security. Paranoia was rampant as the nation geared up for war. The young Japanese American narrator's classmate Denise has moved away to the other side of the room because her former best friend now represents "the Enemy" to Denise, who fears she'll be "giving secrets away" to the Japanese military, thus endangering the American populace.

Possible Responses to *Questions for Discussion and Writing*

1. The internment camps were located mostly in dry, arid (desert) places.

2. Okita's poem gains impact and empathy by being conveyed through the innocent voice of the young girl. We are touched by the unfairness to the child who in no way understands why she is being taken from her home or why her best friend rejects her in such a hateful manner. "I didn't know what to say" (line 21) is her helpless response. The tomato seeds, which would have produced abundantly in her home near Fresno, California, simply "won't grow" (line 6) where the family is being sent. Since water symbolically represents life and spiritual fulfillment, the arid desert of the relocation camp suggests the loss of those vital elements. We fear that the young girl may, like the tomato seeds, find it difficult to flourish there.

3. The narrator feels that her aversion to chopsticks and her love of hot dogs will make her seem truly American, not Japanese, and thus dispel her friend's suspicion that she might be "the Enemy."

4. Denise has been caught up in the anti-Japanese fervor that swept this country following the attack on Pearl Harbor. While she is not justified in rejecting her totally innocent friend, her behavior is quite understandable. Since tomatoes were sometimes called "love apples" (line 4), the seeds can be seen as a gift of love, a long-lasting token of their friendship; but Denise, caught up in her patriotic hostility to the Japanese, would not be likely to nourish the seeds.

Selected Audio and Video Resources for Teaching Poetry

The following list of audio-visual resources is not meant to be exhaustive. There are numerous videos and recordings that can be used to supplement and stimulate the study of poetry. Most of the distributors listed below will send catalogs that give details of their holdings. (For addresses and telephone numbers, see the Directory of Audio and Video Distributors found at the back of this manual.)

W. H. Auden
Recording: 1 cassette
Read by the poet
Available from Spoken Arts

W. H. Auden Reading
Recording: 1 cassette
Available from Caedmon/HarperAudio

Gwendolyn Brooks
Video: 30 min., 1966
Brooks talks about her life and poetry.
Available from Indiana University Center for
　　Media and Teaching Resources

Gwendolyn Brooks
Recording: 1 cassette, 29 min., 1989
Available from New Letters on Air

Robert Browning: My Last Duchess and Other Poems
Recording: 1 cassette
Available from Caedmon/HarperAudio

The Poetry of Countee Cullen
Recording: 1 cassette
Available from Caedmon/HarperAudio

E. E. Cummings: The Making of a Poet
Video: 24 min., 1978
Available from Films for the Humanities & Sciences

Poems of E. E. Cummings
Recording: 1 cassette, 60 min., 1981
Available from Summer Stream

Emily Dickinson: The Belle of Amherst
Video: 90 min., color, 1976
With Julie Harris.
Available from The Video Catalog

Emily Dickinson
Recording: 1 cassette
Available from Recorded Books

An Evening with Emily Dickinson
Video: 60 min., 2 videos: Claire Bloom in
"The World of Emily Dickinson" and Julie Harris in

"A Certain Slant of Light."
Available from PBS Home Video

Poems by Emily Dickinson
Recording: 2 cassettes, 236 min., 1986
Available from Audio Book Contractors

Dickinson and Whitman: Ebb And Flow
Recording: 2 cassettes
Available from Audio Editions

Treasury of John Donne
Recording: 1 cassette
Available from Spoken Arts

Rita Dove
Recording: 1 cassette, 29 min.
Available from New Letters on Air

Poet Laureate Rita Dove
Video: 60 min., color
Available from Films for the Humanities & Sciences

T. S. Eliot: Selected Poems
Recording: Read by the poet. 49 min., 1971
Available from Caedmon/HarperAudio

Robert Frost: A First Acquaintance
Video: 16 min., color, 1974
Examines Frost's life through his poems.
Available from Films for the Humanities & Sciences

Robert Frost Reads
Recording: 1 cassette, 55 min., 1965
Available from Audio-Forum

The Poetry of Donald Hall
Recording: 1 cassette, 26 min., 1964
Available from Audio-Forum

Poetic Voices of Thomas Hardy
Video: 20 min., color
Available from Films for the Humanities & Sciences

A. E. Housman: A Shropshire Lad and Other Poetry
Recording: 1 cassette
Available from Caedmon/HarperAudio

John Keats: Odes
Recording: 1 cassette
Available from Audio-Forum

Treasury of John Keats
Recording: 1 cassette
Available from Spoken Arts

Yusef Komunyakaa
Video: 60 min.,1997
Pulitzer Prize winner talks with author Tori Derricotte and reads from his works.
Available from Facets Multi-Media: www.facets.org

Christopher Marlowe: Elizabethan Love Poems
Recording: 1 cassette, 50 min.
Available from Spoken Arts

Ralph Richardson Reads Andrew Marvell
Recording: 1 cassette
Available from Audio-Forum

Sharon Olds: Coming Back to Life
Recording: 1 cassette, 60 min.
Available from Audio-Forum

Wilfred Owen: The Pity of War
Video: 58 min., color, 1987
Available from Films for the Humanities & Sciences

Marge Piercy: At the Core
Recording: 1 cassette, 58 min., 1976
Available from Watershed Tapes

Sylvia Plath
Video: 4 programs (30 min. each), color, 1974
Examination of the poet and her work.
Available from New York State Education
    Department

Sylvia Plath Reads
Recording: 1 cassette, 60 min., 1987
Available from Caedmon/HarperAudio

The Poetry of Adrienne Rich
Recording: 1 cassette, 36 min., 1968
Available from Audio-Forum

Theodore Roethke
Recording: 48 min., 1972
Available from Caedmon/HarperAudio

Anne Sexton Reads Her Poetry
Recording: 1 cassette
Available from Caedmon/HarperAudio

Shakespeare's Sonnets
Video: 150 min., color, 1984
In-depth look at 15 sonnets, with readings.
Available from Films for the Humanities & Sciences

The Sonnets of Shakespeare
Recording: 2 cassettes
Read by John Gielgud.
Available from Audio Editions

Dylan Thomas: A Portrait
Video: 26 min., color
Available from Films for the Humanities & Sciences

Dylan Thomas Reading His Poetry
Recording: 2 cassettes
Available from Caedmon/HarperAudio

The Poetry of John Updike
Recording: 1 cassette, 47 min., 1967
Available from Audio-Forum

Walt Whitman: The Living Tradition
Video: 20 min., color, 1983
Allen Ginsberg reads Whitman.
Available from Centre Productions

Walt Whitman
Recording: 1 cassette
Read by Alexander Scourby.
Available from Filmic Archives

The Poetry of William Butler Yeats
Recording: 1 cassette
Available from Caedmon/HarperAudio

GENERAL COLLECTIONS

Caedmon Treasury of Modern Poets Reading Their Own Poetry
Recording: 2 cassettes, 95 min.
Available from Caedmon/HarperAudio

English Romantic Poetry: Coleridge, Shelley, Byron, Wordsworth
Recording: 3 cassettes
Available from Recorded books

The Harlem Renaissance and Beyond
Video: 31 min., 1989
Available from Insight Media

Medieval and Elizabethan Poetry
Video: 28 min., color, 1989
Available from Films for the Humanities & Sciences

Moyers: The Power of the Word
Video: 6 programs (60 min. each), color, 1989
Bill Moyers talks with modern poets.
Available from PBS

Victorian Poetry
Recording: 3 cassettes
Available from Caedmon/HarperAudio

Voices and Vision
Video: 13 programs (60 min. each), color, 1988
Available from Annenberg Media

With a Feminine Touch
Video: 45 min., color, 1990
Readings by Valerie Harper and Claire Bloom of poetry by women
Available from Monterey Home Video

PART IV WRITING ABOUT DRAMA

Chapter 16 How Do I Read a Play? [pp. 477–81]

Our advice in this chapter focuses on reading drama. A useful activity could be to have your students read a scene to themselves, using the suggestions in this chapter; then play a recording or video of professional actors doing the same scene. Discuss these questions:

Was the actor's performance similar to your interpretation?

Were there any readings that surprised you?

Did the performance change any of your ideas about the scene?

If you show a video, you might also ask students to consider what effect the sets, lighting, costumes, gestures, and movements had on their understanding and response to the scene, reminding them to imagine these elements as they read the plays that are assigned.

Activities for Creative and Critical Thinking

The following projects and writing assignments will help to engage your students in their study of drama.

- How would you stage a television or film production of any play in this book? Items to think about are set design, location, lighting, music, costumes, camera shots, special effects, changes in the script, casting choices.
- Write the detailed stage directions for a particular scene in a play of your choice. Describe the characters' moves and decide what the characters will do with any props or set features. Explain your decisions.
- Put a character "on trial" for actions that he or she took in the play. Some obvious choices would be Antigone, Othello, Troy Maxson, or the women in *Trifles*.
- Write a letter to a character from a play, offering advice or asking questions about the person's motives and behavior.
- Write a prose account of a minor character's thoughts about the play. For example, what does Bono think about the situation in *Fences*?
- Take a poem or short story and transform it into a dramatic script.
- Write a scene that continues, updates, or provides an alternative to the action from a play. For instance, you might write about what happens when Mrs. Hale and Mrs. Peters visit Minnie Wright in jail (in *Trifles*). Or what happens to Raynell in *Fences*?
- Create the "background story" for one of the characters in a play. What crucial events have occurred in this character's life before the play opens?

Chapter 17 Writing About Dramatic Structure [pp. 482–530]

Although dramatic structure is in general quite similar to the structure of traditional short stories and novels, the terminology for describing it is somewhat more technical. Many instructors use these same terms in discussing structure in any literary work. Certainly by now your students will be familiar with most of these concepts.

ANTIGONE by Sophocles [pp. 484–519]

As indicated in the introduction to the play in the text, *Antigone* is the third and last play in the Oedipus cycle. Sophocles could have counted on his audience to know something of the legend of Oedipus; this knowledge allows readers and viewers to recognize and appreciate the series of dramatic ironies and foreshadowings contained in the play. You may want to supplement the brief summary of the Oedipus legend on pp. 483–84 in the text with this longer version:

> In Greek mythology, Oedipus was the son of Laius and Jocasta, king and queen of Thebes. Laius was warned by an oracle that he would be killed by his own son. Determined to avert his fate, he bound together the feet of his newborn child and left him to die on a lonely mountain. The infant was rescued by a shepherd, however, and given to Polybus, king of Corinth, who named the child Oedipus ("Swollen-foot") and raised him as his own son. The boy did not know that he was adopted, and when an oracle proclaimed that he would kill his father, he left Corinth. In the course of his wanderings he met and killed Laius, believing that the king and his followers were a band of robbers; and thus he unwittingly fulfilled the prophecy.
>
> Lonely and homeless, Oedipus arrived at Thebes, which was beset by a dreadful monster called the Sphinx. The frightful creature frequented the roads to the city, killing and devouring all travelers who could not answer the riddle that she put to them. When Oedipus successfully solved her riddle, the Sphinx killed herself. Believing that King Laius had been slain by unknown robbers, and grateful to Oedipus for ridding them of the Sphinx, the Thebans rewarded Oedipus by making him their king and giving him Queen Jocasta as his wife. For many years the couple lived in happiness, not knowing that they were really mother and son.
>
> Then a terrible plague descended on the land, and the oracle proclaimed that Laius's murderer must be punished. Oedipus soon discovered that he had unknowingly killed his father. In grief and despair at her incestuous life, Jocasta killed herself, and when Oedipus realized that she was dead and that their children were accursed, he put out his eyes and resigned the throne. He lived in Thebes for several years, but was finally banished. Accompanied by his daughter Antigone, he wandered for many years. He finally arrived at Colonus, a shrine near Athens sacred to the powerful goddesses called the Eumenides. At this shrine for supplicants Oedipus died, after the god Apollo had promised him that the place of his death would remain sacred and would bring great benefit to the city of Athens, which had given shelter to the wanderer.

Students need to see that the main conflict in the play is not just a political battle; it's also part of the ongoing struggle between members of the cursed family of Oedipus. At the end of *Oedipus the King*, Oedipus blinds himself and goes into exile, being guided in his wanderings by his faithful daughter Antigone. After their father dies in exile, Antigone and Ismene are returned to Thebes, where they are taken in by their uncle Creon. Oedipus's sons, Polynices and Eteocles, share the throne of Thebes for a short time, under the guidance of Creon, their mother's brother. But the two brothers

133

soon tire of sharing, and Creon supports Eteocles for king. Polynices angrily retaliates by joining six other leaders (including Megareus, one of Creon's sons) in an attack on Thebes. This attempt to overthrow the Theban government fails, but it results in the deaths of both Eteocles and Polynices. Once we understand that Polynices is a traitor to Thebes, we can see the merit in Creon's decree to deny him glory by leaving his body unburied. But Polynices is also a Theban, was once a ruler, and is the son of the former king. He is also survived by two sisters, Antigone and Ismene, who are torn between loyalty to Thebes and loyalty to their brother, despite his treason.

It's important to note that Creon was the one who exiled Oedipus from Thebes; he also backed Eteocles for king, providing the spark that ignited Polynices's rebellion. Moreover, Creon has become king himself, now that the sons of Oedipus are dead. In other words, Creon has a lot of personal investment in preventing any further rebellion that might arise from honoring Polynices. It's also important to know that the family obligation to bury the dead and to cry out in mourning was one of the few public roles allowed to women. The conflict in the play, then, can also be seen as a conflict between men and women—between the government's laws (an exclusively male domain) and the tradition of honoring the death of a loved family member (an activity important to women). Antigone takes on male prerogatives when she takes public action, speaks boldly to the king, and argues openly for political change. That is why Creon accuses her of *hubris* and sees her defiance as a challenge to his right to rule. In the end, however, it is Antigone's love that distinguishes her from Creon. He loses the family he rejected, the state he ruled over briefly, and the favor of the gods. Antigone, on the other hand, loses her life, but her stand turns out best for her family, for the gods (whom she honors), and for the state that she had opposed.

Additional Questions for Discussion and Writing

1. What ideas does the play *Antigone* express about duty and obedience? In what ways do these ideas conform or fail to conform to your own concepts of duty and obedience?
2. The Chorus expresses the values of the community. Is Antigone a danger to this community? How far do you believe a community should go to protect its values?
3. Both Creon and Antigone defend rights that they believe are sacred. What rights are in conflict? Is there any room for compromise?
4. Do you sympathize with Antigone or with Creon? What characteristics of each do you find admirable? Do you ever lose patience with either of them? Explain.
5. Is there any justification for Antigone's cold refusal to allow Ismene to share her martyrdom? Explain. Is Ismene entirely without courage?
6. Creon says at the end, "The guilt is mine." Do you agree?
7. What is your judgment of Antigone as the tragic heroine? One critic has questioned her "total indifference to the rights of the city" and claims that no one in the play really praises her, except her fiancé. She herself says that if the gods allowed her to suffer death for her stand then she would know she was wrong. Was she wrong?
8. Can *Antigone* be read as a justification for civil disobedience? Explain.

Analyzing Dramatic Structure [p. 520]

1. Individual responses to this question will vary.
2. This opening section (lines 1–123) introduces the major conflict of the play and reveals this background information:
   - The sisters are living under a curse (placed on their family because of their father's involuntary incest, we later learn).
   - Antigone and Ismene have lost two brothers who killed each other in a recent battle during which the invaders, led by Polynices, were repelled.
   - One of these brothers was buried with military honors but the other (who led the invaders) was left to lie in the field where he died.
   - Creon, uncle to these two sisters and their dead brothers, is now the king.
   - Creon has decreed that Polynices must not be buried, under penalty of death to anyone who tries.
   - The girls' father, Oedipus, put out his eyes when he learned that he had unknowingly married his own mother.
   - The girls' mother, Jocasta, hanged herself when she learned that she had unwittingly married her own son.
3. From the Chorus we learn the following:
   - Thebes won the battle, repulsing at dawn the invaders who were roused to fight by Polynices.
   - God favored the Theban warriors by sending a thunderclap when the first invading soldier scaled the wall.
   - Again we are told that the brothers both died in combat.
4. The sentry serves to let the audience know that someone has attempted to bury Polynices, in defiance of Creon's law. This character also serves to emphasize the absolute power of the king by showing the fear he inspires in his followers. Clearly the sentry and his fellow soldiers do not expect Creon to be just or fair. They know that he has a terrible temper and mistrusts everyone.
5. The major conflict involves the clash between duty to one's beliefs or conscience (Antigone's determination to bury her brother) and one's duty to authority and to the state (Creon's decree that Polynices be denied burial).
6. Antigone (whose name is the title of the play) is the protagonist. Our sympathies are always with her. Creon is the antagonist, causing the conflict by his unjust ruling. Although Antigone can accurately be called a heroine (she gives her life for what she believes to be right and holy), Creon is not precisely a villain because his intentions are not evil. Clearly misguided by pride and ambition to be a strong ruler, he does relent and try to save Antigone once he sees his wrongdoing.
7. Identifying the climax in this play is somewhat difficult because the plot takes several turns *after* the climax. But press your students to decide at what point the remainder of the action is predetermined (i.e., when clearly the die is cast). This turning point occurs when Creon declares that Antigone must die for not obeying his law. This act signals the turning point because the remaining actions result from this injustice.

   Some might reasonably argue that the climax occurs when Creon rejects the plea of Tiresias to spare Antigone and Tiresias then pronounces his curse. But since we do not know exactly when Antigone kills herself, Creon might have been too late

135

even at this point to forestall the fateful chain of events leading to Antigone's death and his own downfall.

8. The climax does come unusually early in this play, but Sophocles maintains suspense by having Tiresias reason with Creon. The audience keeps hoping that Creon will relent in time to avoid the tragedy. Then the series of reported deaths surprises the audience—as well as Creon, who is shattered by losing his son and his wife in rapid succession.

9. The catastrophe in the extended denouement of this play begins with the report of Antigone's suicide, followed by Haemon's suicide, followed by Eurydice's suicide, the news of which prompts Creon's utter collapse. The outcome becomes inevitable once Creon has caused Antigone's death, thus depriving his son of his bride. Haemon's death causes Eurydice's suicide since she is thus deprived by her husband's willfulness of her last living son.

10. Your students might state the play's theme as "Pride goeth before a fall." Certainly, the major theme of this and many other Greek dramas warns against *hubris*, overweening pride, a character flaw which makes human beings think they know better than the gods. Also important in *Antigone* is the implication that one must stand up for one's beliefs and resist unjust laws. Antigone's refusal to allow Ismene to share her punishment underscores this idea, suggesting that because Ismene lacked the courage to stand up for her convictions, she should not be allowed to share Antigone's martyrdom.

11. Ismene's willing conformity provides a sharp contrast with Antigone's brave defense of what she considers right and just. Ismene simply accepts that the law was "made for the public good."

    Haemon serves as a foil for his father, Creon. The young man boldly stands up to his father and voices reason in contrast to Creon's inflexible, authoritarian stance. His suicide upon finding his beloved Antigone dead suggests fidelity, tenderness, sensitivity—traits entirely lacking in his father until Haemon's death.

12. Eurydice seems to be in the play primarily to show that, as Tiresias prophesied, everyone blames Creon for the deaths of the young people. Her suicide leaves Creon alone, and her dying curse places the guilt squarely on his head as "the murderer of her sons.

The structure of the play may be diagrammed this way:

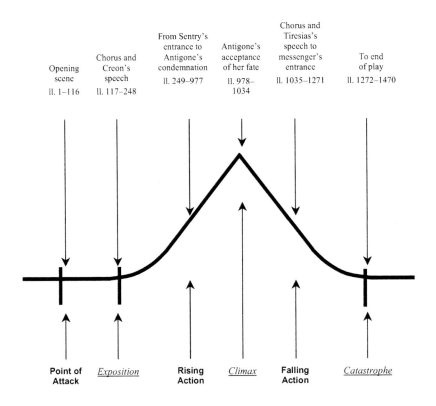

| Opening scene ll. 1–116 | Chorus and Creon's speech ll. 117–248 | From Sentry's entrance to Antigone's condemnation ll. 249–977 | Antigone's acceptance of her fate ll. 978–1034 | Chorus and Tiresias's speech to messenger's entrance ll. 1035–1271 | To end of play ll. 1272–1470 |

Point of Attack — *Exposition* — Rising Action — *Climax* — Falling Action — *Catastrophe*

Avoiding Unclear Language [pp. 524–25]

Have students look through several essays they've written recently—for any of their classes—and ask them to identify any examples of Engfish, jargon, and abstractions they used. How would they revise these usages? Bring in further examples of pretentious language and jargon from a variety of sources (textbooks, journal articles, committee reports, and the like) and discuss ways to improve the clarity and fluency of the language. Also make sure that unclear language is one of the elements that students look for in peer reviewing. The three points discussed in this section—Engfish, jargon, and abstract words—should give peer reviewers something definite and productive to focus on.

Sample Student Paper [pp. 525–30]

Since this student paper employs an approach to *Antigone* that your students might not have considered, you may want to let them respond to the "Questions for Discussion" (p. 530) after you have gone over with them in class the standard questions concerning the rhetorical components of the essay: Is the introduction effective? Is the thesis clearly stated? Are the paragraphs adequately developed? Are the sentences clear? Is the conclusion emphatic? Is the entire paper unified? Is the argument convincing? This last question should spark disagreement, which the discussion questions will allow you to explore.

Questions for Discussion [p. 530]

1. Since the writer focuses on the gender issue as her thesis, one could not say that she overemphasizes it. She acknowledges in her second sentence that she is not going to deal with "the more obvious conflict between the state and the individual." She deliberately chooses to discuss an aspect of the play that many readers might overlook.

2. Because the student was working within a 700-word limit for her essay, she was not able to include all of the evidence that might be used to support her thesis. During the argument between Creon and Haemon, Creon denigrates females: "never lose your sense of judgment over a woman / The warmth, the rush of pleasure, it all goes cold / in your arms, I warn you . . . a worthless woman / in your house, a misery in your bed" (723–26). The implication of his speech is that Haemon is interested only sexually in Antigone, and that once his ardor cools, she will make him miserable with her aggressiveness. Creon's contempt for women as mere sexual objects is first voiced crudely when Ismene expresses dismay that the king would condemn to death his own son's bride and Creon retorts, "there are other fields for him to plow" (642). Creon also tries to disparage Haemon's arguments by saying to the Chorus, "This boy, I do believe, is fighting on her side, the woman's side" (822–29) and calling him a "woman's accomplice!" (837) and a "woman's slave" (848).

   If the student had been given a less restrictive word limit, she might have discussed Eurydice as providing yet another example of the conflict between male and female. Although we know little about the marital relationship between Creon and Eurydice, we can be certain that she blames her husband for the deaths of her sons and curses him as their murderer. (Women, traditionally, have been opposed to war. Men make war, in which women's sons are killed.)

3. Antigone's purpose is more noble than mere sexual rivalry, but then, so is Creon's, supposedly. Although Antigone resents Creon, she clearly resents his power as a male: "Lucky tyrants—the perquisites of power! / Ruthless power to do and say whatever pleases *them*" (566–67). And in her final speech she places the blame for her death on men: "I alone, see what I suffer now / at the hands of what breed of men— / all or reverence, my reverence fore the gods!" (1032–34).

4. The student who wrote the essay naturally found the best evidence for her thesis ("The antagonist, Creon, is fighting to retain control over Antigone, not only as king over subject but also as man over woman") by analyzing the character of Creon. His misogynistic attitude forms the basis for her argument, since no other characters in the play appear openly anti-female. Her conclusion—that his fear of being beaten by a woman causes his rash action—is tied only by implication to his pride: "Creon's pride has made him blind to his mistake" (last sentence, next to last paragraph of the essay). She might well have stated this connection outright, thus emphasizing that her reading of the play supports and illuminates the usual

138

interpretation. She argues that pride causes Creon's fall: her paper attempts to explain why he was so touchy, stubborn, and insecure in his pridefulness.

As a matter of background information, you might want your students to know that during the period in Greek history before this play was written, the state was governed by a matriarchy. Once women were ousted from control, it became expedient to keep them from regaining power. Scholars believe that the political threat that women perhaps posed underlies Sophocles' presentation of Creon as a tyrant unjustly persecuting an assertive woman of noble blood who shows qualities of leadership. Antigone's insistence that the citizens are on her side suggests that she already has followers.

Making Connections
→Compare Antigone to Nora in *A Doll's House* and the women in *Trifles*. How do these women deal with the laws and conventions of the male-dominated societies in which they live?

Videos
→*Antigone*. 88 minutes, b&w, 1962. With Irene Papas. In Greek, with subtitles. Available from Insight Media and Filmic Archives.
→*Antigone*. 95 minutes, color, 1991. With Carrie O'Brien and Chris Bearne; directed by Arlena Nys. Available from Insight Media.
→*Antigone*. 120 minutes, color, 1988. Third part of the BBC production of the Theban Plays. With Juliet Stevenson, John Shrapnel, and John Gielgud. Adapted and translated by Don Taylor. Available from Films for the Humanities & Sciences.

Chapter 18 Writing About Character [pp. 531–83]

Analyzing characters provides a convenient and rewarding way of getting at the intent of a play. Students enjoy talking about the characters and speculating on their motives. For further exploration of character, you will find at the end of this chapter a casebook including selections from professional critics offering diverse interpretations of Amanda's character.

What Is the Modern Hero? [pp. 531–32]
Discussion of both *hero* and *tragedy* (or *tragic*) will reveal rather loose and broad-ranging definitions of these terms. It might help to ask students to distinguish between *heroic* and *courageous* or *bold* (are heroes ever *foolhardy*?) and between *tragic* and *sad* (or even *pathetic*). Some discussion of the limits and problems with abstract value words may also be necessary. Asking students to write out definitions of abstract terms—with examples or illustrations—and then to compare answers can be an enlightening, if sometimes perplexing, activity. Another useful prereading activity for this chapter is ask students to name a modern-day hero and defend or explain their choice.

139

Miller's definition of tragedy—"being torn away from our chosen image of what and who we are"—seems overly broad, one that can be applied to almost anybody. If Miller's concept is applied to the characters in *Fences*, it's possible to see most of them as displaced and at odds with the cosmos (or society). How useful, then, is this definition? Some readers may pity Rose but will not say that she is tragic. Even Troy's single-minded determination, which is akin to Antigone's in some ways, seems, to some, more foolish and misguided than heroic or tragic. Perhaps there are no modern heroes.

FENCES by August Wilson [pp. 533–79]

Fences is August Wilson's most popular play. It's set in the front yard of a ramshackle two-story brick home in Pittsburgh around 1957—on the brink of the civil rights movement. The play's action delineates the problems facing African Americans whose legal freedoms had not yet become a social reality. "Part of the reason I wrote *Fences*," August Wilson has said, "was to illuminate that generation, which shielded its children from all of the indignities they went through." Some critics and readers see *Fences* as a black version of Arthur Miller's *Death of a Salesman* because of the theme of father-son disillusionment and the death of an average American head of household. But the play is not about people who just happen to be black; it's about people who are what they are because they are blacks living in an unjust society run by whites. Wilson includes a number of details to stress that his play is about the black experience: the account of American history that precedes the play (pp. 533–34); the fact that Troy's sons choose to pursue athletics and music (Wilson says these are the only fields fully open to blacks); and the story that Troy tells to begin the play, about one of his co-workers getting away with stealing a watermelon by acting dumb. This is the type of story that slaves told one another (but not to whites) and often involved a slave appearing ridiculous while he was stealing from the white master.

One commentator has called this play "an elegy based on multiple failures of the American dream." Blacks of Troy's day were supposed to subscribe to American ideals (to serve in the army in time of war, for example), but they also had to sit in the back of the bus and accept the fact that they were barred from decent jobs. Troy is a baseball player who was too old to join a major league team when integration came to professional baseball. And when his friend Bono says, "Troy just came along too early," Troy acerbically replies, "There ought not never have been no time called too early." He is now working as a trash collector and fighting the company to let African Americans drive the trucks as well as pick up the trash.

Although the play focuses on black urban life, it also has larger, more universal themes that speak directly to all American families. Troy Maxson is a hardworking man who has a deep sense of responsibility to his family. But as Rose tells him, "The world's changing around you and you can't even see it." This failure to recognize and own the changes that have overtaken him puts Troy in the company of many dramatic protagonists who struggle futilely against the forces of life and the world. Enduring the indignities and degradation of racism throughout his life, Troy has tried to build a stable home for himself, a defense against the world. But the family life that had been Troy's salvation has also hemmed him in, and he risks it for the possibility of some happiness with a younger woman—and loses. In the end Troy is cut off from his wife, his sons, his friends from work, and his brother; in a pointless gesture to control life and fend off death, Troy completes the fence that symbolizes his confinement. *Fences* ends with a funeral scene that is both mournful and joyous, capturing the protagonist's conflict.

Questions for Discussion and Writing

1. Some commentators see Troy's relationship with Alberta as the turning point in Troy's life, and his confession to Rose as the turning point in the play. Do you agree with these interpretations?
2. Re-read the historical summary that Wilson gives at the beginning, entitled "The Play" (pp. 533–34). What themes and concepts does it establish, and how are these ideas carried out?
3. Why doesn't Troy want his son to play football in college? Are the reasons he gives the real ones?
4. Why is the song about Blue given so much prominence?
5. How do you think the play would be different if the characters were white?
6. Analyze the play's emphasis on boundaries, borders, and margins, both physical and metaphorical.
7. Write an essay in which you discuss Troy as both victim and victimizer.

Videos

→*August Wilson*. 51 min., color and b&w, 1990. An interview with Wilson and excerpts from his plays. Available from Films for the Humanities and Sciences.

→*August Wilson*. 29 min., color, 1989. From Bill Moyers's *World of Ideas* series. Available from PBS Video.

→*A Conversation with August Wilson*. 22 min, color, 1992. Interview with Edwina Moore. Available from California Newsreel.

Analyzing the Characters [pp. 579–80]

1. Some deceptions include the following:
   - Cory's not working at the A & P (serious deception since it estranges him from his father, although it's understandable since it's the only way the boy is able to play football, on which he bases all his hopes and dreams).
   - Signing papers to put Gabe away in an institution (a serious, indeed a nefarious action, since Troy believes Gabe deserves his freedom but commits him anyway to get the government money).
   - Watching the game at Taylor's (serious deception since it's Troy's cover for his philandering).
   - Lyon's talent as a musician (a self-deception that seems fairly harmless except that it allows him to avoid getting a job, so his wife has to support him).
   - Troy's talent as a baseball player (we can't be sure but probably involves some self-deception about his ability, which is reinforced by his friend Bono).
   - Walking 200 miles to Mobile (we can't really know, but it seems like the kind of harmless embellishment that is typical of Troy's stories).
   - The wholesale animosity of whites (mostly this comes from Troy concerning sports, so it's probably partly self-deception, partly exaggeration, and partly a very damaging truth).

- Troy's fantasy self-image when he's with Alberta (a damaging self-deception since he convinces himself that in his heart, he's doing right).
- Troy's betrayal of Rose with Alberta (a fatal deception which kills his loving relationship with Rose).
- Gabe's identity (harmless deception resulting from his war wound; Gabe appears to be the happiest person in the play).
- Playing the numbers (would be harmless if they had more money, since it gives them hope, but Troy considers even two nickels a week damaging).
- Troy's encounter with Death (a harmless and typical deception on Troy's part, as he insists that the self-aggrandizing story is just a telling of the facts).
- Rose tries to erase her doubts about Troy (a necessary self-deception since this rationalization allows her to remain with her hugely flawed husband when she has no other options).
- Other people's beliefs that Gabe either needs or doesn't need to be put away (Rose thinks he would be better cared for at the hospital; Troy believes Gabe should not lose his freedom but sends him anyway in the end; Lyons thinks Gabe is an all right guy, as does Bono; the police make money every time they arrest Gabe for disturbing the peace; we can't judge for sure whether any of these characters sees Gabe without some degree of self-deception).
- Why Gabe moved out (readers can't be sure where the truth lies, but Troy could easily be deceiving or self-deceived in believing that Gabe moved out because his new landlady wanted the government rent money; Rose believes what Gabe himself says—that he wanted his own space with his own key).
- Troy pretends no anger toward Gabe (a beneficial deception, like a white lie, because Gabe gets nervous when he senses Troy's anger but feels fine again when Troy tells him he's not mad).

2. The scene could be played to bring out Rose's genial tolerance of her husband's bluster; Troy's dominance throughout the scene; and Bono's almost subservient admiration for Troy.

3. Troy perfectly fits Miller's concept of tragic heroism. His inability to see how the world has changed drives a wedge between himself and his son. Rose tries to tell him, "They got lots of colored boys playing ball now," and Bono chimes in, "You right about that, Rose." But as several characters complain throughout the play, Troy doesn't listen to anyone but himself (another tragic flaw). Thus Cory loses his chance to go to college and perhaps realize his dreams. Troy's refusal to forget the past is rooted in his own missed chances to play professional baseball: "I decided seventeen years ago that boy wasn't getting involved in no sports. Not after what they did to me in the sports." This inability to change with the times causes the "disaster" Miller describes as "inherent in being torn away from our chosen image of what and who we are in this world." This same displacement underlies Troy's rationalization of his infidelity. When he's with Alberta, he says, "I can be a part of myself that I ain't never been." And in the chilling scene in which he whips his father away from raping the young girl, he truly achieves heroic stature: "Right there is where I become a man . . . at fourteen years of age."

Almost all of the characters suffer a similar displacement between their self-concept and their actual roles in the world. Lyons, of course, is an obvious example.

Wilson tells us in a stage direction: "Though he fancies himself a musician, he is more caught up in the rituals and 'idea' of being a musician than in the actual practice of the music." "I just stay with the music," he says, "cause that's the only way I can find to live in the world."

Even Rose, who seems the most well-adjusted person in the play, finally is driven to complain, "I gave eighteen years of my life to stand on the same spot with you [Troy]. . . . Don't you think it ever crossed my mind to want to know other men? That I wanted to lay up somewhere and forget about my responsibilities? . . . I took all my feelings, my wants and needs, my dreams . . . and buried them inside you." By the end of the play she has become reconciled to her circumscribed existence: "But that's what life offered me in the way of being a woman and I took it. I grabbed hold of it with both hands."

Gabriel's tragic displacement is complete and has a physical cause—the metal plate in his head. Fortunately, he's oblivious to the problem, so he's about the only one in the play who has no regrets and seems quite happy.

Cory's self-image of being a college graduate with a good job is dashed by his father's refusal to allow him to be recruited to play college football. At the end of the play he is a corporal in the marines, but this role is not what he envisions for himself, so he plans to leave the service, even though Lyons warns him that there still are no good jobs available. He also still feels overshadowed by his father: "Everywhere I looked, Troy Maxson was staring back at me . . . hiding under the bed . . . in the closet. . . . I don't want to be Troy Maxson. I want to be me." Since he finally agrees to go to his father's funeral, we can assume that perhaps he'll break free finally and be able to find himself.

4. Money has prominence in the play because it's always scarce. We first see Troy and Bono on "payday" (celebrating with their "ritual" pint of booze and conversation). Lyons shows up to borrow ten bucks from his dad, as he does regularly but also seems to repay regularly out of his wife's earnings. At the end of the play, though, he's borrowing $20 instead of $10, and after his divorce, he has taken to "cashing other people's checks" for money and ends up in the workhouse. Troy always gives him a hard time about a grown man borrowing instead of earning money, but he gives it to him nonetheless. Troy passes his own pay envelope to his wife, who apparently has charge of the family finances. This same arrangement holds true at Bono's as well, but when large purchases are made, the men make them and take credit for them: Bono buys Florence's refrigerator and Troy will someday pay to have the roof tarred. As he tells his son in no uncertain terms, "this is my house," that "he done paid for with the sweat of his brow." It's clear that he who earns the money makes the rules in this social setting.

Playing the numbers serves as entertainment ("It's something to do," says Rose) and gives hope to people who have little hope otherwise of ever having enough money. Troy, who earns the one or two nickels per week that Rose spends on the numbers, considers it "throwing your money away" but is at least generous enough that he doesn't forbid her playing.

The money that figures most prominently in the play is Gabriel's money from being wounded during the war. Troy "swooped down on" the cash settlement of $3,000 and used it to buy himself a house (yes, the same one he tells Cory he "paid

143

for with the sweat of his brow"). He then had Gabe come live there and turn over his regular government check every month as rent. Troy sees it as taking care of his brother, except when he gets to feeling guilty about having appropriated it.

Money is especially short at the time of the play in Troy's household because Gabe has decided to move in with Miss Pearl, and she's now receiving the checks that used to go to Troy. The local judge and police department also profit from Gabe's injury by fining him $50 every so often for disturbing the peace. Troy has to pay to bail Gabe out and sees the whole procedure as a scam.

The most pernicious use of Gabe's government money comes near the end of the play when Troy has Gabe committed to the state hospital in order to get part of Gabe's check every month. When Rose accuses him, Troy vehemently denies having done so: "I told you I ain't signed nothing, woman!" But Rose responds, "Troy, I seen where you signed the paper. . . . You done went down there and signed him to the hospital for half of his money. . . . You gonna have to answer for that."

Troy needs the money, of course, to support the woman he's gotten pregnant and the child when it comes. If the family hadn't had enough money before, they are certainly strapped now. But even before this new expense occurred, Troy seems too generous with his son Lyons and too penny-pinching with his boy Cory. The youngster, Cory, wants his dad to buy the family a TV and is sure he can afford to, but Troy says no. If he had $200 he would have to get the roof fixed, and he won't buy a TV on credit because "I ain't gonna owe nobody nothing if I can help it." Troy feels responsible for feeding and clothing the boy but nothing beyond that. His attitude is so far removed from our child-centered society today that he seems quite uncaring to the modern reader. At the end of the play when he makes Cory leave home, he seems downright cruel.

5. Rose's closing monologue suggests a somewhat hopeful way of looking at the play. She begins by explaining to Cory that his father "wanted you to be everything that he wasn't . . . and at the same time he tried to make you into everything he was." She admits that "He wasn't always right," but she's certain that "he meant to do more good than he meant to do harm," even though "Sometimes when he touched he bruised." This explanation may not be much comfort to Cory, who's trying to get out from under his father's dark shadow, but he does ultimately attend the funeral, which suggests at least the beginning of forgiveness. Rose, however, has convinced herself that giving her life over to Troy was a good thing—at least it seemed so before he betrayed her with Alberta. After that, "me and your daddy had done lost touch with one another." Ironically, from that betrayal comes the birth of Raynell, who provides a certain measure of salvation to Rose: "Like I'd been blessed to relive a part of my life," she says. The hope for fostering a new generation is clear in the conclusion of her speech.

6. Responses will vary but Troy presents the most obvious choice because of his overpowering stage presence. But some may want to disqualify him from being considered a hero because of his many morally wrong choices throughout the play: betraying Rose, alienating Cory, swiping Gabe's money, and committing him to the state hospital (at that time also called an insane asylum). Rose might be a better choice. Hers is a quiet kind of heroism, which involves selflessly ignoring her own wants and needs in order to care for the needs of others. Certainly we can see a large

144

measure of heroism in her agreeing to raise her husband's love child as her own: "I'm gonna give her the best of what's in me," she vows. And at the end, her convincing Cory to forgive his father gives the play a semblance of a hope to mitigate the tragedy of Troy's misspent life.

The Exercise on Providing Quotations (p. 583) will also produce some valuable and productive prewriting for a critical analysis of one or more of the characters.

Ideas for Writing [pp. 581–82]

Use the ideas for responsive writing as the bases for small group discussions and collaborative writing. These topics are all designed to lead students to a deeper understanding of the play as they approach it from different angles.

Ideas for Critical Writing

1. Students can use the material from their prewriting assignment in exploring this topic.
2. Responses will vary, but probably it's a bit of all three.
3. The legacies include personality traits and behaviors that were passed to Troy from his father and then from Troy to Cory.
4. If you want to make the job a bit easier for your students, you might suggest that they consult the list of mythical and archetypal sources on page 132 of their textbook.
5. Your students may need to do additional research on life in the 1950s in order to write cogently on this assignment.
6. This topic will allow students to probe deeper into Troy's egocentric personality as they seek a reason for his not even noticing the good that his win for labor over management will do for other black men.

Exercise on Providing Quotations [p. 583]

Quotations to support generalizations:

1. Throughout the play, Rose confronts Troy only on minor flaws, while supporting his self-image as a good, strong, capable man:
   - Troy, don't nobody wanna be hearing all that stuff. (Act 1, Scene 1, p. 778)
   - Troy lying. . . . He ain't paying no ten dollars a month to nobody. (Act 1, Scene 1, p. 779)
   - Well, everybody got their own way of looking at it I guess. (Act 2, Scene 1, p. 801)
   - Ain't no sense you blaming yourself for nothing. Gabe wasn't in no condition to manage that money. You done what was right by him. (Act 1, Scene 2, p. 784)
   - I don't know if he was right or wrong . . . but I do know he meant to do more good than he meant to do harm. (Act 2, Scene 5, p. 815)
2. Though they are affected by an inhospitable environment, the characters also worsen their situations through their own questionable choices:
   - TROY. That's the only way I got a roof over my head . . . cause of that metal plate [in Gabe's head]. (Act 1, Scene 2, p. 784)
   - TROY. I decided seventeen years ago that boy wasn't getting involved in no sports. Not after what they did to me in the sports. (Act 1, Scene 3, p. 789)

145

- ROSE. That was my first mistake. Not to make him leave some room for me. . . . I didn't know to keep up his strength I had to give up little pieces of me. (Act 2, scene 5, p. 815)
- LYONS. Aw, Pop, you know I can't find no decent job. Where am I gonna get a job at? You know I can't get no job. (Act 1, Scene 1, p. 779)
- CORY. It ain't your yard. You took Uncle Gabe's money he got from the army to buy this house and then you put him out. (Act 2, Scene 4, p. 810)
- CORY. Mr. Stawicki done already hired somebody else 'cause I told him I was playing football. (Act 1, Scene 3, p. 788)

3. Troy's strategies to make Rose agree to mother his illegitimate child consist of crass manipulation and self-serving sentimentality:
   - She ain't but a wee bittie little old thing.
   - She innocent . . . and she ain't got no mama.
   - It felt right in my heart.
   - And right now your daddy's scared cause we sitting out here and ain't got no home. Oh, I been homeless before. I ain't had no little baby with me.
   - She's my daughter, Rose. My own flesh and blood. I can't deny her no more than I can deny them boys. You and them boys is my family. You and them and this child is all I got in the world. (Act 2, Scene 3, pp. 806–07)

4. The fence has several symbolic meanings in the play:
   - BONO. Nigger, why you got to go and get some hard wood? You ain't doing nothing but building a little old fence. Get you some soft pine wood. (Act 2, Scene 1, p. 798)
   - BONO. Some people build fences to keep people out . . . and other people build fences to keep people in. (Act 2, Scene 1, p. 799)
   - ROSE [sings]. Jesus, be a fence all around me every day / Jesus I want you to protect me as I travel on my way. / Jesus, be a fence around me every day (Act 1, Scene 2, p. 781)
   - TROY. All right . . . Mr. Death. . . . I'm gonna build me a fence around what belongs to me. And then I want you to stay on the other side. See? You stay over there until you're ready for me. (Act 2, Scene 2, p. 806)

5. Evidence from the play suggests that Raynell is destined for a life of misery and self-deception:
   - ROSE. Girl, get in here and get dressed. What are you doing?
   - RAYNELL. Seeing if my garden growed.
   - ROSE. I told you ain't gonna grow overnight. You got to wait.
   - RAYNELL. It don't look like it never gonna grow. Dag!
   - ROSE. I told you a watched pot never boils. . . .
   - RAYNELL. This ain't even no pot, Mama. (Act 2, scene 5, p. 812)
   - ROSE. Raynell, get in there and get them good shoes on.
   - RAYNELL. Mama, can't I wear these? Them other one hurt my feet.
   - ROSE. Well, they just gonna have to hurt your feet for a while. You ain't said they hurt your feet when you went down to the store and got them.
   - RAYNELL. They didn't hurt then. My feet done got bigger. (Act 2, scene 5, p. 814)

Although these reactions seem typical for a child, they also sound a lot like her father's stubborn insistence on getting his own way and justifying his actions.

ANTHOLOGY OF DRAMA

OTHELLO, THE MOOR OF VENICE by William Shakespeare [pp. 584–669]
Othello differs in several important ways from the other three major Shakespearean tragedies that it is usually ranked with. The protagonist is not a prince or king (as in *Hamlet*, *Macbeth*, and *King Lear*); he is a recently married general. There are no supernatural visits, no fully developed subplot, little comic relief, and few minor characters serving as foils. The cast of *Othello* is small and the plot is concentrated. The action takes place in a few days in only two locations, unlike the years and far-reaching locales that are spanned in the other major tragedies. While all four plays share a thematic fascination with evil, *Othello* is the most focused on one particular form of evil—sexual jealousy. Othello's tragic fall does not threaten the social order: the catastrophe centers on the destruction of a specific, personal love through jealousy. The play is confined to an unusual degree to the fate of three main characters: Othello, Desdemona, and Iago.

Most students will be impressed with the rapid action and the tension of the tightly constructed plot. But they may have problems with the characters and their motives, especially those of Iago and Othello. Iago's envy for Cassio is clear, but the reasons for his jealousy of Othello are less certain. Critics have argued repeatedly about the plausibility of Iago's motivation. Some have said that it is insufficient and that his character is inconsistent. Coleridge used the phrase "motiveless malignity" to account for Iago's behavior. Others have found adequate cause in Iago's suspicions of his wife's fidelity (presuming she was having an affair with Othello), his sexual attraction to Desdemona, and his envy for Othello's position and success. While students may have reservations about the credibility of these motives, they should have little trouble seeing how cunning and crafty the villain is in his manipulation of people and circumstances. Iago belongs to a select group of villains who seem to delight in evil for its own sake. He takes pleasure in deceiving almost everyone in the play and amazes us with his virtuosity. Also, Iago may be so adept at working self-hatred in others because he suffers from it himself.

As for Othello, students may wonder why someone who appears to be intelligent, strong-willed, even-tempered, and honorable can fall so easily for Iago's schemes and deceptions. They may question how such a good character can be driven to such evil deeds. That Othello is black is a key force behind Iago's success. He is also a military man, simple and inexperienced in the ways of love and civilized society. As an outsider, both by race and temperament, Othello is not able to believe in the admiration and esteem that the sophisticated Venetians proclaim for him. When Iago persuades Othello to see himself as alien, the resulting loss of self-regard is devastating. His jealousy arises from a deep suspicion that others cannot love him, since he does not consider himself lovable. Because Othello has loved Desdemona as an extension of himself, his destruction of her is a destruction of himself. The murder of Desdemona is

147

actually a prelude to his suicide. The horror and pity of *Othello* comes from the spectacle of a noble love made filthy by self-hatred, but the play's special terror arises from the fact that the savagery of the two central characters cannot be satisfactorily explained.

Possible Responses to *Questions for Discussion and Writing*

1. Through Act 3, scene 2, Othello is a grandly positive character. He is a leading figure in the Venetian establishment, a respected military man, and a loving husband. He acts with restraint and dignity when confronted by Brabantio, Roderigo, and the officers that Brabantio has gathered (1.2). Othello's response to Brabantio's insults and charges is both eloquent and persuasive: even the Duke says, "I think this tale would win my daughter too" (1.3.171). Desdemona confirms the mutuality of their love, revealing it to be both spiritually satisfying and sexually vigorous.

   With his suicide Othello acknowledges his fault and in doing so may recover something of his former nobility. He honestly admits that he "lov'd not wisely, but too well" and was "Perplex'd in the extreme" (5.2.345, 347). He shows a vestige of his pride when he refers to his former service to the state; and when he identifies with the "malignant . . . Turk" (5.2.354) he once slew, his death retains a moment of honor and atonement.

2. The attraction between Othello and Desdemona seems to be based, to a large degree, on their differences. Othello is very different from the Venetians (like Roderigo) who have courted Desdemona: he is an older black man who has had adventures and experiences that she has never been exposed to. Likewise, Desdemona is apparently unlike any woman Othello has known: refined, virtuous, tenderhearted—as well as young and beautiful and white. They are exotic and mysterious to each other. These differences and mysteries are also largely responsible for the tragedy that comes into their lives, since they account for the insecurities that Iago exploits to fuel Othello's jealousy. The differences are a source of wonderment for Desdemona (she is sure that the noble Othello must still love her) and a source of doubt for Othello (how can he be sure that someone like Desdemona can truly love him?). As Brabantio says to him, "Look to her, Moor, if thou has eyes to see; / She has deceiv'd her father, and may thee" (1.3.291–92).

3. As the embodiment of evil and villainy, Iago must destroy the one person in the play who stands for everything he does not: innocence, purity, loyalty, and virtue. He is a complete cynic who cannot stand to see someone who is truly virtuous. Some readers also think Iago is jealous of Desdemona because, like Cassio, she has displaced Iago from Othello's regard and affections.

4. Desdemona is simply too innocent and trusting for her own good. She has been bewitched, in a way, by Othello and has also become dependent on him. (She ran away from her home to marry Othello and then left with him, away from Venice to the military outpost in Cyprus.) The same cultural dissonance that makes Othello susceptible to Iago's lies also affects Desdemona. Having firmly and courageously defied the prejudices of the only society she had ever known, Desdemona is incapable of betraying her love and devotion to Othello. She recognizes that his jealousy is ignoble, but she continues to give him her love to its fullest extent, saying, " my love doth so approve him, / That even his stubbornness, his checks and frowns, / . . . have grace and favour in them" (4.3.19–21).

5. The protagonist's race was not very important in the play's main source, but it is frequently mentioned by Shakespeare, especially in Act I, where the nature of Venetian society is stressed. The obvious racist caricature offered, even before Othello appears, would be the same stereotypes that many in Shakespeare's audience held at that time. Othello's race helps establish him as an outsider in Venice, and this status makes him susceptible to Iago's wiles. The Moor is fatally naïve about Desdemona's world; and when Iago assures him, "I know our country disposition well" (3.3.202), Othello is ready to accept, at face value, the outrageous claim that adultery is commonplace among Venetian women. Also, once his mind has been poisoned by Iago's charges, Othello is not capable of understanding Desdemona's worth: he has seen and heard Venice's prejudice, but does not fully appreciate her courage in opposing it.

6. Suggest that students begin by defining "reason" and "instinct." One way to frame (and limit) this issue would be: Does Iago rely mainly on reason or on instinct to manipulate Othello and the other characters in the play? Students could also focus on the conflict between reason and instinct in Othello. Or they might identify Othello as a man of instinct and Iago as a man of (perverted) reason, and develop an interpretation around that conflict.

7. Two "marriages" parallel that of Othello and Desdemona. Cassio is linked with Bianca, and although they are not formally married, the comparison is promoted by the fact that Iago substitutes Bianca for Desdemona when he uses the handkerchief to deceive Othello. Moreover, Bianca's jealousy of Cassio (which seems justified) contrasts with Othello's jealousy (which seems incredible). The marriage of Iago and Emilia plainly lacks affection, let alone love, but is marked by sexual jealousy, at least in Iago's overheated imagination: he remarks several times that he suspects his wife of adultery with either Othello (1.3. 369–71 and 2.1.276–77) or Cassio (2.1.287–88)—although both suspicions seem as preposterous as the claims about Desdemona's infidelity.

8. The answers to questions 2 and 5 above provide a number of points that could be used in developing an essay on this topic. Add the observation about Othello as a military man: he has succeeded as a soldier (an all-male environment) but has trouble understanding the civilian world, especially since the duplicitous Iago is his chief intermediary between these two worlds.

Additional Questions for Discussion and Writing

1. What incident first incites Iago to vengeance against Othello?
2. Where in Act I is Othello's race mentioned in a derogatory manner? What are the implications of these slurs?
3. What is Roderigo's relation to Iago?
4. What is Brabantio's initial reaction to the news that Othello and Desdemona are together?
5. Describe how Iago begins to succeed in his evil plans in the third scene of Act II.
6. How does Iago plant the seed of suspicion in Othello's mind (Act III)?
7. How does Cassio's personality make him susceptible to Iago's manipulation?
8. Contrast the Iago-Emilia relationship with that of Othello and Desdemona (see Act III, scene iii).

9. Explain the role of chance or fate in the tragedy.
10. How do you interpret Iago's statement "I am your own forever" (end of Act III, scene iii)?
11. What is Bianca's function in the play?
12. When Othello, enraged by Iago's insinuations, grovels at the villain's feet, is he a tragic figure or merely pathetic?
13. What new trick does Iago devise to incite Othello's jealousy in the first scene of Act IV? Why does Othello fall for such an obvious deception?
14. Compare and contrast Desdemona with Emilia. Why is Desdemona so passive in the last part of Act IV?
15. What mistakes does Iago make in the first scene of Act V? How do these mistakes ensure his own fate?
16. Analyze Othello's speech at the start of scene ii, Act V. Why must he kill Desdemona quickly, rather than listen to her pleas?

Making Connections
→Write an essay in which you compare the tragedy of Othello with the tragedy of Antigone.
→Compare Desdemona with Nora Helmer or Antigone.

Videos
→*Othello*. 93 minutes, b&w, 1952. With Orson Welles and Suzanne Cloutier; directed by Orson Welles. Available from Corinth Films and Filmic Archives.
→*Othello*. 166 minutes, color, 1965; 16 mm film. With Laurence Olivier, Maggie Smith, Frank Findlay, and Derek Jacobi. Available from Swank Motion Pictures.
→*Othello*. 208 minutes, color, 1982. With Anthony Hopkins, Bob Hoskins, and Penelope Wilton. BBC Shakespeare. Available from Filmic Archives, Time-Life, Inc., and Insight Media.
→*Othello*. 198 minutes, color, video. With John Kani, Joanna Weinberg; directed by Janet Suzman. Available from Films for the Humanities & Sciences.

A DOLL'S HOUSE by Henrik Ibsen [pp. 670–722]
Though it would not shock many people today, *A Doll's House* shocked its first audiences by rejecting socially sanctioned roles. Nothing could seemingly justify a wife's walking out on her marriage, away from her children, leaving a husband who abused her only mentally. When Ibsen is able to do so, he makes a powerful statement about personal freedom and development. We can understand Nora's transformation from a powerless child to an adult groping for a reason for existence and principles to live by.

In the first act, Nora is shown as a bubbling and happy childlike doll who depends on her husband to do the thinking. Torvald keeps her in this dependent state and repeatedly emphasizes her dependence by calling her "my little squirrel," "my little skylark," and "my pretty little pet." He foreshadows later difficulties when he says, "There's always something inhibited, something unpleasant about a home built on credit and borrowed money." He cannot allow her to grow up. Nothing will spoil his doll and model dollhouse if he allows no change in her.

150

Nora reveals the shallowness of her thoughts and her background as a rich and spoiled child when her old friend Christine shows up looking for work. Though Christine is careworn and desperately poor, Nora is unable to stop talking about her own good fortune. When Krogstad arrives to fill in the details of Nora's forgery, she still looks down on him, even though they have committed the same crime. By the end of the first act, Nora's happy bubble has been punctured, and we see the tension begin to grow.

Nora spends Act II urgently trying to retain her secure little world, but despite her best efforts, her forgery is destined to come to light. Her mind now operates in two modes. Her childlike thinking assures her that her husband will forgive her the small crime because she did it to save his life. This thought comforts her, and she is eager to see the confirmation of his love. But her slowly awakening adult mind tells her that Torvald is more worried about his own reputation than about her feelings.

Act III shows the beginning of a much healthier relationship between Christine and Krogstad than prevailed in the past. In contrast, the marriage of the Helmers is rapidly deteriorating. When Nora's forgery is finally revealed and her husband betrays his self-centeredness, she makes the break that will allow her to grow.

Possible Responses to *Questions for Discussion and Writing*

1. In the early conversations between Nora and Torvald, the power relations seem to be clearly delineated. Nora is portrayed as a frivolous, airy-headed wife, while Torvald is the affectionate, condescending father figure who is amused at his wife's unworldliness. He definitely appears to be the patriarch of the family.

2. Many students will realize that Nora is going to leave her husband in Act III, when she looks at him "with a growing look of coldness in her face," as she realizes that he has no empathy with her sacrifices in trying to save his life. He sees her only as the harbinger of his humiliation in front of others. This idea builds throughout the scene, incorporating her disgust at his relief and forgiveness when public exposure is not forthcoming.

3. The main antagonist could be seen as the oblivious, bullying Torvald. Alternatively, it could be Krogstad, who struck such a harsh bargain with Nora when she was in need, although he is rehabilitated by love. The whole environment of oppressive marital relationships in the period (or the current period), and the unforgiving system of medical care for the poor can also be seen as antagonists.

4. The climax, at which the die is cast and something must come out into the open, could be identified as occurring when Krogstad puts the damning letter into the letter box. Everything after this point hinges on the reception of this letter.

5. Torvald's arguments all insist on the possibility that the marriage can go back to its earlier stage, when Nora is childlike and Torvald is professorial and fatherly. Moreover, Nora has seen the shallowness of Torvald's values, as he rejects her until it becomes clear that he will not be publicly disgraced due to her actions. Nora's sense of identity, meanwhile, has progressed beyond wishing for a restitution of the status quo.

6. Ibsen is attacking a certain kind of marriage, in which true communication is rare, and each partner is acting a role in a stable power system. He also criticized a system in which money determines well-being: both in Nora's sacrifice for Torvald's health, and in Mrs. Linde's sacrifice of true love for financial help in her earlier choice of a husband.
7. Students will vary in whether they believe that a person like Nora, with such an ingrained background as a dependent wife, will be able to blossom into a full human being. Some might think that she will soon find another patriarch to marry and to be subservient to. More optimistic students may believe that Nora has reached a true turning point and will seek independence and maturity from now on. She certainly has proven, through her secret years of industry to repay her debt, that she can support herself if necessary.
8. Students can identify which characters (and there are several) cling to illusions. Some seem to be destroyed when their illusions are shattered, and others seem to seek the reinstatement of these illusions and the rejection of any lessons they have faced. Torvald's last remarks can be interpreted as ambiguous in this regard.

Additional Questions for Discussion and Writing

1. Looking back on the first act, what foreshadowing can you see?
2. Why is it dramatically appropriate for Nora to borrow the money from Krogstad?
3. Which characters provide background information? Do they help to develop the main characters?
4. Is Nora a victim of circumstances, or does she cause problems for herself and her husband?
5. How much role-playing is there in the Helmers' marriage? Do Nora and Helmer know that they are playing roles? Do they become aware by the end of the play?
6. Examine the theme of weakness and corruption and how these traits are passed down from generation to generation. Consider Krogstad and his sons, Nora and her father, and Dr. Rank.
7. Do you find this play out of date? Write an essay explaining why or why not.
8. In his biography *Henrik Ibsen*, Michael Meyer says this play is not so much about women's rights as about "the need of every individual to find out the kind of person he or she really is, and to strive to become that person." Support or refute this interpretation.

Making Connections

→Compare Nora Helmer with Antigone. Which one is most heroic in your opinion? What would Antigone do if she were in Nora's place? Or compare Nora to Rose in *Fences*. How do these wives deal with their husbands' attempts to dominate and control?

Videos

→>*A Doll's House*. 89 minutes, b&w, 1959. With Julie Harris, Christopher Plummer, Jason Robards, Jr., Hume Cronyn, and Eileen Hacket. Available from MGM/United Artists Home Video.

→*A Doll's House.* 85 minutes, color, 1989. With Claire Bloom, Anthony Hopkins, Sir Ralph Richardson, Denholm Elliott, Anna Massey, and Dame Edith Evans. Available from MGM/United Artists Home Video.

→*A Doll's House.* 98 minutes, color, 1973. With Jane Fonda, Edward Fox, Trevor Howard, and David Warner. Available from Prism Entertainment.

TRIFLES by Susan Glaspell [pp. 723–32]

Susan Glaspell wrote this play at a time (1916) when women did not often write for the stage. The play's feminist point of view is also remarkable for its time. While the action centers on a murder investigation, the playwright skillfully introduces a second investigation, conducted by the two women who accompany the men inquiring into John Wright's death. At the beginning of the play Mr. Hale remarks that "women are used to worrying over trifles," but it is just such trifles that are the substance of the women's investigation.

The men hunt in vain for clues to the murder; the women quickly find what the men have missed. Their discovery is the result of their feminine sensibilities, which enable them to recognize the importance of what they find—a bird with a broken neck. They realize that Wright must have killed it and that the bird's death was probably Mrs. Wright's motive for murdering her husband. Glaspell also introduces the idea that the truly "awful thing" was not the murder of John Wright but the lonely and isolated life his wife had been forced to endure. Because they neglected Minnie Wright, the women feel implicated and decide to hide the incriminating evidence.

The play emphasizes the essential differences between men and women in rural life. The men are insensitive to the nature of women's lives. More important, their adherence to the letter of the law precludes a merciful administration of justice. The two women, with their sense of a higher purpose, band together to protect another woman from the injustice of man's law when applied to women. (At the time this play was written, women were not allowed to vote or serve on juries.)

A year after Glaspell wrote this play, she rewrote it as a short story, titled "A Jury of Her Peers." Although the story is close to the play (after the first page, much of the dialogue is identical with that in the play), the women take more central roles earlier in the story than in the play. The story also takes us inside Mrs. Hale's mind to learn of her guilt for not having visited Mrs. Wright. The story seems to focus more on justice than on the "trifles" overlooked by the men. Perhaps this shift in thematic emphasis is why the author changed the title.

Possible Responses to *Questions for Discussion and Writing*

1. The setting is stark, gloomy, and cold. It conveys the hard life that Mr. Wright imposed on his wife and sums up the relationship between the Wrights.
2. The men are conventional, efficient, officious, and condescending toward the women. They are so smugly certain of their own authority that they overlook the kind of evidence (the "trifles" of the title) that could be used to convict Mrs. Wright.
3. The women recognize the identical knots that Mrs. Wright used on her sewing and on her husband. In the last line of the play, Mrs. Hale reveals that key piece of evidence to Mr. Henderson, but as far as he's concerned, that's "not it."

153

4. Minnie Foster used to wear a white dress with blue ribbons and sing in the choir. All of the joy in her life was strangled out by the confining marriage and isolated existence that she had to endure with Mr. Wright.
5. Encourage students to define what they mean by "the right thing." Do the women choose to hide the evidence because they empathize with Minnie Wright or because they feel guilty that they didn't help her out? In other words, do they do the right thing for Minnie? for themselves? for women in general? for the cause of justice?

Additional Questions for Discussion and Writing
1. Make a list of the events that occurred (or that you speculate might have occurred) before the play begins. Why did Glaspell choose to begin the play where she did?
2. How does the first entrance of the characters establish a distinction between the men and the women? What do the different reactions to the frozen preserves tell you?
3. Why does Glaspell include Mrs. Peters's speech about the boy who killed her cat?
4. Susan Glaspell wrote a short story version of *Trifles* and changed the title to "A Jury of Her Peers." What is the significance of each title? Why do you think she changed the title? Which one do you prefer?
5. Could it be argued that this play is immoral? Write an essay in which you explain your answer to this question.

Making Connections
→Compare Mrs. Peters and Mrs. Hale with Rose in *Fences*. Which women seem to have the most control over their lives?

Video
→*A Jury of Her Peers*. 30 min., color, 1980. Filmed version of *Trifles*, directed by Sally Heckel. Available from Women Make Movies.

BEAUTY by Jane Martin [pp. 733-37]
As a pre-reading activity, ask students to do a short write about these sayings, which the play seems to be exploring and questioning: "The grass is always greener on the other side of the fence"; "Beauty is only skin deep"; "Beauty is in the eye of the beholder." What do these proverbs mean? Is there any truth to them? After reading the play, then ask students to comment on what the play seems to be saying about these proverbs.

The play seems to be straight-on satire about the cultural obsession with physical beauty and sexual attractiveness. But the point of the satire is not that simple. The two trade more than bodies; they trade brains and personalities. As Carla/Bethany says, "I wanted to be beautiful, but I didn't want to be you." And Bethany/Carla says, "You have my brain. You poor bastard." Also, could the combined names (with the slash marks) suggest that the characters represent two sides of the same person? The theme would then involve a claim about self-knowledge or self-acceptance.

Possible Responses to Questions for Discussion and Writing
1. It attacks the obsession with physical beauty, sexual attractiveness, and the preoccupations of outward appearances. It also delivers a strong comment about

154

envy—the human tendency to be unsatisfied with what one has and to want what others have. A lot of advertising is based on creating and exploiting this tendency.

2. Carla fits the dumb blonde stereotype; Bethany is the "plain Jane" type. Whether both are equal objects of the satire is an issue that might spark some disagreement, as will the question of who gets the better deal. It seems that Carla is more self-aware and realistic about herself; she seems less obsessive and thus not the primary target of the ridicule. But as Bethany points out, Carla's self-criticisms must be taken with a grain of salt: "you're just trying to make us feel better because we aren't in your league."

3. She thinks that it's just a trick, that it doesn't really cost Carla anything to denigrate her own advantages.

4. Corresponding male stereotypes might be the technogeek and the dumb jock; or a bumptious egghead (Barney Frank) vs. a handsome smooth-operator (Mitt Romney, John Edwards). The two adult brothers in the TV sitcom "Two and a Half Men" (played by Jon Cryer and Charlie Sheen) present another example of contrasting male stereotypes. Students may prefer to rewrite the script themselves, rather than just explain how to adapt it.

SURE THING by David Ives [pp. 738–46]

This play experiments with the intriguing idea of applying instant replay to real-life encounters. What would happen if we could immediately revise what we say until we get the response we want? This is the fantasy that David Ives plays with in *Sure Thing*. In following this notion to its dramatic limits, the playwright manages to portray a variety of characters and explore a range of emotions in a brief one-act, two-character play. Ives takes the formulaic "boy meets girl" scene and complicates it in unexpected ways. The result is witty and insightful, as well as very funny. As students read they should look for the elements of traditional dramatic structure that Ives uses: point of attack, exposition, rising action, climax, falling action, denouement.

This is a play that students will enjoy acting out. Ask for volunteers, stop the play at several points, and call for a different duo to continue. You might divide the class into groups and have each group work on a section of the play. Then the groups could choose a couple to present their approach to the scene. It might also be fun to mix up the gender assignments: have a female play Bill and a male play Betty, or have the parts portrayed by two males or two females.

Possible Responses to *Questions for Discussion and Writing*

1. A café, as opposed to a bus stop, conveys intent. This setting says the characters are sociable and are looking to hook up with someone (both say they come to the café a lot).

2. The dramatic premise—applying instant replay to a social encounter—makes it easy to arrive at the "right moment." Time is repeatedly readjusted to give the characters multiple chances to "get it right."

3. It signals that a speaker has made a faux pas, and the scene will be replayed to give the person another chance to get it right. In some productions, the listener rings the bell (or simply says "ding") to tell the speaker to try again. This approach underscores the influence of the listener on the speaker's attempts to be the perfect catch.
4. The plot follows the traditional scheme of boy meets girl, boy almost loses girl (many times), boy finally gets girl. Or you could put it the other way around: girl chases boy, girl almost loses boy, girl gets boy. The conflict involves the struggle to find an acceptable mate. It is resolved when both characters re-fashion themselves enough to meet the other's requirements. (Authenticity and honesty have nothing to do with this match.) The climax occurs when the two start to speak simultaneously (p. 745), and the bell stops interrupting their conversation. At the end Betty says "Sure thing" (the play's title), and they then speak together once more: détente has been achieved.
5. This approach will allow more students to participate in the performance.

Additional Questions for Discussion and Writing

1. Is the title ironic? The same phrase—"sure thing"—is also used several times in the play. Does it always mean the same thing?
2. Do you think Bill and Betty are genuinely well matched or are they simply the product of self-revision?
3. Which character is the protagonist? What does the protagonist want? Is the other character the antagonist? Or is the antagonist some social force or convention?
4. How would you describe the comedy in this play? Is it romantic or farcical? Write an essay in which you explain why the play is funny.
5. Write another scene between Betty and Bill that takes place after they come out of the movies.

Making Connections

→Compare Ives's comic treatment of love and romance to the treatment of these same subjects in Raymond Carver's story "What We Talk About When We Talk About Love."
→Compare the encounter between Bill and Betty with that of Jake and Mariana in the story "Love in L. A." by Dagoberto Gilb, focusing on the elements of performance and revision.

CRITICAL APPROACHES FOR INTERPRETING LITERATURE
[pp. 747–52]

Since our emphasis in this text is on writing, using literature as a rich source of content, we discourage lengthy forays into the world of literary criticism. However, students may find good ideas about how to approach a work of literature from reading this Appendix, especially when they are stuck for a topic. If they have not had a literature class yet, they may be unaware that these schools of thought exist. Another time the Appendix may be useful is when you see a student paper or comment that has the seeds of one of these critical approaches already within it, and reading about the approach can focus the discussion.

In this edition of *Literature and the Writing Process*, we have labeled those writing prompts that pertain to specific critical approaches. In these prompts students are directed to review the relevant material is this appendix as a way to help them explore and develop the topic.

Useful Reference Works

Brunel, Pierre, ed. *Companion to Literary Myths, Heroes, and Archetypes.* Trans. Wendy Allatson, Judith Hayward, and Trista Selous. London; New York: Routledge, 1996.

Cirlot, J. E. *A Dictionary of Symbols.* 2nd ed. Trans. Jack Sage. New York: Barnes & Noble, 1995.

Cooper, J. C. *An Illustrated Encyclopaedia of Traditional Symbols.* New York: Thames and Hudson, 1990.

Eagleton, Terry. *Literary Theory: An Introduction.* Anniversary ed. Minneapolis: U of Minnesota P, 2008.

Frazer, Sir James and George W. Stacking. *The Golden Bough: A Study in Magic and Religion.* 1922. Rpt. New York: Penguin, 1998.

Guerin, Wilfred L. *A Handbook of Critical Approaches to Literature.* 5th ed. New York: Oxford UP, 2005.

Harmon, William. *A Handbook to Literature.* 11th ed. Upper Saddle River: Prentice, 2009.

Lentricchia, Frank, and Thomas McLaughlin. *Critical Terms for Literary Study.* 2nd ed. Chicago: Chicago UP, 1995.

Preminger, Alex, and T. V. F. Brogan, eds. *The New Princeton Encyclopedia of Poetry and Poetics.* Princeton: Princeton UP, 1993.

Tresidder, Jack, ed. *The Complete Dictionary of Symbols.* San Francisco: Chronicle, 2005.

Urdang, Laurence, and Frederick G. Ruffner, Jr., eds. *Allusions: Cultural, Literary, Biblical, and Historical: A Thematic Dictionary.* 2nd ed. Detroit: Gale, 1986.

Walker, Barbara G. *The Woman's Encyclopedia of Myths and Secrets.* Edison: Castle, 1996.

Directory of Audio and Video Distributors

For further information, consult the *Educational Film & Video Locator of the Consortium of College and University Media Centers,* published by R. R. Bowker; or the *Film & Video Finder*, published by the National Information Center for Educational Media.

Annenberg Media
P. O. Box 2345
South Burlington, VT 05407
www.learner.org

Audio Book Contractors
P. O. Box 40115
Washington, DC 20016
202-363-3429
www.audiobookcontractors.com

Audio Editions
P. O. Box 6930
Auburn, CA 95604-6930
800-231-4261
www.audioeditions.com

Caedmon/Harper Audio
P. O. Box 588
Dunmore, PA 18512
800-242-7737
www.harpercollins.com

Caedmon Records
    See Caedmon/Harper Audio

Corinth Films
3117 Bursonville Rd.
Riegelsville PA 18077
610-346-7446
www.cornithfilms.com

Coronet/MTI Film & Video
    See Phoenix Learning Group
Filmic Archives
448 Pepper St.
Monroe, CT 06468
800-261-1920

Films for the Humanities & Sciences
P. O. Box 2053
Princeton, NJ 08543-2053
800-257-5126
www.films.com

Indiana University Instructional Support Services
Franklin Hall, Room M114
Bloomington, IN 47405-1223
812-885-2853

Insight Media
2162 Broadway
New York, NY 10024
212-721-6316, 800-233-9910
www.insight-media.com

Learning Corporation of America
    See Phoenix Learning Group

Listening Library
    See Random House Audio

MGM/United Artists Home Video
1350 Avenue of the Americas
New York, NY 10019
212-707-0300
www.mgm.com

Monterey Home Video
566 ST. Charles Drive
Thousand Oaks, CA 91360
800-424-2593
www.montereymedia.com/video

National Public Radio
Listener Services
635 Massachusetts Ave NW
Washington, DC 20001
202-513-3232
www.npr.org

New Dimensions Radio
P. O. Box 569
Ukiah, CA 95482
800-935-8273
www.newdimensions.org

New Letters on Air
University of Missouri at Kansas City
5100 Rockhill Rd.
Kansas City, MO 64110
816-235-1168
www.newlettere.org/onTheAir.asp

PBS Home Video
1320 Braddock Place
Alexandria, VA 22314
703-739-5380, 800-645-4727

Phoenix Learning Group
2349 Chaffee Drive
St. Louis, MO 63146
800-221-1274
www.phoenixlearninggroup.com

Pyramid Media
P. O. Box 1048
Santa Monica, CA 90406
800-421-2304
www.pyramidmedia.com

RCA/Columbia Home Video
    See Sony Pictures Home Entertainment

Random House Audio
400 Hahn Road
Westminster, MD 21157
800-726-0600
www.randomhouse.com/audio

Recorded Books
270 Skipjack Rd.
Prince Frederick, MD 20678
800-638-1304
www.recordedbooks.com

Smithsonian Folkways Recordings
600 Maryland Ave. SW, Suite 2001
Washington, DC 20024
800-365-5929
www.folkways.si.edu

Sony Pictures Home Entertainment
10202 W. Washington Blvd.
Culver City, CA 90232
www.sonypictures.com/homevideo

Spoken Arts
195 South White Rock Road
Holmes, NY 12531
800-326-4090
www.spokenartsmedia.com

Time-Life Video
Customer Service
1450 East Parham Rd.
Richmond, VA 23280
800-950-7887
www.TimeLife.com

Video Learning Library
15838 North 62nd Street, Suite 101
Scottsdale, AZ 85254
800-383-8811
www.videolearning.com

Warner Home Video
4000 Warner Blvd.
Burbank, CA 91522
818-954-6000
www.warnerbrothrs.com

Women Make Movies
462 Broadway, Suite 500
New York, NY 10013
www.wmm.com